Readings of the Particular

The Postcolonial in the Postnational

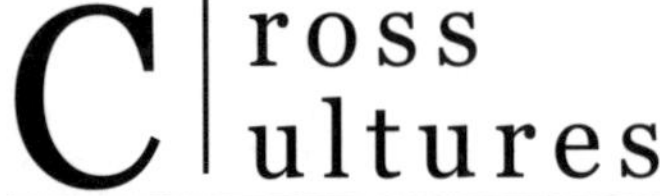

Readings in the Post / Colonial Literatures in English

89

Readings of the Particular

The Postcolonial in the Postnational

Edited by
Anne Holden Rønning and
Lene Johannessen

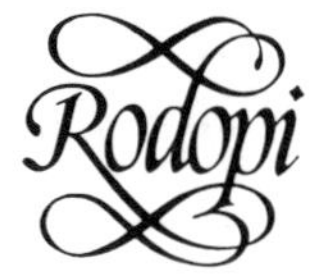

Amsterdam - New York, NY 2007

The paper on which this book is printed meets the requirements of "ISO 9706:1994, Information and documentation - Paper for documents - Requirements for permanence".

ISBN-13: 978-90-420-2163-1

Printed in The Netherlands

Table of Contents

II Performing Possibilities

III Poetic Sites of Intertextuality

Introduction

THIS COLLECTION OF ESSAYS has been assembled with the aim of throwing light on transculturality and the identities and masks that people put on, in writing as much as in life. It is a follow-up to the first Norwegian collection of essays on colonial and post-colonial writing, *Identities and Masks*,[1] published in 2001. In an increasingly global world, all of us are becoming transcultural in some form or other. This is far from a new phenomenon, but illustrative of the problematic and scale of contemporary border-crossings.

As the world turns postnational, postcapitalist, transcultural and even post-human, what position is left for the postcolonial? If it is true, as Negri and Hardt claim in *Empire*, that our time is characterized by "a decentred and deterritorializing apparatus of rule that progressively incorporates the entire global realm within its open, expanding frontiers,"[2] where in this description does the postcolonial fit? One can understand those who see postcolonial studies and theories in a state of crisis; who perceive the overlap with globalization theories and methodologies as detrimental to the continued development of the area. In addition to this, postcolonial studies have come to encompass such a wide range of inquiries that it can be difficult to see what the field really is. Coupled with an increasingly market-driven academe, one may have some sympathy with Graham Huggan when he says that, "like other commodified terms

---

[1] *Identities and Masks: Colonial and Postcolonial Studies*, ed. Jakob Lothe, Anne Holden Rønning & Peter Young (Kristiansand: Høyskoleforlaget, 2001).

[2] Michael Hardt & Antonio Negri, *Empire* (Cambridge MA: Harvard UP, 2000): xii.

used largely for academic purposes, postcolonialism has taken full advantage of its own semantic vagueness."[3] Arif Dirlik's criticism is more disciplinary and ideological:

> It is tempting, and not entirely misleading, to suggest that the postcolonial is what postcolonial intellectuals do, and postcolonial intellectuals in our day represent a wide range of intellectual and political positions unified only by a common interest in the politics of cultural identity. Conversely, it would seem that the very deployment of the vocabulary of postcolonial criticism is sufficient qualification for postcolonial identity, further complicating the politics of postcoloniality. This may be quite in keeping with the spirit of overcoming boundaries and binarisms, but the intellectual confusion it creates is self-evident.[4]

Dirlik may have a point. The confusion he refers to resides in an interest that often seems based on nothing more that locating and identifying mechanisms and structures of power-relations and oppression. In addition, we should remember that the location of the postcolony and its discourse is, and perhaps always was, uncertain, encompassing both the colony in its process of self-construction and the relationship it inherits and must negotiate with the former colonizer. The idea of the national is, moreover, itself becoming increasingly difficult to comprehend and define; the provenance of the aesthetic accordingly comes up against complex conceptual, epistemic and cultural boundaries. Finally, the "Empire," hovering above cultural production as at once homogenizing and diversifying, still awaits consistent responses. In a situation where power-relations and cultural governance are mixed up in questions of Empire and the marketplace, the exact nature and function of the postcolonial is far from clear.

And yet, in the midst of postnationalism, postcapitalism, globalization and occasionally extreme forms of cultural relativism, the particularities and significance of regions and their histories and discourses persevere. The past decade is certainly not lacking in illustrations of their manifes-

---

[3] Graham Huggan, *The Post-Colonial Exotic: Marketing the Margins* (London: Routledge, 2001): 1.

[4] Arif Dirlik, *Postmodernity's Histories: The Past as Legacy and Project* (Boston MA: Rowman & Littlefield, 2000): 8.

tations, beyond any answerable presupposition. Theories and methods of globalization may have much to offer, but in their global reach they also have limitations. Theirs is by definition a "top–bottom perspective," but, however spectacular such a bird's-eye view, it can only rarely give an accurate or complete picture. This is where postcolonial theories may yet have something to offer, despite the deplorable situation Dirlik describes.

Key elements in colonial and postcolonial discourse and criticism have always involved a focus on belonging, on identity, on expressing, explaining and analyzing present and past dynamics between peoples and cultures. Historically, these considerations arose out of social and political realities of specific times and places, relying heavily on knowledge of the particularities of location and the complex discourses thus refracted. This still underlies postcolonial literatures and theories, even if they are sometimes subsumed under more general parameters. In the concern with the particular, postcolonial theories shed light on processes of cultural globalization on a fundamental level. Engaging with and problematizing issues of transculturalism and the refraction of local cultural practices in the diaspora, postcolonial literature and theory are a corrective and complement to the grand narratives of globalization.

We use the word 'transcultural' to emphasize the increasing complexity of the realities postcolonial theories engage with, the very same complexity that made "Empire" possible, and one that has assumed a geographical and demographic dimension unimaginable fifty years ago. Marie Louise Pratt explains transcultural as describing "how subordinated or marginal groups select and invent from materials transmitted to them by a dominant or metropolitan culture."[5] She also stresses the fact that she sees transculturation in terms of "co-presence, interaction, interlocking understandings and practices."[6] The prefix 'trans-', then, suggests an ongoing process that privileges the dialogic principle over the monologic.

The process of transculturation and the focus on the particularities of the realities underlying various locations form the background for this

---

[5] Mary Louise Pratt, *Imperial Eyes: Travel Writing and Transculturation* (London & New York: Routledge, 1997): 6.

[6] Pratt, *Imperial Eyes*, 7.

volume of critical essays. In different ways and from their different perspectives and disciplines, scholars from Africa, Europe, and North America engage with the specificities of the postcolonial aesthetic and the realities that foster its various modes of expression. The readings in this collection crystallize the simultaneously common and distinct concerns of literatures from places as different as England, Scotland, France–Algeria, the USA, South Africa, Native Canada, to mention a few. As imperial forces and the marketplace's drive for hegemony persist with undiminished energy, the aesthetic of postcolonial specifics is one of the important counterweights to conflation – hence, control.

❧

The book opens with a "Prelude," an essay by Wenche Ommundsen, who takes up cultural citizenship in imagined diasporic communities. She suggests "a cultural approach to notions of citizenship invites an examination of the play of identities, masks and performed selves [...] and [...] a reappraisal of the imagined communities to which they owe their allegiance." What she calls her "airport fiction" is the parable she employs to illustrate the complexity of cultural citizenship. Airports are the site where citizenship encounters a variety of cultural responses, thus exposing the imaginary nature of diasporic notions.

I Novels and Their Borders

Taking her cue from Samuel Huntington's "The Clash of Civilizations?" and Said's response, "The Clash of Definitions," Priscilla Ringrose examines the idea of 'glocality' in relation to the descendants of North African migrants in France. More specifically, she examines the depiction of identity in the literature of writers who grew up in families where one or both parents emigrated to France from the Maghreb. Rather than arriving at one way of reading and representing this history, Ringrose concludes that immigrant protagonists internalise fictions of conflict; "some create alternative fictions, while yet others, by stepping out of the bipolar dynamic, open out into [a] multicultural borderless world."

In "Allegories of Ambivalence: Scottish Fiction, Britain and Empire," Alan Freeman discusses the Scottish novel tradition as simultaneously active participant in *and* marginalized Other to the imperialistic State. Freeman examines key nineteenth-century examples, by Sir Walter Scott and Robert Louis Stevenson, and work by the leading contemporary novelist William Boyd. He shows how major narratives of the expansionist age are structured around binary relational values, which, in effect, allegorize that ambivalent status.

The inherent and bothersome fictiveness of self-construction is at stake in Ute Kauer's discussion, which, focusing on André Brink's work, examines the interrelatedness of history and storytelling in his post-apartheid novels. It is the role of cultural memory and the construction of hybrid identities, particularly the re-invention of the formerly marginalized female voices, that are forefronted. Brink's project, Kauer argues, questions a re-imagining of the nation that ignores spaces of cultural memory. These cannot necessarily be easily harmonized.

Another powerful storyteller from South Africa is Bessie Head. In a close analysis of the short story "The Wind and a Boy," Johan Schimanski focuses on her fiction as essentially border writing. Through analyses of the cultural, spatial, temporal, epistemological and textual borders involved in selected instances of the articulation process, he engages in a dialogue with Head's writing as it refracts some of the central problems of (post)colonial borders in Africa, especially Southern Africa.

Zakes Mda is a remarkable addition to the impressive list of writers from South Africa; starting off as the author of about thirty plays, he has in recent years turned to writing novels. David Bell focuses, with reference to Mda's *Ways of Dying*, *She Plays with the Darkness* and *The Heart of Redness*, on traditional African modes of narrative, custom, costume and cosmology as constitutive of a site of language-thought empowerment. His analyses conclude that Mda's handling of "death and dying" must be seen as a contribution to the debate on the African Renaissance.

Self-construction is the main concern in Ulla Rahbek's essay, which explores Jean Rhys's "On Not Shooting Sitting Birds" for the controlling mechanisms operating within such construction – control of memory, of authorship, of selfhood, and eventually of hermeneutics. "The focus in the story," Rahbek maintains, "is both on how characters try to exercise control over themselves and others, and, by extension, on how the reader attempts to control text, characters and author." In her reading, she demonstrates how labels such as 'modernist', 'colonialist', and 'feminist' do not necessarily amount to more than further attempts at control.

II Performing Possibilities

If the novel genre has been particularly conducive to experimentation with different traditions, styles and ideologies, the medium of film is certainly no less so. Isaac Julien is a member of the Sankofa collective, a group of black British filmmakers who took their name from the mythical African bird signifying 'the act of looking into the past to prepare for the future'. One of Julien's most acclaimed films is *Looking For Langston* (1988). In his essay on spectation and its limitations, Asbjørn Grønstad discusses the problematic dynamic of vision. Exploration of the site of vision, the rerouting and decolonization of the appropriating gaze, is here carried out in relation to "the dreamy meditation on the logistic of desire and the homoerotic gaze."

The activity of imaging and spectating has, as we know, very much also been a Western activity in its interaction with its 'Others'. This activity, only one among many, has also left its mark on performance in African theatre. Evelyn Lutwama explores the three stages African theatre has gone through, the precolonial, the colonial and the postcolonial, arguing that Western accentuation of male dominance is particularly noticeable. This survey concentrates on West, East and Southern African communities and their theatre traditions, but its key concerns extend beyond these locations. The present postcolonial feminist struggle for equality is taking over the political struggle for independence of past decades, but the questions remain: Whose portrayal of whom, where and how?

Moving now to the North American continent, Canada and its theatre tradition has had to grapple with some of the same issues. In her essay on the need for producing Canadian drama, Anne Nothof examines the history of "national drama" as "inclusive, diverse, multi-ethnic, and indigenous." This overview of Canadian theatre history centres on the issue of national identity, not an easy enterprise in a country imbued from its inception with changes and shifts, presently counting its population as originating in 210 different countries. The correspondence between the stage and the nation, then, lies very much in the efforts of both to create an imagined space in which some shared sense of identity can be located.

Nothof's essay is an informative background for the two more detailed explorations that Susan Knutson and Kristina Aurylaitė embark on. Knutson focuses on the renowned writer George Elliott Clarke, a black Nova Scotian. She emphasizes Clarke's identity as a writer with roots in pre-Confederation Canadian history, his work foregrounding the prevalence of mixed cultural heritages as a national feature in what is ultimately a call for social justice. In her analyses of the relation between Clarke's *Execution Poems* and Shakespeare's *Titus Andronicus*, Knutson argues that the widespread presence of Shakespeare in Canadian drama underscores the Empire's appropriation of Shakespeare for its colonial purposes. Central to this discussion is the complexity of Canada's claim to postcoloniality.

Daniel David Moses and Tomson Highway are well known to most readers of North American plays. Kristina Aurylaitė considers the tension and potential of spatial intersections in her analysis of Moses's *Coyote City* and Highway's *The Rez Sisters*, how, in the vein of Henri Lefebvre's treatise on the configuration of social space; "both plays allow their characters to [unsettle] the precise boundary line between the white and the Native spaces […] allowing for a possibility of change, development and becoming." Her discussion suggests that a new spatial configuration of the border zones between Native Canadian and Euro-Canadian has a mobilizing and transforming influence.

III Poetic Sites of Intertextuality

In his readings of David Dabydeen's poem "Turner" and his second novel, *Disappearance*, Erik Falk embarks on a voyage into amnesia as a site for production and renewal. Falk contends that "the loss of memory, history and identity at stake in these texts in no way equals absence, but in itself constitutes a history that must, ultimately, be 'forgotten' for a new and unpredictable future to be possible." In the course of these considerations, it also becomes clear that in both texts the eventual return home for the protagonists is a challenge to history, and so must necessarily also be a kind of new production "of material and concrete new connections."

As the title of his essay indicates, Charles Armstrong considers William Butler Yeats's ambivalent role in relation to the Irish case as colony. "Many Masks, Big Houses: Yeats and the Construction of an Irish Identity" problematizes Yeats's position by positing that "there is some uncertainty whether he should be cast among the camp of the dominating or the subjected powers, or whether he is of essence a more liminal figure." Armstrong thus joins those who have, for instance, criticized Said's essay on Yeats and his relation to colonialism – "Yeats's survival and canonization rests on the mutual amplification of his various assumed identities of nation builder, aesthetic modernist and mystic sage."

Paul Muldoon is, along with Seamus Heaney, one of the major Irish poets assuming Yeats's legacy. In his exploration of the relationship between these two, Ruben Moi argues that Muldoon's poetic is "a distinct alternative to Heaney's aesthetic and conceptualization of Northern Ireland." Moi demonstrates how Muldoon employs imperial cultural encounters to comment on the Northern Ireland situation from a global perspective to present "the other Other."

Concluding this section, Jacquelynne Modeste explores intertextual relationships between Richard Wright's *Native Son*, Ralph Ellison's *Invisible Man*, and Albert Murray's *The Seven League Boots*, indicating how the organizing themes in these landmark works of the African-American literary tradition stylistically parallel the structure of jazz music. Moreover, they intersect, Modeste argues, with "the ways in which a rejection of cultural traditions casts one as an outsider in his own community, reinforces negative self-images, and constricts possibility, whereas cultural connections can serve to promote group consciousness and serve as platforms of opportunity upon which individual potential can be realized."

We would like to express our thanks to Gordon Collier for his excellent editorial input and indexing, and the Faculty of Arts, University of Bergen, for financial assistance in bringing out this publication.

ANNE HOLDEN RØNNING and LENE JOHANNESSEN

❧

❧ Prelude

Have Culture, Will Travel

❧ Cultural Citizenship and the Imagined Communities of Diaspora; a Fiction

WENCHE OMMUNDSEN

IN HIS RECENT ESSAY "Outline of a General Theory of Cultural Citizenship," Bryan Turner argues that "cultural citizenship and the cultural underpinnings of modern citizenship remain neglected aspects of contemporary studies of citizenship."[1] To some, this perceived neglect comes as something of a surprise. Issues such as cultural belonging, cultural difference, multiculturalism, culturalism and national culture have been high on the academic agenda in the last decade and one can only speculate that disciplinary boundaries have prevented them from migrating from cultural studies, sociology, communication studies and anthropology to citizenship studies. If Turner is right, however, a renewed interest in culture within citizenship studies might have profound implications for the discipline as a whole, particularly in its potential to destabilize the central concepts of culture and citizenship themselves. In the context of diasporic, transnational and transcultural populations, as I hope to demonstrate in this essay, a cultural approach to notions of citizenship invites an examination of the play of identities, masks and performed selves in which individuals as well as groups must engage, and, beyond that, a

---

[1] Bryan S. Turner, "Outline of a General Theory of Cultural Citizenship," in *Culture and Citizenship*, ed. Nick Stevenson (London: Sage, 2001): 12.

reappraisal of the imagined communities (national or supranational) to which they owe their allegiance.[2]

The term 'diaspora', literally denoting a 'scattering of seeds', traditionally referred to the scattering of a specific people: "the exile of the Jews from their historic homeland and their dispersion throughout many lands, signifying as well the oppression and moral degradation implied by that dispersion."[3] In recent years the term has taken on much wider, and also more contested, meanings. "Today," writes William Safran, "'diaspora' and, more specifically, 'diaspora community' seem increasingly to be used as metaphoric designations for several categories of people – expatriates, expellees, political refugees, alien residents, immigrants, and ethnic and racial minorities *tout court*."[4] In his influential definition, Safran wants to retain a number of characteristics attributed to more traditional notions of diaspora, including notions of an original 'centre', a collective myth of the homeland, a sense of alienation and insulation from the host society and a myth of eventual return. More recently, however, a number of critics have questioned the relevance of these characteristics to contemporary diasporic populations,[5] or have even argued that the current popularity of the concept of diaspora has the effect of masking the complexity and fluidity of national and cultural belonging.[6] Their concerns are central to this discussion of cultural belonging within overseas Chinese

---

[2] My use of the term 'imagined community' gestures towards Benedict Anderson's influential outline of the origins and development of the nation-state, but will be expanded to include communities owing their existence to a differently imagined sense of belonging, both within and beyond the boundaries of the nation-state. See Anderson, *Imagined Communities: Reflections on the Origin and Spread of Nationalism* (London: Verso, 2nd ed. 1991).

[3] William Safran, "Diasporas in Modern Societies: Myths of Homeland and Return," *Diaspora* 1.1 (1991): 83.

[4] Safran, "Diasporas in Modern Societies," 83.

[5] See, for example, James Clifford, *Routes: Travel and Translation in the Late Twentieth Century* (Cambridge MA: Harvard UP, 1997), and Paul Gilroy, "'It ain't where you're from, it's where you're at…': The Dialectics of Diasporic Identification," *Third Text* 13 (Winter 1990–91).

[6] Ien Ang, *On Not Speaking Chinese: Living Between Asia and the West* (London: Routledge, 2001).

communities: the notion of diaspora is 'tested', so to speak, against another term denoting belonging, that of cultural citizenship.

Cultural citizenship may, in the simplest terms, be taken to mean a certain 'fit' or compatibility between the cultural attributes of an individual, or a group, and those of the society in which they live. It is a complex concept, taking in rights, responsibilities and competencies as well as the more intangible issues of identity and belonging which have been the subject of intensive debates within cultural studies in the past decade. In the case of diasporic or transnational peoples, it is further complicated by the fact of their multiple cultural and/or civic allegiances (to home and host nations in the first instance, but frequently also to the cultural space of diaspora itself). Turner argues that cultural citizenship is something we should be able to measure:

> It should be possible to create indices which could be constructed to measure to what extent location, education, social class, gender, race and linguistic knowledge stand in the way of full access to and participation in either the high or low cultural spheres of any particular state or society.[7]

"State or society" here seems to refer primarily to nation-states, and Turner names two distinct "cultural spheres" within such states, high and low. He may not, of course, have intended these to be exclusive. I would argue, however, that cultural configurations in today's world are so complex that instruments for measuring cultural citizenship would need to be of immense precision and flexibility. The relationship between culture and citizenship was never simple, but while it traditionally tended to be taken for granted that nation-states could both assume and impose a degree of cultural uniformity, today's multicultural nations have developed complex, often contradictory policies and practices for dealing with cultural difference. At the same time, "imagined communities" other than the nation make different, sometimes competing claims for cultural allegiance: supranational formations such as the European Union; global organizations (NGOs or multinational corporations); the "homeland," real or

---

[7] Turner, "Outline of a General Theory of Cultural Citizenship," 27.

imaginary, of diasporic or transnational populations; the transnational space of diaspora itself. Although I suspect that rumours of what Arjun Appadurai[8] has referred to as the "terminal crisis" of the nation-state have been greatly exaggerated, the domain of culture, to an even greater extent than the civil, political and social spheres, is surely one that is increasingly marked by multiple, overlapping and constantly diversifying modes of belonging. This essay, while generally endorsing Turner's call for the elaboration of methodologies aimed at identifying and assessing the parameters of cultural citizenship, gestures towards some of the complexities we might encounter along the way. I have chosen to focus on a diasporic population because diasporas, with their national, transnational and post-national sites of cultural allegiance, are frequently cited as models for cultural belonging in a globalizing world: to Khachig Tölölyan, they are "the exemplary communities of the transnational moment."[9]

My account here of the complexity of cultural citizenship in diaspora takes the form of a parable – what I would like to call my 'airport fiction'.

To most, the term 'airport fiction' evokes novels of the kind usually found at newsagents' stalls in airports: thick volumes with the author's name in large embossed letters, promising enough romance, suspense or action to tackle the discomfort, boredom and, in these uncertain times, anxiety of the longest intercontinental flight. This fiction has little to offer in either the romance or the nail-biting department, and the author is unlikely ever to see her name in embossed capitals. It is, however, mercifully short, and if some of what is lacking in character and plot development is made up by its evocation of, and contribution to, a number of current debates within diaspora and citizenship studies, the fiction will have fulfilled its purpose.[10]

---

[8] Arjun Appadurai, *Modernity at Large: Cultural Dimensions of Globalization* (Minneapolis: U of Minnesota P, 1996): 21.

[9] Khachig Tölölyan, "The Nation-State and its Others: In Lieu of a Preface," *Diaspora* 1.1 (1991): 5.

[10] I develop my ideas on these issues in more conventional academic form in two related essays; see "Tough Ghosts: Modes of Cultural Belonging in Diaspora," *Asian Studies Review* 27.2 (2003): 181–204, and "Cultural Citizenship in Diaspora: A Study of Chinese Australia," in *Asian Diasporas: Cultures, Identities,*

❧

Let us, then, imagine an airport – no, make that three airports. The first seems familiar – in fact, it is almost identical to Tullamarine, Kingsford Smith, or the airport of any other capital city welcoming international travellers to the nation-state of Australia. There is the well-known bin for disposing of unwelcome foodstuffs, passport control, sniffer dogs, baggage trolleys which refuse to separate, and red and green customs lanes. But there is a difference. After having had their baggage checked, their surplus alcohol confiscated and their wooden souvenirs sprayed, the weary travellers have another room, and another checkpoint, to pass on their way to waiting relatives or business appointments. "Cultural citizenship," says a large sign over the door, "please have your form and your cultural baggage ready for inspection and wait until called." By chance, all these travellers seem to be of Chinese origins, though their flights have originated in a number of different countries (Singapore, Malaysia, Indonesia and Vietnam as well as Hong Kong, mainland China and Taiwan) and some have come all the way from Europe and America.[11] The majority have Australian passports and all of them have been "cleared" by immigration officials. They shuffle forward slowly and have to hand in their forms at a place designated as the "language barrier." From this point on they are organized into different lines depending on language and other cultural competencies. However, as the form exists only in English, there are already long delays. One People's Republic of China (PCR) national, who is arriving in Australia for the first time, is not impressed. "I thought Australia was a multicultural nation," he argues through a volunteer interpreter, "why then is English the only acceptable language?" "Multicul-

---

Representation, ed. Shawn Wong & Robbie Goh (Hong Kong: Hong Kong UP, 2004): 77–94. This work is all based on empirical research conducted within the Chinese diasporic community in Australia in 2000 and 2001 and greatly assisted by research fellow Dr Ouyang Yu.

[11] "The sources, socio-economic backgrounds and circumstances of Chinese immigrant arrivals in Australia have been much more diverse than those of Chinese communities in the other great contemporary immigrant-receiving countries"; *Floating Lives: The Media and Asian Diasporas*, ed. Stuart Cunningham & John Sinclair (St Lucia: U of Queensland P, 2000): 37.

turalism doesn't mean you don't have to speak English," explains the official, "unless, of course, you just want to work in a restaurant or factory with other Chinese, but then you would hardly be a cultural citizen of Australia, would you? If you take my advice, try to get up to speed with English as soon as possible. Fortunately" (and he points to the little girl at the man's side), "the kids pick it up very quickly – in a few years she will practically have forgotten Chinese." "But I don't want her to forget," the man complains, "the language is an important part of her heritage." "Don't worry," the official answers, "when she has forgotten you can send her to Saturday school to pick up a bit of Chinese – enough to get by." The man is clearly unhappy, but he is holding up the queue and has to move on.

At the next desk the travellers first have to show their educational credentials. They are impressive. The majority have university degrees, and among the younger generation, HSC/VCE scores and university participation-rates are well above the national average for Australia.[12] Their credentials are carefully scrutinized, however, and many, particularly those from the People's Republic of China, are stamped "Not Recognized in Australia" or "Requiring Further Investigation." Then they are asked to give a statement about their "cultural capital." "Is that the same as money?" someone asks. "Not quite," answers the official, "but money helps." He then launches into a lecture about how everything, including culture, is commodified these days, thus working as items of exchange within the late-capitalist system. The travellers are much too tired to make much sense of what he says. He issues each of them with a certificate of "socio-economic status," which, it would seem, gives a combined score for education and economic circumstances. Many of the mainlanders, who had initially ticked "professional" on the form, find themselves demoted to lower rungs on the social scale.

The next official is a jolly lady who asks them to show her their cultural heritage. "I write poetry," one of them says, "and occasional essays on contemporary Chinese culture." "I am a painter," says another, "my

---

[12] HSC (Higher School Certificate) and VCE (Victorian Certificate of Education) are secondary-school diplomas on which university entry is based.

work deconstructs Western postmodernism from the position of an alternative Asian modernity." The woman does not know what to do with this. "Don't you have any Chinese stuff?" she asks, "you know, dragon parades, lion dances, New Year celebrations?" A couple have brought beautiful costumes, and exotic customs, but on the whole, it would seem, they are a pretty disappointing lot when it comes to culture. The woman makes a final attempt: "What about food, then?" she asks. Fortunately, they are all knowledgeable about Chinese food, and most profess to be passable cooks. Relieved, she stamps their form and allows them to pass to the final checkpoint near the door.

This last check seems to be a mere formality: their signatures are verified and the forms collected. But by now one of the travellers has become curious, and not a little agitated. "What about race?" she asks, "you seem to have checked everything else – and I have heard about 'White Australia' and all that, you know."[13] The official reassures her: "No, no, that was all in the past. We have a colour-blind citizenship policy now." She is not convinced. "So why is it that everyone in this room is East Asian? Are there no other travellers?" He explains slowly, as if to a three-year-old: "That's because this is the Chinese room – we sort people according to culture now."[14] "Is there a European room, then, and another one for South Asians, or people from the Middle East?" "There used to be a room for Europeans," he explains, patiently, "Greeks, and Italians, you know. But we don't bother much about those any more. They sort themselves

---

[13] The 'White Australia Policy', which covered a number of measures aimed at preventing people of non-European backgrounds from settling in Australia, was introduced in 1901, at the moment of Federation, and remained in place until the 1960s.

[14] Unwittingly, he gestures towards the discourse of 'culturalism' –see Jon Stratton, *Race Daze: Australia in Identity Crisis* [Sydney: Pluto, 1998) – defined by Étienne Balibar in his influential essay "Is there a 'neo-racism'?": 'It is a racism whose dominant theme is not biological heredity but the insurmountability of cultural differences, a racism which, at first sight, does not postulate the superiority of certain groups or peoples in relation to others but 'only' the harmfulness of abolishing frontiers, the incompatibility of life-styles and traditions"; Balibar & Immanuel Wallerstein, *Race, Nation, Class: Ambiguous Identities* (London: Verso, 1991): 21.

out." And as if to prove his point, he gestures towards his colleagues, many of whom, it appears, are of southern European origins. Then he lowers his voice: "About the others," he says, "well, there's the big room next door. That's by far the busiest these days. I suppose you have heard about detention centres, the Pacific Solution, temporary protection visas and all that..."[15] She nods, "but what kind of questions do you ask them, how are they sorted?" He looks around, this time rather nervously. "It's pretty confidential, security reasons, you see, so I don't really know," he whispers, "but I think it's mostly about religion. And for some reason, clothing seems to have become an issue as well...." Realizing that quite a few are now listening to him, he checks himself, looks around nervously, and suddenly becomes very officious. "Welcome to Australia," he says, to no one in particular, and quickly waves the whole group through into the bright sunshine.

❧

The second airport, and the realm to which it provides access, does not really look like any we have encountered in the world of nation-states and geographical borders. It is oddly deterritorialized, and seems to be floating somewhere above ground.[16] At the same time, it would seem, it is present in almost every country of the known world. You know that this is no ordinary airport as soon as you get there by the fact that there is no passport control. In fact, it would seem that passports, or any other reminder of national belonging, are positively discouraged. "Welcome to the Chinese diaspora," reads a large sign in both English and Chinese in the entrance hall. The place looks more like a shopping mall (tax-free, of

---

[15] He is referring to the immigration crisis caused by the Tampa incident in 2001, when asylum seekers were rescued from a sinking boat by the Norwegian freighter Tampa, but subsequently denied entry to Australian territory. The incident caused a major political debate in Australia, as well as widespread international condemnation of the country's immigration policies.

[16] It has become a critical commonplace to refer to diaspora as a 'floating', 'ungrounded' or 'deterritorialized' space; see, for example, *Ungrounded Empires: The Cultural Politics of Modern Chinese Transnationalism*, ed. Aihwa Ong & Donald Macun Nonini (New York & London: Routledge, 1997).

course) than an airport, and the boundary between the airport and the diaspora itself is blurred. “Greater China Emporium,” reads the name over the entrance, “outstanding Asian values.” In order to get in, one has to pass a checkpoint for ethnic credentials. Here, each visitor has to present their Chineseness, which is duly weighed, measured, and classified. Some of the visitors are clearly nervous about their qualifications. One woman, who looks like the cultural critic Ien Ang, does not seem to know what she is doing there in the first place. “I don’t speak Chinese,” she says, “I don’t think I have come to the right place.”[17] “No worries,” the officer reassures her, “we’re not very strict about that.” And before she has the time to change her mind and turn around, he grabs her and drags her in. Others are not so lucky. A non-Chinese-looking man is trying to argue his case. “My wife is Chinese,” he says, “I observe all the traditions,” but to no avail. Sadly, he watches his wife and children disappear on the other side of the barrier. Another man does not give up as easily. “I am a sinologist,” he shouts, “I speak Mandarin and know three other dialects. I bet I know more about Chinese culture than anyone else in this room.” The officer shakes his head firmly. “I have my orders,” he says, “only Chinese people can be admitted.” The two men join a group of other rejects. Their situation, as it turns out, is not so bad. They are led to a viewing platform overlooking the mall, where they are given a copious amount of informative pamphlets as well as refreshments, and where they are invited to join a guided tour which twice a day takes non-Chinese visitors around the major cultural attractions of the diaspora. Although they are barred from entering certain premises, their experience of the diaspora is not, in the end, so very different from that of most Chinese travellers.

The emporium is divided into two sections, entitled “The Past” and “The Future.” The past consists of a replica Chinatown, complete with gambling houses, opium dens, Peking opera, brothels, and innumerable restaurants and shops. Everything is for sale, from the most exotic foodstuffs to the finest antiques and handicrafts. There is also an abundance of

---

[17] In her recent book *On Not Speaking Chinese: Living Between Asia and the West*, Ang spells out the implications, for notions of cultural belonging, of looking Chinese, but not speaking Chinese.

books and videos on Chinese history and culture. The future looks very different, more like a real-estate agent's catalogue. It consists of a street lined with huge modern houses, and office buildings in which groups of impeccably dressed men and women are negotiating business deals. One house has an "Open for Display" sign in front and a banner over the door reading "Chinese aspirations." Inside, visitors are offered brochures and free consultation on a number of topics: business opportunities, modern Confucian ethics, upward social mobility, investment in educational credentials, the language of the American business school, and where to get the best piano or violin lessons for children.

Having come to the end of the past and future displays, a group of travellers set out in search of the present. "I'm afraid that's still under construction," an apologetic official tells them. "Constructing the past was a major undertaking, and the future is not without problems of its own. Fortunately we had generous corporate sponsorship. The present, however, is proving problematic. We hired a group of scholars, but they have not been able to come to an agreement. They filed not one, but half a dozen reports, none of which has been approved by our sponsors." She allows them to peep into a room with a hastily scribbled notice reading "The Present. Please be quiet." on the door. Inside, the room is anything but quiet. An animated conference is under way, a cacophony of voices all competing for attention. A couple sign up for the conference and rush in to register their views; the others beat a hasty retreat.

As the travellers approach the exit, some of them take out their credentials and look for further guidance. But the officials all seem to have disappeared, and before them the diaspora is barely distinguishable through a thick haze. They make their way, some striding bravely, others advancing slowly and with trepidation.

☙

The final airport hails the travellers as "global citizens," "world citizens" and "cosmopolitans." On the inside, it looks much like a normal airport, featuring billboards advertising the latest in communication technology, luxury goods and exotic holiday resorts. Its outside 'world' seems to be a compacted version of the one we know, consisting primarily of global cities and the networks that connect them. Opinions differ greatly as to the exact location of this airport. Some regard it as a kind of space-station, in orbit around the globe; some argue that it exists only in the dimension of cyberspace, others that it has no reality, tangible or electronic, but is merely an idealistic intellectual construct. Some view it as a utopic, others a dystopic, fiction. Seen from a distance, its would-be citizens all look much the same: predominantly Western, affluent, and dressed in the uniform of the international business community. On closer inspection, one discovers a number of less uniform sub-groups: the international jet-set in the latest designer gear, the scholars, who clearly have little respect for the dress-code, the students, who affect an air of sophistication but who obviously do not know their way around. The Chinese are initially nowhere to be seen, but on closer inspection there are quite a few, and they seem to be in a hurry. Many rush past in the astronaut lane, a fast track specially designed for the most frequent travellers.[18]

Apart from obligatory portable computers and mobile phones, the citizens of the world travel light. The cultural citizenship assessment protocol seems much more efficient than the obstacle race employed by most nation-states in order to determine eligibility. It consists of a point-scoring system, in which points are added, and in some cases subtracted, for particular items of cultural competence or cultural baggage. Once you get used to it, the system is simple enough. Would-be citizens score points for each language they speak, but the languages are not all equal. The scores for English-language competency are the highest; the others rate according to their relative importance in global communication. Chinese, as it turns out, has recently been upgraded to category B, and competent speakers are awarded a score well above that given for most other non-Western languages. Applicants without basic English literacy, however, incur penalty points which make it virtually impossible for them to reach the required total score. Other cultural competencies are scored in a similar manner: a degree of familiarity with the high and low cultural spheres

---

[18] 'Astronaut' is a term frequently used for Chinese businessmen who commute between their businesses in Hong Kong or Taiwan and their homes in Canada, the USA or Australia. See, for example, Ong & Nonini, ed. *Ungrounded Empires*.

of the Western world are requisites, but a wider cultural repertoire, particularly if it includes knowledge of the arts and practices of exotic peoples, provide important bonus points. If, however, this exotic baggage becomes too heavy, especially if it stands in the way of familiarity with, and acceptance of, the cultural ways of the Western world, the travellers find themselves having to subtract rather than add points.

There is plenty of help available for those who have difficulties understanding the intricacies of the system. "Think of it like this," an official with the rather grand title of "Cultural Diversity Management Consultant" explains, "you need to learn to distinguish between those parts of your baggage that make up your cultural capital, and those that represent cultural liabilities. Our general advice is that you should discard items that exceed the dimensions for business class carry-on luggage." "Are you saying that we need to leave our cultural heritage behind if we wish to become global citizens?" someone asks. "No, no," she answers, "we are all in favour of heritage and cultural diversity. But we can't let it get in the way of the efficient administration of global business, so it must be sensibly managed." And she shows them a clever contraption, much like those multi-purpose gadgets travellers are so fond of, which allows them to pack their cultural heritage tightly for easy storage, but which can be unfolded to display it to maximum effect. The shop where this and a number of similar travel goods are for sale makes a brisk trade. The travellers learn fast, but the score required for full cultural citizenship of the global community is higher than most of them had expected, and many have their application rejected. A privileged few are given the stamp of approval; the rest either have to resign themselves to more narrow cultural spheres or sign up for an ambitious programme of re-education.

Near the exit gate stands an elderly official, muttering to himself and to anyone who can be bothered listening. "The cosmopolitan community is not what it used to be," he complains. "There was a time when it was a moral community of sorts, concerned with values and ideals. Then all these bright young things came along, accusing us of simply reinforcing eurocentric and masculinist values.[19] And then what happened? Nobody can agree on what should replace the old values, and we are left with nothing but commodities. As far as I am concerned, we may as well give up the scoring system altogether and simply count frequent flyer points!" A few of the more scholarly types gather around him. Some agree with him; others challenge him to come up with a definition of cosmopolitan citizenship that is less culturally biased. Soon, however, they forget about him altogether and start networking among themselves. They exchange e-mail addresses and make plans for academic conferences on the paradoxes of global citizenship, and on the tensions between cultural rights and human rights (he offers a useful overview of the paradoxes of cultural equality within notions of world citizenship). They agree that the best location for such a conference would be an exotic holiday resort: after all, there is no reason why their intellectual work should get in the way of the pleasures of the global village. Well pleased with themselves, they disperse, and once again blend into the business-suited throng.

❧

Unlike most airport novels, this is an open-ended fiction, which does not propose to tie up loose ends, locate the precise origins of wayward ideas, or follow each flight of fancy to its destination. By way of conclusion, I simply want to gesture towards a couple of points arising from this exercise itself, the imaginary embodiment of ideas normally reserved for more carefully argued academic debate. First, as I soon discovered, any activity involving cultural categorization will of necessity invite generalization as well as the temptation to stereotype. And yet, as I hope my fiction also indicates, we are dealing here with both individuals and communities whose cultural characteristics are never fixed but always mobile, multi-faceted and contested. Secondly, in the real world, as opposed to this fiction, the travellers find themselves having to negotiate the prerequisites for cultural citizenship of not only one, but often two, three, or even more

---

[19] For a brief history of notions of global citizenship, see Geoffrey Stokes, "Global Citizenship," in *Rethinking Australian Citizenship*, ed. Wayne Hudson & John Kane (Cambridge: Cambridge UP, 2000).

such imagined communities at one and the same time, with different, sometimes conflicting requirements for cultural belonging. Finally, if we accept that Benedict Anderson's famous concept (1991) can be made applicable to formations other than nations, we also have to accept the fact that imagined communities are differently imagined depending on the social, political and legal frameworks within which they are constituted. It follows that membership of a nation-state links cultural belonging to the social, civil and political realm and to rights and obligations which include, but go beyond, spheres of action generally understood as cultural. Cultural 'citizenship' of a diaspora, by contrast, is not accompanied by civic rights and so is cultural in a different, more narrow sense. The notion of *global* cultural citizenship, on the other hand, has the potential to take the term 'culture' onto a plane where it is likely to be understood in relation to major ideological or philosophical debates. By widening the concept of 'cultural citizenship' to include membership in transnational or global communities such as those discussed here, I suggest, we not only reveal the complexity of cultural belonging in the contemporary world, but force a rethinking of the central terms of citizenship and culture, and the interplay between them. To represent, let alone measure, this complexity is not something we can leave to airport fictions, but an undertaking the nature of which we can only start to imagine.

❧

Works Cited

Anderson, Benedict. *Imagined Communities: Reflections on the Origin and Spread of Nationalism* (London: Verso, 2nd ed. 1991).

Ang, Ien. *On Not Speaking Chinese: Living Between Asia and the West* (London: Routledge, 2001).

Appadurai, Arjun. *Modernity at Large: Cultural Dimensions of Globalization* (Minneapolis: U of Minnesota P, 1996).

Balibar, Étienne, & Immanuel Wallerstein. *Race, Nation, Class: Ambiguous Identities* (London: Verso, 1991).

Clifford, James. *Routes: Travel and Translation in the Late Twentieth Century* (Cambridge MA: Harvard UP, 1997).

Cunningham, Stuart, & John Sinclair, ed. *Floating Lives: The Media and Asian Diasporas* (St Lucia: U of Queensland P, 2000).

Gilroy, Paul "'It ain't where you're from, it's where you're at…': The Dialectics of Diasporic Identification," *Third Text* 13.1 (Winter 1990): 3–16.

He, Baogang. "World Citizenship and Transnational Activism," in *Contextualising Transnational Activism: Problems of Power and Democracy*, ed. Nicola Piper & Anders Uhlin (London: Routledge, 2004).

Ommundsen, Wenche. "Tough Ghosts: Modes of Cultural Belonging in Diaspora," *Asian Studies Review* 27.2 (2003): 181–204.

Ommundsen, Wenche. "Cultural Citizenship in Diaspora: A Study of Chinese Australia," in *Asian Diasporas: Cultures, Identities, Representation,* ed. Shawn Wong & Robbie Goh (Hong Kong: Hong Kong UP, 2004): 77–94.

Ong, Aihwa, & Donald Macun Nonini, ed. *Ungrounded Empires: The Cultural Politics of Modern Chinese Transnationalism* (New York & London: Routledge, 1997).

Safran, William. "Diasporas in Modern Societies: Myths of Homeland and Return," *Diaspora* 1.1 (1991): 83–99.

Stokes, Geoffrey. "Global Citizenship," in *Rethinking Australian Citizenship*, ed. Wayne Hudson & John Kane (Cambridge: Cambridge UP, 2000): 231–42.

Stratton, Jon. *Race Daze: Australia in Identity Crisis* (Sydney: Pluto, 1998).

Tölölyan, Khachig. "The Nation-State and its Others: In Lieu of a Preface," *Diaspora* 1.1 (1991): 3–7.

Turner, Bryan S. "Outline of a General Theory of Cultural Citizenship," in *Culture and Citizenship*, ed. Nick Stevenson (London: Sage, 2001): 11–32.

❧

I

❧ Novels and their Borders

'Beur' Narratives of Self-Identity

❧ Beyond Boundaries and Binaries

PRISCILLA RINGROSE

IN 1993, THE JOURNAL *Foreign Affairs* published an article entitled "The Clash of Civilizations?" by Samuel Huntington, Harvard Professor and former Director of Security Planning for the US National Security Council. Huntington argued that in a post-Cold War world, the crucial distinctions between people were not primarily ideological or economic but cultural.[1] The political rifts of the future would occur not so much between nations but between civilizations. The most important dividing line of all would separate Western civilization from the other seven civilizations that Huntington identifies.[2] Huntington claimed that unity among countries within the same overarching cultural values would rise, while conflict across civilizational boundaries would grow.[3]

In a counter-article, "The Clash of Definitions," Edward Said accuses Huntington of perpetuating a Cold-War-style mentality into the twenty-first century.[4] Said objects to Huntington's simplistic definition of

---

[1] Samuel Huntington, "The Clash of Civilizations?" *Foreign Affairs* 72.3 (1993): 22.

[2] Huntington, "The Clash of Civilizations?" 25. Huntington refers here to seven or eight major civilizations. These include "Western, Confucian, Japanese, Islamic, Hindu, Slavic-Orthodox, Latin American and possibly African civilization."

[3] Huntington, "The Clash of Civilizations," 22.

[4] Edward Said, "The Clash of Definitions," in *Reflections on Exile and Other Essays* (Cambridge MA: Harvard UP, 2002): 570.

civilizations as uniform monolithic units, and questions the logic of his assumption that "other civilizations necessarily clash with the West."[5] He shows how Huntington naturalizes the differences between the West and the rest:

> Thus to build a conceptual framework around the notion of us-versus-them is in effect to pretend that the principal consideration is epistemological and natural – our civilization is known is accepted, theirs is different and strange – whereas in fact the framework separating us from them is belligerent, constructed, and situational.[6]

Said prefers to defend the diversity and hybridity of cultures, pointing to the fusions characteristic of contemporary music, and to the rich crossover between different literatures despite "the existence of powerful national and ideological barriers that separate them."[7] But Said claims that the real weakness of Huntington's thesis is its assumption that civilizations are wholly separate from one another, whereas in fact "the overwhelming evidence is that today's world is in fact a world of mixtures, of migrations, of crossings over."[8] He goes on to refer to the crises of identity suffered by nation-states as a result of the massive global flows of migrants, citing the situations in the USA, Britain and France in particular.

Said's vision of the world conforms closely to that of globalization theorists, interested in capturing the complex interactions between global cultural flows and individual lives. Roland Robertson, for example, coins the term 'glocal', an amalgam of global and local, arguing that the two terms are not mutually exclusive.[9] For Ulrich Beck, this concept is useful in its application to an understanding of personal lives as both assuming

---

[5] Said,"The Clash of Definitions," 570.

[6] "The Clash of Definitions," 577.

[7] "The Clash of Definitions," 583.

[8] "The Clash of Definitions," 587.

[9] Roland Robertson, "Glocalization: Time–Space and Homogeneity–Heterogeneity," in *Global Modernities*, ed. Mike Featherstone, Scott Lash & Roland Robertson (London: Sage, 1995): 25

and transcending the local.[10] The 'glocal' individual, in his complex relations to global cultural phenomena beyond his locally lived life, thus transcends the barriers of Huntington's water-tight, sealed-off civilizations.

I propose to examine the notion of 'glocality' in relation to the descendants of North African migrants in France. I will be taking a literary rather than an anthropological approach, looking at the depiction of identity in the literature of writers who grew up in families where one or both parents emigrated from the Maghreb to France. The term 'beur' is used (controversially) to describe the subset of those descendants of migrants whose parents were post-World War II labour migrants.[11] I will show that both Huntington's and Said's very different understandings of culture provide a useful framework for examining the 'glocal' identity of the 'beur' protagonists portrayed in these novels.

In many of the novels, especially those published in the 1980s, the search for identity is represented in terms of a binary clash between global and local, with the local component identified with the French nation and the global component associated with the Maghrebi nation. Here local and global exist in a conflictual relationship mimicking a Huntington-like clash of civilizations. I suggest that more recent works increasingly point to the fact that the *global* aspects of identity are no longer monopolized by the Maghrebi space. I will show how globalization has opened up new identificatory spaces in these novels beyond the Maghrebi and French nations, pointing to a disjunctive world closer to Said's vision.

But whether or not they are conceived within the binary mode, these narratives are all concerned with mobile selves navigating new identifi-

---

[10] Ulrich Beck, *What is Globalization?*, tr. Patrick Camiller (*Was ist Globalisierung?* 1997; Cambridge: Polity, 2000): 73

[11] The use of the term 'beur' has become contentious. In the 1980s, this appellation was favoured by descendants of Maghrebi migrants and was associated with their entry into social and political activism. However, the term has come to acquire negative connotations which evoke the exclusion and marginalization of such communities within French society. See *Cultures Transnationales de France*, ed. Hafid Gafaïti (Paris: L'Harmattan, 2001): 10–11. Alternative terms are now used, such as "descendants of recent Maghrebi migrants to France" or "descendants of North African immigrants." For practical purposes, I have opted to use the term 'beur', but in inverted commas to indicate its problematic nature.

catory waters. As such, they will be related to Anthony Giddens' account of modernity and its relation to the self, according to which the self is conceived as a reflexive project, sustained through a revisable narrative of self-identity.[12] 'Beur' literature demonstrates that, within this open-ended project of self-identity, categories such as national identification may become part of the revisable narrative of the self.

To return to those novels which do favour a bipolar approach, we find that the conflict of cultures is presented, in Huntington-like terms, as inevitable. The battles raging in these novels are internal conflicts between the protagonists' French and Algerian selves. This conflict is phrased most directly in the title of Souâd Belhaddad's novel *Entre-deux Je: Algérienne? Française? Comment choisir...?* (between two selves: Algerian or French? An impossible choice...). Other novels, such as *Zeida de nulle part* (Zeida from nowhere) and *Une fille sans histoire* (a girl without a [his]story), relate to the binary opposition negatively, as their protagonists present themselves as orphans of both cultures. The sense of living between mutually irreconcilable 'civilizations' is captured by terms such as schizophrenia, contradiction and war:

> Living like the French, behaving differently from them. Buried within me, this symptom of schizophrenia shows signs of life. And of death. Schizophrenia. Does that sound too violent? Well, so be it.[13]
>
> I am in the Algerian war. I carry its conflict.[14]
>
> It was simply running away, she knew that, but to live differently and somewhere else, that could perhaps help her to escape all the contradictions from which she suffered.[15]

According to Alec Hargreaves, it is very rare

[12] Anthony Giddens, *Modernity and Self-Identity: Self and Society in the Late Modern Age* (Cambridge: Polity, 1991): 52.

[13] Souâd Belhaddad, *Entre-deux Je: Algérienne? Française? Comment choisir...?* (Paris: Mango, 2001): 45. All translations in this article are mine.

[14] Nina Bouraoui, *Garçon manqué* (Paris: Stock, 2000): 31.

[15] Leïla Houari, *Zeida de nulle part* (Paris: L'Harmattan, 1985): 41.

> [for] international migrants [to] succeed in inculcating in their descendants a level of attachment to pre-migratory cultural codes which is in any way comparable to their own. In most cases, the necessary precondition for this has been a degree of political control amounting to colonial or quasi-colonial authority.[16]

Although this is borne out in the novels examined, it is nevertheless the case that, as far as the autobiographies of *young women* are concerned, the values of the country of origin still maintain a strong hold over the psyche – the global reference-point is still the culture of the home Maghrebi nation. Writing becomes a way of coming to terms with *guilt*, associated with the perception of having to make an impossible choice between two warring cultures, as Souâd Belhaddad explains:

> The taboos which my culture carries — those incessant threats of hell –- were transmitted to me in France. So I have experienced the guilty need to transgress them and the unspeakable pain of freeing myself from them [...].[17]

Belhaddad's autobiographical account, in common with that of many other female 'beur' writers, involves the costly decision to abandon the traditions prescribed by her family, in favour of a 'modern' life-style. According to Giddens, the notion of 'lifestyle' is by its very nature associated with modernity:

> Lifestyle is not a term which has much applicability to traditional cultures, because it implies choice within a plurality of possible options, and is 'adopted' rather that 'handed down'. Lifestyles are routinised practices […] but the routines followed are reflexively open to change in the light of the mobile nature of self-identity. Each of the small decisions a person makes every day – what to wear, what to eat, how to conduct himself at work, whom to meet with later in the evening – contributes to such routines. Such

---

[16] Alec G. Hargreaves, *Immigration, 'Race' and Ethnicity in Contemporary France* (London: Routledge, 1995): xv.

[17] Belhaddad, *Entre-deux*, 9.

> choices (as well as larger and more consequential ones) are decisions not only about how to act but who to be.[18]

In 'beur' autobiographies produced by young women, many small decisions regarding life-style are made by the main protagonists in the build-up to the fateful decision to break decisively with familial tradition (adopting Western-style dress outside the home, entering into clandestine liaisons with the opposite sex, taking part in forbidden activities such as dances). By stepping out of a traditional setting where identity is "handed down," they enter into a world where they have to decide "who to be," where identity is for the making and where choices (whether trivial or consequential) provide material for a particular narrative of self-identity. The act of writing autobiography can therefore be understood as part of this reflexive process of self-construction. As such, the autobiographical narrative itself contributes to the on-going revisable narrative of self-identity. But in Belhaddad's own telling of her story, the choices that provide material for her particular narrative of self-identity are still conceived primarily in binary terms, as if the building-blocks of identity must be acquired from either French or Algerian culture: "I can no longer bear to carry two worlds – inside, outside. Shame inside, showing off outside. The possible and the forbidden."[19]

Belhaddad uses both the term 'guilt' and the term 'shame' to describe her relation to her parents, to parental law, and also to what she calls her "secret desires."[20] According to Giddens, however, there is an important conceptual difference between the two terms. He associates the notion of 'guilt' with traditional modes of life, in contrast to 'shame', which he relates to modernity. Shame, then, has become modernity's new guilt. And, whereas guilt "depends on mechanisms *extrinsic* to the internally referential systems of modernity," shame comes into play "the more self-identity becomes internally referential."[21] Guilt is a form of anguish most prevalent in types of society where social behaviour is governed according to

---

[18] Giddens, *Modernity and Self-Identity*, 81.

[19] Belhaddad, *Entre-deux,* 71.

[20] *Entre-deux,* 43.

[21] Giddens, *Modernity and Self-Identity,*153.

established moral codes.[22] Shame, on the other hand, "is essentially anxiety about the adequacy of the narrative by means of which the individual sustains a coherent biography."[23] So, whereas guilt expresses the inability to follow moral codes imposed from the outside, shame comes into being when the subject becomes aware of the inconsistencies of the self-referential identity he has constructed for himself.

In Giddens' terms, these women writers experience shame as a result of their conscious understanding of the dislocation between the world of their families and that of late-modern society. But they also live with guilt at transgressing parental moral codes, especially as far as sexual norms are concerned. Novels written by men tend to exhibit less angst. Writers such as Azouz Begag, Akli Tadjer and Mehdi Charef adopt strategies such as humour and irony to address cultural duality and alienation. Omar, the "beur" hero of Akli Tadjer's *Les ANI du 'Tassili'* (the unidentified Arabs of the *Tassili*) explains his identity as follows: " – We are like Canada Dry. We have Arab names, we are as dark as Arabs but we are no longer really Arabs!"[24]

The works of these male authors also manifest a dimension which bypasses the binary, bi-national frame of reference, since their protagonists often affirm a *localized* sense of identity. In *Les ANI du 'Tassili',* Omar, who is travelling on a ferry symbolically located between Algiers and Marseille, enthusiastically identifies himself with his French home town, "La Garenne–Colombes", while cynically referring to the French nation's symbolic exclusion of 'beurs' such as him: "I was the naive victim of this trick [customs] form, imagining that being born in La Garenne-Colombes made me French."[25] Not surprisingly, the novel ends with a final invocation of his home-town: "The *Tassili*'s horn sounded three times in the

---

[22] *Modernity and Self-Identity,* 153.

[23] *Modernity and Self-Identity,* 65.

[24] Akli Tadjer, *Les ANI du 'Tassili'* (Paris: Seuil, 1984): 15. The reference here is to a French advert for the drink product "Canada Dry," which claimed that Canada Dry (fizzy ginger-ale flavoured mineral water) looked like alcohol, tasted like alcohol, but did not contain any alcohol.

[25] Tadjer, *Les ANI,* 12.

port… As for me, I could already see my Garenne–Colombes."[26] Another Omar, the young hero of Azouz Begag's novel *Le gone du Chaâba*,[27] when questioned by his teacher about his origins, proudly refers to the local hospital in Lyon where he was born: "She asked me what age I was when I came from Algeria, and so I proudly observed that I had first seen the light of day in Lyon, in its biggest hospital: Grache-Blache (Grange-Blanche)."[28]

Other works produced by descendants of Maghrebi migrants transcend the binary narrative by opening out onto new identificatory spaces provided by the effects of globalization. The sources of these spaces are provided from the global flow of information and media (TV, film and music).

Georgette!, by Farida Belghoul, is about a seven-year-old 'beur' girl who is seriously disturbed by the dislocation between the worlds of school and family. Unable to cope with the way in which school diminishes her family (her father, the family patriarch is emasculated in her eyes when she discovers his illiteracy), she projects a kind of demented anger onto all who surround her; her family, friends and schoolteacher: "This crazy woman is a cannibal. She eats frogs and gobbles me all up. She nibbles at me and the flesh on my bones disappears."[29]

Georgette periodically withdraws into a dream world, drawing her inspiration from the virtual world of TV violence and fantasy. One source of the various virtual identities she borrows is American westerns, which her family consume avidly, all siding volubly with the Indians. Georgette goes about her daily life imagining herself to be as dangerous as an Indian, face and hands adorned with war paint and armed to the teeth, planning strategic retreats.

Although Giddens states that a person's identity is found above all in "the capacity *to keep a particular narrative going*," he points out that the story maintained cannot be "wholly fictive" if the individual is to function

---

[26] *Les ANI*, 190.

[27] "Gone" refers to a young kid from the city of Lyon, "*Chaâba*" to a shantytown on the outskirt of Lyon.

[28] Azouz Begag, *Le gone du Chaâba* (Paris: Seuil, 1986): 201.

[29] Farida Belghoul, *Georgette!* (Paris: Barrault, 1986): 131.

within society: "It [the individual's biography] must continually integrate events which occur in the external world, and sort them into the ongoing 'story' about the self."[30] In Georgette's case, the narrative created privileges events from the fictional world, leading to a story about the self and others which has no relation to 'reality': "Flip, flop, bare feet in the puddles. I've worked it out! Finally, I am the daughter of a Red-Indian Chief, my brother is his son and my mother is a queen. At my side is Michelle, the down-and-out!"[31] If self-identity is a reflexive project sustained through a revisable narrative of self-identity, then Georgette's story illustrates both the purposes and the limits of such an open-ended project. On the one hand, the incorporated fictional elements originating in the global film industry create an inner world which serves to diffract the dual poles of national identity in which she has to negotiate her 'real life', enabling her to escape and counter the French-Algerian double-bind. On the other hand, this new narrative of the self, being based on fiction, cannot realistically be sustained within the external social world.

In another novel, *Boumkoeur*, by the 'beur' Rachid Djaïdani, the Huntington-style binary cultural model of East versus West, French against Algerian, is almost completely replaced by the story of a new subculture. This is neither French nor Algerian, but a multicultural urban *cité*-culture of drugs, violence and coded slang. Ethnic specificity is eroded in a sea of immigrant kids of unspecified origin. Eschewing the level of the national, their identity draws its *local* aspect from neighbourhood multi-ethnic gang affiliations and its *global* aspects from African-American hip-hop, with its rap rhythms:

> He holds out his fist, for the shake, now fist to fist is the way to go, the salute is the evolution of badland population, pumped from black American ghettoes [...]. What comes round goes round, I'm the hip hop hound. Tapping into rapping I swing a salute with a fist like a funk, I'm the kind that does a bunk.[32]

---

[30] Giddens, *Modernity and Self-Identity,* 54.

[31] Belghoul, *Entre-deux*, 86.

[32] Rachid Djaïdani, *Boumkœur* (Paris: Seuil, 1999): 32. I have opted for a loose translation of the original, to convey the rhythm.

According to Giddens, "the more tradition loses its hold, the more daily life is reconstituted in terms of the dialectical interplay of the local and the global, the more individuals are forced to negotiate lifestyle choices amongst a variety of options."[33] He stresses the fact, however, that life-style options are not simply the prerogative of the privileged few – for, while "class divisions and other fundamental lines of inequality, such as gender or ethnicity can be *defined* in terms of differential access to forms of self-actualization and empowerment," the term 'life-style', he claims, also refers to choices made and courses of action followed under conditions of material deprivation, and as such life-style patterns "may sometimes also involve the more or less deliberate rejection of more widely diffused forms of behaviour and consumption."[34]

In the case of *Boumkoeur*, the protagonists' identification with the transnational hip-hop movement provides an example of life-style choices opened up by the effects of the globalization, but which are nevertheless available for those on the margins of mainstream social and political life. Global travel has also opened up new identificatory spaces for many of these writers. Some attempt to escape the cultural duality in which France imprisons them by indulging in what Belhaddad terms geographical bulimia. For Belhaddad the excess of geographical spaces enables her to fashion for herself "an identity which merges all the continents I have embraced."[35] But for her and for half-French / half-Algerian Nina Bouraoui, one particular geographical space stands out, a third space which releases them from the eternal Algerian–French binary. That *third space* is Italy, a land where they feel they can be themselves:

> Everything was so easy. Being. […]. I was not longer French. I was no longer Algerian. I was myself. With my body.[36]

---

[33] Giddens, *Modernity and Self-Identity,* 5.

[34] *Modernity and Self-Identity,* 6.

[35] Belhaddad, *Entre-deux*, 149.

[36] Bouraoui, *Garçon Manqué*, 184.

> In Italian I can be trusting, and can say "I love you" without the feeling of betraying anyone. Or of betraying anything whatsoever.[37]

The fact that the global village provides new identifications has led globalization theorists such as Gordon Mathews to come up with new theories of the cultural shaping of the self and to revise traditional definitions of culture. For much of the last century, the assumption (in Huntington mode) was that cultures existed as separate bounded units, enabling anthropologists such as Clifford Geertz to compare contrasting Javanese, Balinese and Moroccan concepts of the self.[38] In this sense, culture was identified with nation and was equated with "the way of life of a people."[39] But insofar as the source of culture can now be identified, along Said-like lines, as the 'global village', then culture can now be said to equal "the information and identities available from the [global] cultural supermarket."[40]

Mathews proposes a theory of the cultural shaping of the self which takes into account the influences of both nation and global village.[41] He suggests that the self is shaped culturally on three different levels of consciousness. The first and deepest level, which he dubs a taken-for-granted level, refers to the way that we are all unconsciously shaped by the particular language and society into which we are born. The second level of cultural shaping relates to the way in which the nation-state promotes specific social codes of behaviour (through state media, public education, and the like). The third and shallowest level of cultural shaping refers to the wares of the cultural supermarket: i.e. to aspects of culture which we consciously select from an array of global choices.

The effect of the global cultural supermarket on personal culture may be considered nothing more than a superficial exoticization of taste

---

[37] Belhaddad, *Entre-deux*, 129.

[38] Gordon Mathews, *Global Culture/Individual Identity* (London: Routledge, 2000): 2–3.

[39] Mathews, *Global Culture/Individual Identity*, 11.

[40] *Global Culture/Individual Identity*, 11.

[41] *Global Culture/Individual Identity*, 12–16.

(Japanese restaurants, salsa dance classes). But it can equally well be seen to penetrate more deeply. We could cite the case of Europeans who have converted to Buddhism. Or we could take the example of a Third-World country such as Bhutan, until recently a highly isolated society, where the introduction of cable TV has resulted in significant changes in local habits, including "an insatiable appetite for western products, and different attitudes towards love and relationships."[42]

What Mathews contends is that the global cultural supermarket is eroding the cultural norms propagated by the state. He believes that the taken-for-granted aspects of identity inculcated by the nation are shrinking and that the global cultural supermarket is replacing them. As a result of globalization, then, we could say that identity is becoming more and more of a choice.

How does this theory apply to our protagonists? Obviously, the choices offered by the global cultural supermarket weaken the nation-state's cultural claims on all sectors of a given population to a greater or lesser extent. But in the case of descendants of migrants, the experience of two sets of national values, that of the parent(s) country of origin and that of the 'home country', *itself* relativizes the notion of a nation state's exclusive claims on the individual.

In the case of the 'beurs', exposure to French cultural codes interferes with any automatic interiorization of Arab national values. In Mounsi's work *Territoire d'outre-ville* (trans-urban territory), the narrator accords superstitious significance to his grandmother's Islamic faith: "As long as her image spiralled round me, with her prayers, her benedictions and her small hopes – I was saved."[43] Yet ultimately, his experience of French secularism leads him to distance himself from religion: "God has nothing but a poetic value for me."[44] On the other hand, many protagonists voice nostalgia for the lost security which traditional values provide, as Zeida's attitude towards her mother's religious fatalism indicates: "You would

---

[42] David Walsh, "Ancient Bhutan's Encounter with the Electronic Age," *National Institute on Media and the Family* (September 2003): 1. http://www.mediafamily.org/mediawise/abe_mw.shtml

[43] Mounsi, *Territoire d'outre-ville* (Paris: Stock, 1995): 37.

[44] *Territoire d'outre-ville*, 35.

speak, I would listen, wishing desperately that I could be like you, and accept life as it comes, You haven't had a happy life but anything will make you smile. I'm ashamed of myself, the more I rebel, the less I know what I want."[45]

In a number of novels, secondary characters are encountered (often an older brother) who, while not necessarily strictly following the precepts of Islam, nevertheless adopt fundamentalist behaviour-patterns. This adherence to strict religious forms of behaviour can be understood as providing a solution or counterweight to the openness of modern society: "The more 'enclosing' a given religious order is, the more it 'resolves' the problem of how to live in a world of multiple options."[46]

The function of these protagonists is to act as opponents of the quest for freedom on the part of the main (female) characters. These young men are often self-appointed spies and inquisitors who jump on any perceived infringement of familial law. In the case of *Ils disent que je suis une beurette* (they call me a 'beur' girl) by Soraya Nini, the big brother earns the nickname "KGB" because of the sophisticated surveillance techniques he uses to keep tabs on his young sisters: "'You are a whore, I am going to kill you! Everyone is laughing at us now. I am going to do your face in! Then we'll see if you still want to hang around with men!'."[47]

This incident illustrates the extreme segmentation common to the experience of these young women, caught between the strict limits of their domestic situation and the multiple freedoms of life outside the home. Giddens uses the term "lifestyle sectors" to describe a "segment" or "time–space 'slice'" of an individual's overall activities, within which certain modes of behaviour are adopted.[48] He maintains that because of the diversity of modern life, individuals move between different life-style sectors, in which they may adopt very different modes of behaviour. In the case of the 'beurs', this variance can be extreme, and it is often the interference which occurs between a life-style sector and the traditional

---

45 Houari, *Zeida de nulle part*, 38.

46 Giddens, *Modernity and Self-Identity*, 142.

47 Soraya Nini, *Ils disent que je suis une beurette* (Paris: Fixot, 1993): 68–69.

48 Giddens, *Modernity and Self-Identity*, 83.

home setting (as in the example above) that causes conflict and, in some cases, acts as a catalyst for change.

As far as "KGB" is concerned, he appears to experience a different kind of segmentation, whose contradictions are unproblematically assimilated:

> KGB has his own special reading of the pornographic variety. My mother may well have a fit whenever she finds them, stashed under the mattress, and throw them in the bin each time, that does not stop them from constantly reappearing.[49]

These 'fundamentalist' characters, whose lives are subject to contradictions, serve only to underline the ambiguous feelings which the main female protagonists feel towards their religion.

The ambivalence demonstrated by the main characters towards Islamic religious values also applies to their attitudes towards French cultural values. These are not unquestionably internalized, either because they clash with the family's cultural shaping or because they originate in a referential world which necessarily excludes the migrant. In *Le gone du Chaâba*, Azouz Begag uses humour and irony to expose the manner in which the French education system marginalizes his young 'beur' hero. The master speaks:

> "We are all descendants of Vercingetorix!"
> "Yes, Sir!"
> "Our country France, has a surface area of ..."
> "Yes, Sir!"
> The teacher is always right. If he says that we are all descended from the Gauls, then he is right and too bad if we don't have the same moustaches.[50]

National identity for Omar is no longer a fixed, unitary category but a floating sign, with which he can play around with for his own benefit, as an incident in which he is confronted by his Jewish classmates reveals:

---

[49] Nini, *Ils disent que je suis une beurette*, 63.
[50] Azouz Begag, *Le gone du Chaâba* (Paris: Seuil, 1986): 62.

> "Hey, you! Are you an Arab or a Jew?" asked the oldest of the Taboul boys, during play-time. [...] Since the terrible question has been put to me, I have had the time to think of a thousand consequences which my reply might have, in a fraction of a second. I must not give the impression of hesitating.
>
> "I am a Jew!" I said, convinced.[51]

The novel *Une fille sans histoire* by Tassadit Imache demonstrates in a more consequential manner how national identity can detach itself from a given acquisition and enter into the realm of conscious choice. Lil's father is Algerian, but he has never shared any aspect of his culture with her. Because Lil's mother is French, Lil's father regards his own children as racial bastards. The French mother, on the other hand, has made it her life-long ambition to erase all signs of her children's Arabness, overriding their Arab names with French names (Lil was originally named Leila). As a teenager, Lil decides to create an Algerian identity for herself. This is not a national identity as shaped by the workings of the nation-state or enforced by migrant parents, but an identity consciously built up from scratch through the shelves of the local library: "In the days that followed, she borrowed all the books she could find on Algeria from the library of the town where she was boarding. On Algeria's geography. On the origins and the culture of its people."[52]

Ironically, in Lil's attempt to create an Algerian identity from point zero, both definitions of culture come together, that of "the way of life of a people" and that of the "choices available on the supermarket (library) shelves," since Lil shops for, or buys into, *the way of life of a people*. This 'Algerianness' is no longer something she has been born into but a latter-day construction of home. National identity is portrayed as a fictional narrative which can be rewritten at will.

We recall, in conclusion, how Said maintains that the conflict between civilizations is a narrative created by Huntington in the interests of Western supremacy. Similarly, in a more specific context, the sociologist Nacira Guenif Souilamas maintains that the conflict between France and

---

[51] Begag, *Le gone,* 188.

[52] Tassadit Imache, *Une fille sans histoire* (Paris: Calmann–Lévy, 1989): 117.

Algeria is a fiction perpetuated by the French state in the interests of its national self-importance.[53] Both fictions, whether the clash of civilizations or of nations, and however dubiously constructed, are powerful narratives with many adherents. In the literature produced by the descendants of Maghrebi migrants, we see that many of the protagonists construct new narratives of the self by internalizing this fiction, that some create alternative fictions, while yet others, by stepping out of the bipolar dynamic, open out into the multicultural borderless world envisioned by Said.

WORKS CITED

Beck, Ulrich. *What is Globalization?*, tr. Patrick Camiller (*Was ist Globalisierung?* 1997; Cambridge: Polity, 2000).

Begag, Azouz. *Le gone du Chaâba* (Paris: Seuil, 1986).

Belghoul, Farida. *Georgette!* (Paris: Barrault, 1986).

Belhaddad, Souâd. *Entre-deux Je: Algérienne? Française? Comment choisir...?* (Paris: Mango, 2001).

Bouraoui, Nina. *Garçon manqué* (Paris: Stock, 2000).

Djaïdani, Rachid. *Boumkœu* (Paris: Seuil, 1999).

Gafaïti, Hafid, ed. *Cultures Transnationales de France* (Paris: L'Harmattan, 2001).

Giddens, Anthony. *Modernity and Self-Identity: Self and Society in the Late Modern Age* (Cambridge: Polity, 1991).

Hargreaves, Alec G. *Immigration, 'Race' and Ethnicity in Contemporary France* (London: Routledge, 1995).

Houari, Leïla. *Zeida de nulle part* (Paris: L'Harmattan, 1985).

Huntington, Samuel. "The Clash of Civilizations?" *Foreign Affairs* 72.3 (1993): 22–49.

Imache, Tassadit. *Une fille sans histoire* (Paris: Calmann–Lévy, 1989).

Mathews, Gordon. *Global Culture/Individual Identity* (London: Routledge, 2000).

Mounsi. *Territoire d'outre-ville* (Paris: Stock, 1995).

Nini, Soraya. *Ils disent que je suis une beurette* (Paris: Fixot, 1993).

---

[53] Nacira Guénif Souilamas, *Des "beurettes" aux descendantes d'immigrants nord-africains* (Paris: Grasset, 2000): 50.

Said, Edward, "The Clash of Definitions: On Samuel Huntington," in Said, *Reflections on Exile and Other Essays* (Cambridge MA: Harvard UP, 2002): 569–90.

Souilamas, Nacira Guénif. *Des "beurettes" aux descendantes d'immigrants nord-africains* (Paris: Grasset, 2000).

Tadjer, Akli. *Les ANI du 'Tassili'* (Paris: Seuil, 1984).

Walsh, David. "Ancient Bhutan's Encounter with the Electronic Age," *National Institute on Media and the Family* (September 2003) <http://www .mediafamily .org/mediawise/abe_mw.shtml>.

❧

Allegories of Ambivalence

❧ Scottish Fiction, Britain and Empire

ALAN FREEMAN

THIS ESSAY OUTLINES SOME FEATURES of Scottish fiction relating to Scotland's historically ambiguous engagement with Britain and the British Empire, and goes on to examine key nineteenth-century examples, by Walter Scott and Robert Louis Stevenson, and by the leading contemporary novelist William Boyd. Scotland's novel tradition has often been regarded as unsuccessful, but recent 'post-' stages of theory have offered alternative perspectives on its textual strategies. Scots have always occupied a peculiar relation to Britain as both active participant in and marginal Other to the State and its Empire. Major narratives of the expansionist age are structured around binary relational values which, in effect, allegorize that ambivalent status. In our postcolonial era, William Boyd's apparently traditional writing locates British characters pursuing meaning in end-of-Empire and post-imperial environments. Like his predecessors, Boyd exemplifies Edward Said's insights into historical interconnectedness, and the hybridity of the colonial encounter as defined by Homi Bhabha; each author thus dramatizes selfhood as shaped by cultural interaction within Britain and across territories affected by empire.

Ambivalence

The rich seam of colonial analysis was initiated by Said in *Orientalism*, which sets out the basic terms of orientalist projection by European onto non-European cultures:

> Along with all other people variously regarded as backward, degenerate, uncivilised and retarded, the Orientals were viewed in a framework constructed out of biological determinism and moral-political admonishment. The Oriental was linked thus to elements in Western society (delinquents, the insane, women, the poor) having in common an identity at best described as lamentably alien. [1]

While generating its potentially irrecoverable alterity of Oriental from European, the binary process can be seen to extend within as well as between cultures, as the above quotation suggests, in a complex of relations based on gender, class, region, religion, sexuality and sanity, each of which may be cross-cut by further contradictions of inclusion and exclusion. The status of Scotland within Britain has always been ambivalent: neither actively engaged in national resistance, like Ireland, nor equal partner in the new State, it was both colonizer abroad and, partly, colonized at home. Scots were at the forefront of British advance at the expense of indigenous populations across the globe, while remaining in anxious thrall to the dominant values which determined their own movements.

This double-sided pattern has evolved across centuries. Establishing itself as one of Europe's first nations, Scotland, with its wars of independence in the early fourteenth century (led, of course, by Mel Gibson), secured the Declaration of Arbroath (1320), which asserted the autonomy of the Scottish people from the external threat of England's Plantagenet monarchs in the south. This obscured an older internal division: that between the Gaelic-speaking culture which receded to the highlands – the Gaeltacht – and those communities who spoke 'Inglis', the latter enjoying greater links with mainland Europe and the powerful southern neighbour.

---

[1] Edward W. Said, *Orientalism* (London: Vintage, 1978): 207.

While these remained separated by geography, language and custom, the two nations' fortunes were drawn inextricably closer by the Union of Crowns in 1603; a century later, the Union of Parliaments in 1707 put an end to an autonomous Scotland. The unique State of Great Britain added further, recognizably modern dualities to Scots' experience of their Scottishness.

It was the age of Enlightenment and of Jacobite risings, of achievement and assimilation. The greatest minds produced by the Scottish education system included David Hume, Adam Smith, Adam Ferguson, William Robertson and William Reid. A distinctive world-view emerged from the new social sciences which developed in the universities and the intellectual life centred on neoclassical Edinburgh. In the model of history formulated by Hume and Robertson, humanity progressed, step by step, from agrarian simplicity to technologically advanced, urban civilization. Contemporary Scotland was deemed to be on the leading edge of this linear movement, permitting some to crow in celebration of their anointed nation: "We look back on the savage condition of our ancestors with the triumph of superiority."[2]

Not everyone was impressed. Urbane condescension among the English elite was scarcely dented by ideas from the economically subordinate north, and Samuel Johnson could mock Scotland in his dictionary: "Oats – a grain which in England is generally given to horses, but in Scotland supports the people."[3] In these decades, the Scottish 'cultural cringe' was enshrined, boastful assertiveness being matched by, or covering over, assumed inferiority. Hume had felt so humiliated by ridicule of his Scots accent in his first travails in England that he tried to mimic polite English speech (failing dismally). Along with the coffee-houses in which leading thinkers could share ideas, there also flourished clubs dedicated to teaching educated Scots to ape genteel English diction. This was merely the bourgeois concomitant of the fate suffered by those from the Gaeltacht who fought against the absorption of the old nation into the new Britain.

---

[2] Thomas Warton, quoted in William Ferguson, *Scotland: 1689 to the Present* (Edinburgh: Oliver & Boyd, 1968): 215.

[3] Samuel Johnson, *A Dictionary of the English Language* (1755; New York: Levenger, 2003).

To its opponents, Jacobitism and the fanatical Highlanders who supported it in the dramatic uprisings of 1715 and '45 were the very epitome of historical anachronism. The final defeat of Charles Edward Stuart's retreating forces at Culloden in 1746 was the last military battle fought on British soil; one consequence was the brutal pacification of Highland communities. This was an internal colonization carried out by Lowland Scots and English in the name of the new Britain.

Curiously, as the old Scotland was being superseded by the modernity of which its historians were so proud, a kind of ersatz alternative arose in its place. Before Walter Scott or the long, slow expulsion of the Gaels in the first half of the nineteenth century known as the Highland Clearances, Scottish identity became associated with the symbols of its own, now virtually defunct, Other. As recently as 1745, when Highlanders marched into unprepared Edinburgh and then into England, propagandist prose and ballads circulated:

> Thieves and Rogues come at his Back
> Those *Amorites* from North,
>   A bare-ars'd nasty lousy pack
> Come o'er the Water of Forth [4]

Such specifically Orientalist representation had accompanied Gaelic–Inglis relations for centuries. Just as Scotland embodied the unacceptable Other in England, so, for Lowland Scots and English alike, Gaels were the hordes at the gate, with their barbarous tongue, ragged clothing, and savage conduct. As with images of Native Americans in the nineteenth century or African Americans in our own time, the Celts in this image titillate as well as threaten polite society, their exposed flesh and physical energy conveying a hint of sexual potency as well. But in the wake of Highland demise and the growing drift of Lowland Scots abroad, the ugly stereotype graduated into the positive Other beloved of antiquarian nostalgia – bearer of the naturalness, loyalty and physical courage rendered

---

[4] From *The Original and Conduct of the Young Pretender* (1745), quoted in William Donaldson, *The Jacobite Song: Political Myth and National Identity* (Aberdeen: Aberdeen UP, 1988): 40.

redundant by encroaching materialism. Scottish reality was determined by imperatives in the wider economic world, but so, too, was the means of preserving a sense of national identity: the only refuge from the British present was this symbolic, vestigial Celtic Otherness. National sentiment might take the form of the kitsch appropriations on which the modern tourist industry is founded – the pastiche kilt worn by George IV on his State visit to Edinburgh in 1822, the fiction of clan tartans – but, also, they were genuine totems for a people disoriented by the great European advance.

As a new stage in history got underway, these people spread far and wide. "Between the Battle of Waterloo and the end of the American Civil War in 1865, the British Empire grew by an average of 100,000 square miles per year," writes Arthur Herman, summarizing the distances Scots traversed:

> At each turn, a coterie of Scots or men and women of Scottish descent took the lead. They operated sheep farms in New South Wales, grew rye and barley in Lower Ontario, worked in lumber camps in British Columbia, trapped beaver and otter along the Mackenzie River, managed coffee plantations in Ceylon, sold ships' stores in the Falkland Islands, guarded the Officers' Club in Mysore – and traded opium in Hong Kong and Canton.[5]

Ambivalence about that experience is encapsulated in the very title of Herman's book: *How the Scots Invented the Modern World, or, the True Story of How Western Europe's Poorest Nation Made Our World and Everything In It*. Written by an American historian of Scottish descent, it is characteristically ironic, boastful but wry, suggesting uncertainty about whether or not this narrative requires the endorsement of others, doubt about whether the scale of the Scottish diaspora betokens triumph or defeat. The author goes on to detail the ambiguous achievements of Scots emigrants to Britain's colonies: the hard work, ingenuity and fortitude required to succeed in farming and trade; the misappropriation of land and

---

[5] Arthur Herman, *How the Scots Invented the Modern World, or, the True Story of How Western Europe's Poorest Nation Made Our World and Everything In It* (New York: Crown, 2001): 294.

resources; and the cruelties of the oppression visited on colonial 'subjects'. Scots, in fact, earned a reputation for harsh, authoritarian rule, especially in the plantations of the Caribbean and the American South, where, notoriously, in later resistance to the forward march of Enlightenment, Scottish families would help found the Ku Klux Klan. As the sun slowly set on the Empire in the twentieth century, Scots' disaffection with their Britishness was mostly polarized between incompatible parties of nationalism and socialism, a habit still predominant in the recently reconstituted Scottish parliament of devolution.

The study of literature, like the evaluation of this history, has reflected a similar insecurity. Scottish education has come to value indigenous culture in ways unthinkable in the past, yet Scottish literature remains not only little known outside Scotland, but not even read by the majority of staff in departments of English literature in Scottish universities. However, as we move beyond the duality of over-endorsement or excessive disavowal, the study of fiction has benefitted from placing texts in the broader theoretical perspectives which have developed in the post-imperial decades. How might the transcultural theories of Said and Bhabha refine readings of Scottish novels?

Edward Said points to the omissions prepetrated by texts, the salient contextual information which may be elided in works of the realist tradition. Most broadly, the prioritization in much Western literature of beauty, personal emotion and the Universal Human Condition occludes the particularities of historical struggle, dominance, and exploitation. More specifically, Said elaborates as follows on the significance of space in the novels of Jane Austen:

> After Lukacs and Proust, we have become accustomed to regarding the novel's plot and structure as constituted mainly by temporality that we have overlooked the fundamental role of space, geography and location.[6]

---

[6] Edward W. Said, "Jane Austen and Empire," in *Raymond Williams: Critical Perspectives*, ed. Terry Eagleton (London: Polity, 1989): 156.

Said goes on to emphasize the expanse of geographical and social space that these elements trace in their interconnection with the rapidly changing economic structures of British society and its increasing dependence on the fruits of Empire. This sense of interconnection is useful when relating Scottish narrative to history. Cairns Craig invokes the spatial dimensions of Scots' experience to reconsider the question of why Scottish fiction is not the same as its English counterpart. Scotland, he writes, became an unbounded nation:

> There can be no coherent narrative of the nation not because the nation lacks narrative development but for precisely the opposite reason: its narrative spills out over many territories; it cannot be accommodated within the continuities demanded by the genre of a national history.[7]

Where Austen's concern with a recognizable, unitary community requires elision of the wider interconnections that shape the fate of her heroines, we find that Scottish novelists lend greater emphasis to the increasingly transnational trajectories of Scots' experiences as they journeyed outwards along those routes of connection. The arc of diaspora becomes a structuring element in narrative.

But the mediated condition of Scottishness predicates a further complexity when the Scot as European colonizer encounters the non-European 'Other'. Homi Bhabha's concept of hybridity has particular relevance here. Bhabha shifts attention from the content of the otherness imposed by colonizers on the colonized to the subtleties and instabilities which occur in the border territories between them. This applies to reality as well as to consequent forms of writing. For Bhabha, colonial identity is a condition shaped by fear and desire. The 'Other' is separated, but retains a desired quality, and a symptom of this process is that each side in some way mimics the features of the other. The result is a new hybrid formation; colonizer and colonized are each altered by the relation: "The *menace* of mimicry is its *double* vision which in disclosing the ambivalence of

[7] Cairns Craig, *The Modern Scottish Novel: Narrative and National Imagination* (Edinburgh: Edinburgh UP, 1999): 237.

colonial discourse also disrupts its authority."[8] An inevitable consequence of the encounter is paranoia, aggressive projection leading to its contrary, the sense of persecution by the colonized. This, too, is an experience beyond bounds, with the potential to destabilize the already insecure status of the Scot as Briton. These perspectives illuminate many Scottish novels, both in identifying characteristic uses of space and in examining ambiguities of identity in the border encounter.

Fiction of the Colonial Age: Walter Scott and Robert Louis Stevenson

As Britain rose to world prominence in the nineteenth century, key Scottish writers worked with some of these issues in their fiction. Where Jane Austen elides the geographical connections on which her fictional worlds were built, Walter Scott, in the historical novel, and Robert Louis Stevenson, in his idiosyncratic Gothic tales, do the reverse, spectacularly foregrounding the contrasting lands across which history's dramas are played. Scott portrays the collision between noble tradition and modern efficiency out of which historical advance is forged, an innovation which earned the praise of Georg Lukács and provided the template for a genre which extends from *The Last of the Mohicans* to the recent film *The Last Samurai*.[9] In Walter Scott's *Waverley* (1814), set during the last Jacobite rising, Edward Waverley is a dreamy young Englishman sent to Scotland to improve his worldly education. While there, he is captured by Highland bandits and finds himself participating with the clans in the insurrection. In the spatial/temporal metaphor of the Enlightenment historians, Scotland was a nation not only made up of two cultures but also undergoing two separate stages in historical development. To cross the Highland Line in space was not only to leave one culture for another, it was to travel temporally from the present into the past. This is exactly the way Scott uses his non-heroic protagonist, whose wavering loyalties enable sympathetic

---

[8] Homi Bhabha, *The Location of Culture* (London: Routledge, 1994): 88.

[9] See Georg Lukács, *The Historical Novel*, tr. Hannah & Stanley Mitchell (Harmondsworth: Penguin, 1981); James Fenimore Cooper, *The Last of the Mohicans* (1826; Oxford UP, 1992).

portrayal of both sides of the conflict. The form directly embodies Said's geographical interconnectedness, as vast, separating distances are spanned and the opposed communities harmonized in the new economy. Waverley's movement follows a map of the economic dynamic behind social change.

Moreover, the writing exemplifies the construction of new identities out of the struggle. Scott's Romanticism finds voice in the rich evocation of lost Celtic tradition, but this is a perception filtered through the mountainous grandeur of the Gaeltacht. The projections this involves accommodate his sympathetic British/Scottish perspective. For example, Edward encounters Flora Mac-Ivor, sister of the clan chieftain Fergus, amid the sexualized backdrop of a glistening waterfall:

> The rocks now receded, but still showed their grey and shaggy crests rising among the copse-wood. Still higher, rose eminences and peaks, some bare, some clothed with wood, some round and purple with heath, and others splintering into rocks and crags. [...] Here, like one of those lovely forms which decorate the landscapes of Poussin, Waverley found Flora gazing on the waterfall.[10]

Highland scenery is inscribed with energies suppressed in polite society, Celtic culture is equated with nature's bounty. As a highly rewarded representative of the new Britain, Scott demonstrates Bhabha's border-line anxiety, guilt about the destruction of the Gaels, and projection of desire onto them, as in this scene; but, in so doing, he attributes to Gaeldom precisely the valour and martial threat that justify its repression by the State. Ultimately, the author displaces Highland culture into the compensatory realm of art: as we see, this description locates its subjects firmly within an imaginative frame (the metaphorized mountain, the landscapes of Poussin), and Flora and Fergus will be immortalized in portraiture after their demise. This leaves the narrator to reconcile the lost past with the thriving present. How better to do so than by naturalizing the new political

---

[10] Walter Scott, *Waverley, or, 'Tis Sixty Years Since* (1814; Harmondsworth: Penguin, 1972): 176.

topography? Describing how an influx of wealth and commerce has transformed Scotland since Culloden, he observes:

> But the change, though steadily and rapidly progressive, has, nevertheless, been gradual; and, like those who drift down the stream of a deep and smooth river, we are not aware of the progress we have made until we fix our eye on the now-distant point from which we set out.[11]

Far from the dirt and noise of industry, this progress flows inevitably across nature's contours. The momentum of modernity is onwards, ever onwards; however virtuous older Scottish traditions might be, they cannot withstand this impetus, and pragmatism dictates their dismissal. Scots could savour the rewards of their Britishness while retaining the strictly cultural patriotism centred on the images so colourfully depicted by Scott. Thereafter, visions of nation in Scotland – as in Ireland – would feature a sense of absence at its centre, and be sustained by the persistent elegy to its perceived demise known as the Celtic Twilight. But the dead do not always go away, and figures of the depressed may not be so obliging as to fade into the past, even in Scott. The vast sweep of his epics allegorizes historical advance, but it is an advance accompanied by expanding areas of instability and doubt.

Such instabilities are the norm in Robert Louis Stevenson's best stories. Where Scott offers grand spectacle, Stevenson's Gothic mode features strange spatial disjunctions, unreliable narrators, and troubling indeterminacy at the point of colonial contact. He summarized the settings used in his best work, *The Master of Ballantrae*, thus: "scene Scotland – the States – Scotland – India – Scotland – and the States again; so it jumps like a flea."[12] The story also hinges on the 'Forty-Five Rebellion, but, far from this being a narrative resolution of national duality, dispersal and threat are the key motifs. Having joined the rising on behalf of Bonnie Prince Charlie following the arbitrary toss of a coin, James, the eldest son

---

[11] Scott, *Waverley*, 340.

[12] Robert Louis Stevenson, *The Master of Ballantrae* (1892; Oxford UP, 1983): Introduction, ix.

of the Durie family of Ballantrae, is banished in the rebellion's aftermath, leaving the title of Master, and his fiancée, to his brother Henry. The main narrator is the family retainer MacKellar, who shapes his material to suit his disapproval of the elder brother, while accounts by James's disreputable accomplices provide as much inconsistency as MacKellar does. If this suggests a binary opposition between two versions of Scotland, it is one in which the beaten Scottish Other keeps returning to haunt those at home. Additionally, far from embodying a traditional nobility, James exudes the dangerous charm of the Byronic anti-hero, and his dissolute habits drain the estate of its wealth, drawing his brother and MacKellar across continents in pursuit of him. By the end, he appears to have died and to lie buried in the American wilderness, though even this is unclear.

Conversely, where Scott's river naturalizes the linear flow of progress, in Stevenson it transports characters into uncharted imaginative territories. One narrator, another uprooted Jacobite, the Irishman Burke, recounts his journey with James:

> The town of Albany was at that time much concerned in contraband trade across the desert with the Indians and the French. This, as it was highly illegal, relaxed their loyalty, and as it brought them in relation with the politest people on the earth, divided even their sympathies. In short, they were like all the smugglers in the world, spies and agents ready-made for either party.[13]

They travel from order and stability to amorality and menace. The geographical expanses of America may represent the menace of the unknown, but it is the Europeans who fill them with chaos, creating then crossing borders on their expedient way. As the passage continues,

> Our Albanian, besides, was a very honest man indeed, and very greedy; and, to crown our luck, he conceived a great delight in our society. Before we had reached the town of New York we had come to a full agreement, that he should carry us as far as Albany upon his ship, and thence put us on a way to pass the boundaries and join the French.[14]

---

[13] Stevenson, *The Master of Ballantrae*, 62.

[14] Stevenson, *The Master of Ballantrae*, 62.

Their odyssey allegorizes the instability of Scotland and Scottishness. Stevenson's colonial encounter follows Said's lines of interconnection, but, in keeping with Bhabha, its binary clarity slips and slides as James brings the wilderness back home with him. Centreless Scotland comes under threat from the encounter with Otherness. For example, MacKellar describes overhearing James speaking in the strange tongue of his sub-continental-Indian servant Secundra Dass:

> I drew nearer, and stood like a man dreaming. Here was certainly a human voice, and that in my own master's house, and yet I knew it not; certainly human speech, and that in my native land; and yet listen as I pleased, I could not catch one syllable. An old tale started up in my mind of a fairy wife (or perhaps only a wandering stranger), that came to the place of my fathers some generations back, and stayed a matter of a week, talking often in a tongue that signified nothing to the hearers; and went again, as she had come, under cloud of night, leaving not so much as a name behind her.[15]

Alien diction uttered in the intimacy of his master's house activates in MacKellar the frisson of Otherness repressed within his national boundaries: the ancient, the gypsy, the female, the fairy, all tending in his mind towards the unnameable silence of nullity. Where movement across countries leads to a final harmony in Scott's *Waverley*, the emigration of Stevenson's Scots does not consolidate Scotland, it attenuates it, allowing the irresistible back-flow of a menacing Other to rush in from the outside. Ballantrae might be the counterpart of Jane Austen's community, but where her social hierarchies are sustained by discreetly draining the resources from the global network whose centre they occupy, in this case the opposite again occurs – the home is depleted by the atavist on its highly visible edges. In this novel, the Scottish dispersal bestows paranoia and dread amid the collapse of meaningful structures of nation, home, family and self.

---

[15] Stevenson, *The Master of Ballantrae*, 152–53.

Fiction of the Post-Colonial Age: William Boyd

Echoes of Said and Bhabha, Scott and Stevenson resound in the writing of William Boyd, whose characters seek structure in lives stretched across the moral and political contours of a world emerging from the age of empire. Reflecting the basic facts of his own expatriate upbringing, William Boyd's novels are often set in late- or postcolonial locations such as East Africa or the Caribbean; the action often takes place during wars; the characters usually portrayed are rootless Britons adrift in a changing world; and the design of fictions mostly resembles that of the nineteenth-century *Bildungsroman*, or at least a disjointed, updated version of it. John James Todd, the protagonist of *The New Confessions*, recounts his life as miserable middle-class private-school boy, British soldier, bohemian film-maker, and elderly, frail recluse. Leaving Scotland for England, Todd traverses the battlefields of two World Wars, Western Europe in crisis, and is drawn, via Mexico, to the beacon of modern exiles, the USA, only to flee again, this time driven out by McCarthyism and personal feuding.

Todd's voyage across the century corresponds to British imperial fortunes in the same period, but his transnational tale owes much to his Scottish background. He makes direct use of Stevenson's spatial analogue to summarize the flea-like trajectory of his own life: "The geography of my early life, its fixed points and certainties, were hopelessly out of date now."[16] A binary relation develops between departures from Scotland and disruptive returns. Todd finds the moral and imaginative parameters of his homeland inadequate to encompass his sense of self as he evolves from bourgeois opportunist into avantgarde artist in Berlin and Paris; but as well as the necessary structuring opposition against which that nomadic life can be played out, Scotland provides at times a comforting solidity and a refuge from the vagaries of that cosmopolitan existence. Todd's voyage also features a series of connections with and separations from his friend Karl–Heinz, the German prison guard who provides him with his first copy of Rousseau's *Confessions*. Their coming together occurs in counterpoint to Todd's reluctant Scottish resumptions, British and Ger-

---

[16] William Boyd, *The New Confessions* (Harmondsworth: Penguin, 1987): 312. Further page references are in the main text.

man united as friends and filmmaking colleagues across Europe's major political divide.

Todd's defamiliarizing journey involves two sorts of anxious transcultural configuration. The first is his obsession with the *Confessions*, the second is his postmodern, americanized identity. Rousseau serves as a template for the order Todd attempts to impose on the emotional trauma caused by war and economic migration. The autobiographical framework is selfconsciously moulded by Todd to fit that of Rousseau, and his filmmaking career revolves around producing his own version of the *Confessions*: "Rousseau and his autobiography delivered me. I never forgot that precious, exceptional gift. The book, as you will see, was to become my life" (208). This permits Todd to write himself as the Romantic outsider above and beyond the constraints of bourgeois morality. In his narrative, art and passion transcend mortal error, validating the global meanderings of his rootless hero, who is recast as a citizen of the world. We discover, however, that Todd is out of step with that world, not because of its bourgeois strictures, but because he is clinging to a redundant nineteenth-century value-system.

His experience in the trenches of World War One foreshadow later difficulties. In the midst of that conflict, Todd is bewildered by a twentieth-century kind of Scottishness, the obverse of Scott's Romanticism. In this vision, national pride is compatible with British identity and commercial imperatives, but not with categories of conflicting industrial class, and so projects out from its colourful nostalgia another Other, that of the industrial proletariat. The patriotic but socially opportunistic Todd and his upper-class colleagues are confronted by an entire battalion of such aliens:

> These were the 17th/3 Grampians, a Bantam battalion, every man under the army's minimum height of five foot three inches. Kite and Somerville-Start were both taller than six feet.
>
> 'What the fuck are youse cunts looking at?' One of the men said in a powerful Scottish accent.
>
> '*What?*' Kite said, unable to conceal his astonishment. (148)

But, whereas for Stevenson's MacKellar foreign diction is equated with ancient Scottish superstition, to Todd the speech of these proletarian men is heard as an intimidating sub-linguistic growl; they represent animal threat. "We waited our turn uneasily," Todd continues of their first confrontation,

> like lanky anthropologists amongst a pygmy tribe. We stood head and shoulders above these tiny dirty men. They seemed more like goblins or trolls than members of the same race as ourselves. (148)

Adopting a position of part Enlightenment social scientist, part Scandinavian Romantic, he can only construe his fellow Scotsmen according to the degree of discomfort they evoke in him. When heading for the German lines, the Bantams' transgression against formal grammar and semantics will be followed by actual physical attacks on their British class enemies. Todd's later obsession with Rousseau represents an untenable defence against history: the avantgarde film director remains more the Romantic Scot than he realizes, facing the future via nostalgia for a fantasy of the past. Where Rousseau the transcendent itinerant lived in his chosen way thanks to aristocratic benefactors in Old Europe, the narrator's artistic life comes to depend on a different sponsor, Hollywood.

Here the real twentieth-century parallel between Todd's life and art creeps up on him unnoticed: the shift from modernist Europe to postmodern USA. He joins the exodus from a Europe under the shadow of Nazism, mixing with fleeing actors and artists, financiers and chancers, all contributing to the great heterogeneous milieu of America. Although that nation might be defined in opposition to indigenous native tribes, to corrupt Europe, or to its own undemocratic South, there never was an American people, only variants of migrant populations. This twentieth-century encounter is not between white colonizer and non-white colonized; it is the displaced Europeans who find themselves re-configured as the altered, inferior, Old-World types. "I went swimming in the sea with Ernest's two older boys, Clancy and Elroy," Todd recounts of another German friend, adding:

> ('They Yamericans now,' Ernest would say, 'Europe finish.'). I tinkered with my script of *The Confessions: Part II*. I felt oddly unreflecting and unbothered about things. One reason for this is that

> Europe might as well have vanished from the map of the world as far as life out here on the Pacific littoral was concerned. (418)

Like Kafka's Amerika, Ernest's Yamerica exists as much in minds as on maps. The émigrés occupy each side of the new equation, but remain detached from both: Yamerica names an identity no longer coterminous with political borders, a product of flux, a condition of exile. Once more, as the above passage intimates, landscape again allegorizes change. Where Scott's narrator used his river image to assess historical progress, here West Coast climes act for their new arrivals as a buffer against historical memory. Free of the tribulations of war, adrift in the seasonless sunshine and wealth of Los Angeles, Todd initially sinks into the torpid ease of the core-less self. This leaves the history from which so many residents are in flight liable to replacement by the fantasy versions in which Hollywood specializes.

But more troubling times lie ahead for him as the prevailing psychology of the newly dominant nation is unleashed by McCarthy's House Un-American Activities Committee. To escape persecution at the hands of the committee, Todd becomes an accessory to murder, necessitating one more flight, this time to a remote Mediterranean island, where he writes his memoir while looking fearfully over his shoulder. Recounting completion of his film of the *Confessions* in the midst of investigation, the proud creator describes its dramatic denouement, the death of Rousseau:

> Then dozens of stones are hurled through the panes. Glass breaks. Shards fly. We are back in Motiers, the mob is stoning his house. A rock catches Jean-Jacques on his forehead, blood flows. He clutches his chest in monstrous agony and falls to the floor. Therese comes in. The room is exactly as it was. Exquisite moonlight floods the tranquil room. Jean–Jacques lies on the floor, dead. End. Credits. (550)

This should be the artist's valediction to his idol and affirmation of his own life. But there is one problem: his ending is fiction, not fact. The real Rousseau died unpleasantly, but in privacy, as a result of illness; Todd's Rousseau is publicly lynched by the hysterical mob. Todd has sought integration of his fragmented life via transcendent art but, ultimately, his redemptive narrative becomes symptomatic of the perceptual pattern it is intended to counter. Victimized by both a personal enemy and a political system based on competitive exploitation, he fashions an autobiography that becomes a contemporary parable. Our global paradigm is framed by Hollywood, generating its ahistorical entertainments tailored to suit national ideology, and by Washington, imposing Cold War and then Christian–Muslim binaries on the fluidities out of which the USA could grow. Todd's Rousseau is shaped by a perceived threat from external, nameless, numberless Others; like his tormentors, Todd has become materialist, individualist and hollow, destabilized by competitiveness and the cyclical process of projection. His *Confessions* allegorizes the paranoiac, hybrid self normalized by placeless transnationalism. Boyd seems able to dramatize provisional, insecurely bounded identity via his own peculiarly Scottish perspectives. "After all," Todd concludes, awaiting a mysterious figure who has been inquiring after him, "this is the Age of Incompleteness. John James Todd, I said to myself, at last you are in tune with the universe" (572).

Being in tune with the universe has never, for Scots, entailed being at one with the metaphysics of nation. Fiction has always marked Scotland's status as marginal Other and agent of Empire; the best of it exploits national and personal identities discontinuous with designated boundaries, driven by imperatives of larger historical change. During the age of British expansion and the realist novel, Scots were both orientalized and Orientalist in their world-view. Scott and Stevenson allegorize their alienation from, as much as their participation in, Empire, utilizing the structuring elements of time and space to embody dispersal and instability across that brave new world. In our own era of globalized, hybrid cultures, Boyd portrays the citizen of the world residing in permanent exile from it: we are all Yamericans now.

❧

WORKS CITED

Bhabha, Homi K. *The Location of Culture* (London: Routledge, 1994).

Boyd, William. *The New Confessions* (Harmondsworth: Penguin, 1987).

Cooper, James Fenimore. *The Last of the Mohicans* (1826;. Oxford: Oxford UP, 1992).

Craig, Cairns. *The Modern Scottish Novel: Narrative and National Imagination* (Edinburgh: Edinburgh UP, 1999).

Donaldson, William. *The Jacobite Song: Political Myth and National Identity* (Aberdeen: Aberdeen UP, 1988).

Eagleton, Terry, ed. *Raymond Williams: Critical Perspectives* (London: Polity, 1989).

Ferguson, William. *Scotland: 1689 to the Present* (Edinburgh: Oliver & Boyd, 1968).

Herman, Arthur. *How the Scots Invented the Modern World, or, the True Story of How Western Europe's Poorest Nation Made Our World and Everything In It* (New York: Crown, 2001).

Johnson, Samuel. *A Dictionary of the English Language* (1755; New York: Levenger, 2003).

Lukács, Georg. *The Historical Novel*, tr. Hannah & Stanley Mitchell (Harmondsworth: Penguin, 1981).

Said, Edward W. *Orientalism* (London: Vintage, 1978).

Scott, Walter. *Waverley, or, 'Tis Sixty Years Since* (1814; Harmondsworth: Penguin, 1972).

Stevenson, Robert Louis. *The Master of Ballantrae* (1892; Oxford: Oxford UP, 1983).

❧

The Need to Storify

❧ Re-inventing the Past in André Brink's Novels

Ute Kauer

History and Storytelling

"Stories or history?' – 'Not much difference, is there?'."[1] This brief exchange between her grandmother and the heroine of André Brink's novel *Imaginings of Sand* exemplifies the preoccupation with fact and fiction underlying most of Brink's post-apartheid work. The blurring of the borderlines between history and storytelling can, of course, be classified as a typically postmodern phenomenon. Since Hayden White, it has become a commonplace in historical theory that historical narratives are "verbal fictions"[2] and not representations of objective truth, and fiction itself has thoroughly illustrated and played around with the postmodern truism of reality's fictitious character. Nevertheless, to talk about the "global postmodern" is still a highly problematic approach, as the relations between 'centre' and 'periphery' are still very much based on an uneven distribution of power (as the terms themselves suggest). Postmodernism is more or less a Western phenomenon. Still, André Brink's work is obviously very much influenced by elements of Occidental postmodernism, which serves to underline his hybrid status as

---

[1] André Brink, *Imaginings of Sand* (San Diego CA, New York & London: Harcourt Brace, 1996): 88. Further page references are in the main text.

[2] Hayden White, *Tropics of Discourse: Essays in Cultural Criticism*. (Baltimore MD & London: Johns Hopkins UP, 1978): 82.

a South African writer: coming from an Afrikaner background and now writing mainly in English, he incorporates Western as well as African traditions in his work, and neither emerges unchanged. His approach is indeed transcultural, and his writing-practice aims at a dialogue between European ideas and South African identities. In an interview, Brink stresses the fact that he once experienced this kind of hybridity as a form of schizophrenia, but sees it now as enriching, because the different identities "can complement each other, and [...] in the end, you don't want to deny either of them as a part of yourself."[3]

Now, the preoccupation with the past in Brink's novels is not only an expression of postmodern or Western influences in his work but is also tied up with the South African context. The role of literature in South Africa has undeniably changed in the post-apartheid years, as Susan Gallagher points out: "from resistance to reconstruction, from protest to construction, from anger to reconciliation."[4] What does this mean for the relation of history and storytelling, for presenting the past in fiction? As Brink himself points out, South African fiction during apartheid faced the "need to record, to witness, to represent,"[5] as the media were not fulfilling this function. Now, after apartheid, the past no longer has to be represented, but instead reimagined or "reinvented," to use Brink's terminology. The "need to storify" arises because the silences of the past have to be addressed; different versions have to be made available in order to confront the reader with the possibility – and the responsibility – to choose.[6] The use of the term "responsibility" indicates that Brink is not talking about a typically postmodern arbitrariness, but is, rather, proposing new and different understandings of identity and history, beyond a hegemonic concept of the past, beyond conclusive or totalizing narratives. History and storytelling are thus not dichotomies but collaborate in the construc-

---

[3] John Higgins, "What You Never Knew You Knew: An Interview with André Brink," *Pretexts: Literary and Cultural Studies* 8.1 (1999): 7.

[4] Susan Vanzanten Gallagher: "The Backward Glance: History and the Novel in Post-Apartheid South Africa," *Studies in the Novel* 29.3 (1997): 382–83.

[5] André Brink, *Reinventing a Continent: Writing and Politics in South Africa.* (Cambridge MA: Zoland, 1998): 236.

[6] Brink, *Reinventing a Continent*, 243, 244.

tion of hybrid identities. The interplay of fact and fiction enables the "powerful act of appropriating the past through imaginative understanding" which is, according to Brink, "necessary for the sanity of the whole community."[7]

In this essay, I will try to explore the interrelatedness of history and storytelling in Brink's post-apartheid novels, concentrating first on the role of cultural memory and the construction of hybrid identities and, second, on his reinvention of the formerly marginalized female voices.

Cultural Memory and Hybrid Identities

A reinvention of the past implies an appropriation of cultural memory. The silences of the past, the silenced voices, leave blanks in the cultural memory of a nation. Filling those blanks with different versions of the past saves the marginalized voices from collective forgetting. "The past is not simply there in memory, but it must be articulated to become memory,"[8] as Andreas Huyssen comments in the course of his reflections on the tension between fact and representation in memory. Brink's second-latest novel, *The Other Side of Silence*, is a case in point. The fate of Hanna X is recovered from collective forgetting by imagining it, by shaping the "threadbare facts of history,"[9] as the narrator calls it, into a story. The narrator describes how the German woman Hanna X (he is not able to recover her last name) is shipped to the German colony in South-West Africa, how she is discarded, raped and mutilated. Quite literally, Hanna is unable to tell her own story: her tongue has been cut out. She is silenced, physically and by collective forgetting. By telling her story, her fate is re-inscribed in both African and European memory. "The mode of memory is *recherche* rather than recuperation,"[10] in Andreas Huyssen's terminology. Thus, an imaginative reconstruction of the past does not

---

[7] Brink, *Reinventing a Continent*, 244.

[8] Andreas Huyssen, *Twilight Memories: Marking Time in a Culture of Amnesia* (New York & London: Routledge, 1995): 3.

[9] André Brink, *The Other Side of Silence* (Orlando FL: Harcourt, 2002): 148. Further page references are in the main text. Brink has since published the magical-realist novel *Praying Mantis* (London: Secker & Warburg, 2005).

[10] Huyssen, *Twilight Memories*, 3.

repeat history but opens it up to the present. André Brink's novels exemplify Huyssen's claim, since Brink searches for a past that might enable the construction of hybrid identities. Several characters in the novels experience a sense of displacement, which is counteracted or even resolved by storifying the past. Hybrid identities need a hybrid past, or, rather, the possibility of choice. Brink's negotiation of this part of German colonial history indicates that this might be true beyond the South African or postcolonial context.

In the case of Brink's novel *Imaginings of Sand*, the heroine Kristien, an expatriate, also represents such a hybrid identity. Her former home country and her new home, England, are both alien territories. "And it will need a miracle, or an act of faith [...] to make me part of the – a – real world again" (42), she states at the beginning. The miracle is initiated by her grandmother's storytelling. The stories give Kristien the feeling of "recovering something," as she realizes (96), precisely because they question the importance of facts, of official history. The grandmother's ironical paradox – "I can remember things that never happened" (4) – does not resolve the heroine's doubts about the 'real' nature of the events, it encourages them. This does not, however, necessarily imply a postmodern dissolution of the real or of the past. In Linda Hutcheon's sense, the storifying of the past draws attention to "the act of imposing order on that past, of encoding strategies of meaning-making through representation."[11] Ordering experience in the form of narrative enables Kristien to relate to the past of her home country, to make it her own. Ironically, the fictions of her grandmother make her part of the "real world" again. As the authors of the volume *The Self We Live By*, Holstein and Gubrium, point out, the postmodern self is basically left with two options: merely reacting to or transforming the crisis of identity. Possible reactions are either to save the authentic self from postmodern dissolution, or to "dismiss the self as an empirical reality."[12] Brink aims at a transformation of the crisis,

---

[11] Linda Hutcheon, *The Politics of Postmodernism* (London & New York: Routledge, 1989): 67.

[12] See James A. Holstein & Jaber F. Gubrium, *The Self We Live By: Narrative Identity in a Postmodern World* (Oxford: Oxford UP, 2000): 57.

by attempting to find new subjectivities, whereby identity becomes largely a narrative with multiple options, instead of being a fixed entity.

Flip Lochner, the narrator of *Devil's Valley*, also experiences a sense of displacement in his cultural environment. As a disillusioned journalist, he sets out to explore the isolated community of Devil's Valley, to write "a little tract of history," as he claims.[13] All he gets from the different inhabitants of the valley, however, are stories that contradict or complement each other. His desperate search for facts, for written documents, proves to be a wild-goose chase: there are no written records in the valley, cultural memory rests on oral traditions only. Instead of facts, he gets magic, apparitions and superstitions which question his whole world-view – as he observes exasperatedly, "One prepares to face the threats one knows, not the fucking unknown" (8). Again, the constructions of meaning and identity are dependent on the process of storifying. In the end, the "lies of stories" (299) that constitute cultural memory appear more real than written records. Facing the unknown means, for Flip Lochner, confronting himself with the process of history-making, instead of searching for the truth, for a master-narrative that explains the past. In the end, he realizes that even collecting all the stories would not make up a complete history (368). Brink does not present this uncertainty as a loss – constructing the past has a utopian dimension: "We fabricate yesterdays for ourselves which we can live with, which make the future possible" (299).

The elements of magical realism in the texts, especially in *Devil's Valley* and *Imaginings of Sand*, have been criticized as "New Age supernatural gloss"[14] and "far-fetched alternative medicine."[15] It is true that, as well as blurring the boundaries between dream and reality, myth and historical fact, the novels indeed present supernatural apparitions. In *The Rights of Desire*, the ghost of Antje of Bengal haunts the house of the first-person narrator. In *Devil's Valley*, people who are long since dead

---

[13] André Brink, *Devil's Valley* (London: Secker & Warburg, 1998): 9. Further page references are in the main text.

[14] Review of *Imaginings of Sand* by Richard Bernstein, "A Personal but Political Novel of South Africa," *New York Times Review of Books* (11 Dec 1996).

[15] Review of *Devil's Valley* by Lorna Sage, "Escape From Paradise," *New York Times Review of Books* (21 March 1999).

frequently appear. Even in his second-latest novel, *The Other Side of Silence*, less haunted by ghosts and apparitions than Brink's other works, the spirits of all the dead women materialize in the dark. Now, even if this kind of device seems slightly contrived at times, all the ghosts fulfil a certain function, beyond simply giving the texts a New Age or supernatural atmosphere: they are all reminders of forgotten stories. Antje of Bengal wants her story to be told, and the dead women from the graves also try to reach the "other side of silence," or, in Hanna's words in *The Other Side of Silence*: "She knows they are the women from the unmarked graves outside, the nameless ones, forgotten by everyone, relegated to obscurity as if they had never existed" (131). Their stories have to be told, have to be included in cultural memory. As Sandra Chait points out, the rewriting of the past is essential for a society in transition:

> The transfer of political power from oppressor to oppressed brings in its wake the appropriation and reworking of mythological material. As new governments rewrite their people's history, so too do their novelists and poets recover and re-vision the cultural identity embedded in their people's myths.[16]

I would not, however, agree with Chait's conclusion that the appropriation of mythological material functions necessarily as "historical catharsis"[17] and thus offers an easy way out of historical responsibility. On the contrary, what the ghosts and mythological figures in Brink's novels demand is to be recognized, to be part of cultural memory. The majority of the ghosts that people Brink's texts are female, and only by demarginalizing the female voices of the past can history offer points of identification for all the members of a multicultural society. Brink's re-inventing of history and myth does not function as a justification or catharsis but displays a utopian quality. It is not an easy way out of responsibility, but allows a mode of historical imagining that offers new perspectives on the present. Literature must explore the improbable in order to offer new insights into

---

[16] Sandra Chait, "Mythology, Magic Realism, and White Writing After Apartheid," *Research in African Literatures* 31.2 (2000): 17.

[17] Chait, "Mythology, Magic Realism, and White Writing After Apartheid," 17.

the present and the future: "Only by dreaming and writing the *impossible* can life be made possible once again."[18]

Counteracting Silence: The Female Past

Dreaming the impossible implies that former versions of the past are questioned and complemented by new readings. It is precisely in this imaginative re-creation of the past that the process of transculturation can take place. Mary Louise Pratt explains the term 'transculturation' as follows: "Ethnographers have used this term to describe how subordinated or marginal groups select and invent from materials transmitted to them by a dominant or metropolitan culture."[19] Pratt also sees the concept of transculturation very much in terms of "copresence, interaction, interlocking understandings and practices."[20] The clarification is important, as the prefix 'trans-' suggests an end-product somewhere beyond the different cultures. Cultural interaction does not, however, result in a vacuum or in a homogeneous 'third culture' made up of marginal and dominant rudiments. In the process of interaction between different cultural groups, the retelling of the past functions to familiarize the unfamiliar, in Hayden White's terminology.[21]

For Brink, the female would appear to be the unfamiliar and marginalized Other. Most of his post-apartheid novels offer extensive revisions of the traditional gender discourse. *Imaginings of Sand* is the most obvious example, as the whole of South African history is retold from a female point of view. Male and female histories are presented as dichotomies, as the men's past is the master-narrative: "Theirs the monuments for the ages; ours, at most, the imaginings of sand" (330). Solidified expressions of a (male) heroic past are contrasted with the shifting and transitory impressions women have left on history. But finding a means of expression is essential in order to survive. Whereas Kristien's displace-

---

[18] Brink, *Reinventing a Continent*, 202.

[19] Mary Louise Pratt, *Imperial Eyes: Travel Writing and Transculturation* (London & New York: Routledge, 1997): 6.

[20] Pratt, *Imperial Eyes*, 7.

[21] See White, *Tropics of Discourse*, 86.

ment is turned into a feeling of solidarity in the end, her sister Anna is not able to break the silence: she kills her whole family. Violence is the only means of articulation left to her; it is, as Kristien says, "the only sign she can leave behind" (331). Anna, as the inevitable victim, is the last in a chain of silenced female voices. Finding a means of articulation is a crucial step on the way to liberation. – "countering silence," and, ultimately, "countering death" is, according to Brink, the "primordial function of literature."[22] Anna was not able to break the silence; consequently, she failed to counter death. Her grandmother (and, through her, Kristien) has counteracted the silence through her stories.

Kristien's displacement is also, quite literally, transformed by a new sense of place, of the place that is her home-country. Only a sense of history can connect her to the actual environment, and her grandmother's stories enable her to enter into a "dialogue beyond, or far below, language" (227) with the space that forms her home. Time and place, a sense of history and a sense of space, are necessary to form an image of the nation, "an image to match the name of Africa" (138).

To imagine national communities, we need a sense of historical continuity.[23] This understanding of historical continuity depends on the recognition of temporality, as Huyssen makes clear: "In an age of an unlimited proliferation of images, [...] the search for the real itself has become utopian, and this search is fundamentally invested in a desire for temporality."[24] Recognizing, accepting and appropriating temporality rests on the ability to connect official and personal history. Brink presents the disruption of this connection in his novel *The Rights of Desire*. The ageing narrator is cut off from the present: he was forced into early retirement from his job as a librarian, his wife has died, his children have left the country, and his best friend and neighbour has been brutally murdered. The narrator's world is shaken by the appearance of a young woman, his new lodger. In his passion for the young woman, he equates her body with

---

[22] Brink, *Reinventing a Continent*, 142.

[23] Jan Assmann, *Das kulturelle Gedächtnis: Schrift, Erinnerung und politische Identität in frühen Hochkulturen* (Munich: C.H. Beck, 2000): 133.

[24] Huyssen, *Twilight Memories*, 101.

undiscovered territory: while undressing her, he proclaims: "This was *my* new world, *my* invention."[25] Yet the girl refuses to be re-invented by him; his desire remains unfulfilled. In the end, it is Antje of Bengal's ghost that teaches him how to connect past and present. He has to recognize the female perspective and acknowledge its presence. Whereas Antje's point of view hardly features in his retelling of her story at the beginning of the novel, the recognition of her history induces a sense of the present in him in the end: "There is the world outside [...] which requires me and strongly concerns me. Antje will see to it that I do not avoid it" (306). The importance of including the marginalized female voices is stressed again. Steven Robins puts it this way:

> It remains to be seen whether South Africa's contested past will be remembered in a form that does not privilege particular historical experiences, collective memories, and nationalisms, and elide others.[26]

Acknowledging the female past is an attempt at counteracting a totalized version of collective memory.

Simon During claims that the process of exploring new civic imagery is also part of the "feminization of society."[27] Yet this feminization cannot take place without reproducing stereotypes about the female, and Brink's feminization of history is also not free from clichés and binary opposites that might support an essentialist view of femininity. First of all, in all the novels the superior understanding of historical processes is definitely female. Only the women try to transcend the binaries of fact and fiction, of guilt and reconciliation, of crime and punishment. However, the equation men=stupidity / women=wisdom has led to the allegation that Brink's

---

[25] André Brink, *The Rights of Desire* (London: Secker & Warburg, 2000): 167. Further page references are in the main text.

[26] Steven Robins, "Silence in my Father's House: Memory, Nationalism, and Narratives of the Body," in *Negotiating the Past: The Making of Memory in South Africa*, ed. Sarah Nuttall & Carli Coetzee (Oxford: Oxford UP, 2000): 139–40.

[27] Simon During, "Literature – Nationalism's Other? The Case for Revision," in *Nation and Narration*, ed. Homi K. Bhabha (London & New York: Routledge, 1990): 143.

world is inhabited by too many "cartoon figures."[28] His characterizations may be rather schematic at times, but they also underline Brink's attempt to draw attention to the fact that women are indeed the "new victims of the culture of impunity and disorder,"[29] as Ato Quayson states. Apart from the superior female wisdom, another quality of femininity is noticeable: quite frequently, women represent the unknown, retaining a strongly enigmatic quality. This is true for Ouma Kristina in *Imaginings of Sand*, for the women in *Devil's Valley*, and also for the young woman in *The Rights of Desire*. There is an obvious correlation between women's roles as redeemer and their mysteriousness. The essentialist traits in the characterization of Brink's female protagonists only underline the fact that even in re-imagining a female past one has to rely on existing material. It is not possible to abandon traditional stereotypes completely, only to modify them. In Brink's own words, myth-making is a necessary step in appropriating the past: "Myth may have preceded history, but in the long run it may well be the only guarantee for the survival of history."[30] Thus, Brink's reconstruction of the past offers new metaphors which might complement our understanding of history, without wholly deconstructing existing myths and metaphors. Instead, he proposes counter-myths.

Past, Present, Future: Reimagining the Nation

A sense of national identity depends on the historical imagination of a nation. In a multicultural society like South Africa's, this means that identity has to rest on diversity, not on a homogeneous version of the past. Totalizing narratives of the past, which exclude certain groups from collective memory, fail to provide the basis for such an identity. In post-apartheid literature, the preoccupation with the past is therefore not sur-

---

[28] Richard Bernstein, "A Personal but Political Novel of South Africa," *New York Times Review of Books* (11 Dec 1996).

[29] Ato Quayson, "Symbolisation Compulsion: Freud, African Literature and South Africa's Process of Truth and Reconciliation," *Cambridge Quarterly* 30:3 (2001): 212.

[30] André Brink, "Stories of History: Reimagining the Past in Post-Apartheid Narrative," in *Negotiating the Past: The Making of Memory in South Africa*, ed. Sarah Nuttall & Carli Coetzee (Oxford: Oxford UP, 2000): 42.

prising. It is not only an expression of coming to terms with the burden of past and present violence and oppression, but also a crucial step in the redefinition of the nation. The obsessions with history in literature are thus neither regressive nor escapist, as Huyssen rightly observes:

> In cultural politics today, they occupy a utopian position vis-à-vis a chic and cynical postmodern nihilism on the one hand and a neo-conservative world view on the other that desires what cannot be had: stable histories, a stable canon, a stable reality.[31]

Huyssen is referring here to postcolonial *and* European literatures – indicating that our European societies and nations might be in need of re-imagining as well. The paradigms that used to define our European nations (a common language, history, religion) have been rendered obsolete by the global postmodern condition – or maybe the homogeneity implied in those ideas has always been a myth. André Brink's preoccupation with the past is therefore neither an expression of postmodern nihilism nor an attempt at transcending historical reality. The need to storify does not question the existence of the real, but expresses an urge towards the entertaining of diverse realities. The blanks in the cultural memory of the nation have to be filled in order to intensify "the relationship between the individual and her or his spatial and temporal environment."[32] Brink's versions of the past function as counter-memories, thus creating imaginary openings that enable alternative options for the past and future. To return to Holstein's and Gubrium's analysis of the postmodern self, Brink's transformation of the crisis of confidence "presents us with worlds and identities of our own making, the narrative particulars of which are as limitless as our imagination."[33] Brink's novels suggest that accepting difference rather than levelling it out may, in the long run, prove to be the more demanding and utopian task, and not only for South African literature and society.

---

[31] Huyssen, *Twilight Memories*, 101.

[32] Brink, *Reinventing a Continent*, 245.

[33] Holstein & Gubrium, *The Self We Live By*, 231.

WORKS CITED

Assmann, Jan. *Das kulturelle Gedächtnis: Schrift, Erinnerung und politische Identität in frühen Hochkulturen* (Munich: C.H. Beck, 2003).

Bernstein, Richard. "A Personal but Political Novel of South Africa," *New York Times Review of Books* (11 December 1996).

Brink, André. *Devil's Valley* (London: Secker & Warburg, 1998).

——. *Imaginings of Sand* (San Diego CA, New York & London: Harcourt Brace, 1996).

——. *The Other Side of Silence* (Orlando FL: Harcourt, 2002).

——. *Praying Mantis* (London: Secker & Warburg, 2005).

——. *Reinventing a Continent: Writing and Politics in South Africa* (Cambridge MS: Zoland, 1998).

——. *The Rights of Desire* (London: Secker & Warburg, 2000).

——. "Stories of History: Reimagining the Past in Post-Apartheid Narrative," in *Negotiating the Past: The Making of Memory in South Africa*, ed. Sarah Nuttall & Carli Coetzee (Oxford: Oxford UP, 2000): 29–42.

Chait, Sandra. "Mythology, Magic Realism, and White Writing After Apartheid," *Research in African Literatures* 31.2 (2000): 17–28.

During, Simon. "Literature –Nationalism's Other? The Case for Revision," in *Nation and Narration*, ed. Homi K. Bhabha (London & New York: Routledge, 1990): 138–53.

Gallagher, Susan Vanzanten. "The Backward Glance: History and the Novel in Post-Apartheid South Africa," *Studies in the Novel* 29.3 (1997): 376–95.

Higgins, John. "What You Never Knew You Knew: An Interview with André Brink," *Pretexts: Literary and Cultural Studies* 8.1 (1999): 7–15.

Holstein, James A., & Jaber F. Gubrium, *The Self We Live By: Narrative Identity in a Postmodern World* (Oxford: Oxford UP, 2000).

Hutcheon, Linda. *The Politics of Postmodernism* (London & New York: Routledge, 1989).

Huyssen, Andreas. *Twilight Memories. Marking Time in a Culture of Amnesia* (New York & London: Routledge, 1995).

Pratt, Mary Louise. *Imperial Eyes: Travel Writing and Transculturation* (London & New York: Routledge, 1997).

Quayson, Ato. "Symbolisation Compulsion: Freud, African Literature and South Africa's Process of Truth and Reconciliation," *Cambridge Quarterly* 30.3 (2001): 191–214.

Robins, Steven, "Silence in my Father's House: Memory, Nationalism, and Narratives of the Body," in *Negotiating the Past: The Making of Memory in South Africa*, ed. Sarah Nuttall & Carli Coetzee (Oxford: Oxford UP, 2000): 120–40.

Sage, Lorna. "Escape From Paradise," *New York Times Review of Books* (21 March 1999).

White, Hayden. *Tropics of Discourse: Essays in Cultural Criticism* (Baltimore MD & London: Johns Hopkins UP, 1978).

❧

The Postcolonial Border

❧ Bessie Head's "The Wind and a Boy"

JOHAN SCHIMANSKI

WHAT HAPPENS when national borders meet textual borders – in a postcolonial context, in Southern Africa, in the writings of Bessie Head, in a story called "The Wind and a Boy"?[1] What happens when the borders of a short story are juxtaposed with global borders, with the borders of a post- or neocolonial system, borders which figure what Gayatri Spivak describes as an "international division of labour"?[2] In order to provide provisional answers to these questions, I shall furnish here a brief presentation of an interpretative practice which focuses on the border, a 'border poetics'; and a reading of "The Wind and a Boy," using some of the tools of border poetics and some reflections on the question of the postcolonial border.

---

[1] Bessie Head, "The Wind and a Boy," in *The Collector of Treasures and Other Botswana Village Tales* (London: Heinemann, 1977): 69–75. The present essay is part of a larger project on literature and borders. For a related study of postcolonial borders in Southern Africa, focusing on the juxtaposition of the internal borders of the apartheid state and the borders between realistic prose and poetic metaphor, see Johan Schimanski, "Genre Borders in a Border Novel: Nadine Gordimer's *My Son's Story*," in *Genrer och genreproblem: Teoretiska och historiska perspektiv / Genres and Their Problems: Theoretical and Historical Perspectives*, ed. Beata Agrell & Ingela Nilsson (Göteborg: Daidalos, 2003): 505–13.

[2] See Gayatri Chakravorty Spivak, "Can the Subaltern Speak?" in *Marxism and the Interpretation of Culture*, ed. Cary Nelson & Lawrence Grossberg (Urbana: U of Illinois P, 1988): 271–313.

Border Theory and Border Poetics

One of the first problems a theory of the border must deal with is the very applicability of the term 'border'. Borders may be found within a very wide range of contexts. Even limiting oneself to literary studies, they are often invoked, especially in discussions of transgression and identity. What quickly becomes apparent, at least within the context of a border theory proper, is that the word 'border' is frequently applied where alternatives could have been just as useful: words like 'difference' and 'opposition', for example, depending on what is intended. The problem with using the term 'border' instead of these other terms is that it tends to territorialize difference, even if only within an imaginary mental landscape. One runs the risk of homogenizing bordered-off areas in this landscape, and repressing in the process more network- or rhizome-like models of the world. However, this reductive use of the term 'border' – common and unavoidable as it is – is the bread and butter of border theory. Border theory regularly returns to such questions as how difference is made into borders, how networks are refigured as territories, and what kind of borders are the end-products of these territorializing processes. Are they divides or joins? Places of communication or of non-communication? Of insight or of blindness? Are they precise lines? Zones? Overlaps? Double invaginations?[3] Seams? Floodgates? Are they stable or shifting? Is there something on the other side?

Border theory as such is hampered also by not being a homogeneous academic field (or territory). It is at the present time a fragmentary affair, almost dysfunctionally so, and certainly has little to be mustered in the way of agency. Border theory is a network of approaches crossed by internal divides, laid out by people working in many different disciplines and in different geographical contexts. It focuses on different themes: nations, transgression, border-crossers, scaling, figurality, ethics, subject-formation, rites of passage, identity/hybridity, etc. Many of these themes are

---

[3] A term used by Jacques Derrida in one of his discussions of the border: "La loi du genre" (1980), in Derrida, *Parages* (Paris: Galilée, 1986): 249–87; tr. Avital Ronell as "The Law of Genre" in *Acts of Literature*, ed. Derek Attridge (New York: Routledge, 1992): 211–52.

directly relevant to the study of literary borders, and what one may call border poetics; especially so the study of border-crossing narratives, but also of the way in which borders are figured metaphorically or through other rhetorical devices.

Border poetics can be defined as any approach to literary texts which connects borders on the levels of *histoire*, the represented or presented world, and of *discours*, the text itself, a weave of rhetoric and narrative. Border poetics is sensitive to borders on many levels of the text, the five most important being, I propose: *textual borders*, the edges and divides of the text as discourse; *topographical borders*, borders in the represented space of the setting; *symbolic borders* or, properly, differences which have allowed themselves to be territorialized in a symbolic landscape; *temporal borders*, the passages from one period to another – territorialized time; and *epistemological borders*, borders which positivism imagines as always expanding – knowledge territorialized. But while all border-crossing narratives may be examined for their textual, topographical, symbolic, temporal and epistemological dimensions, I must underscore the fact that this five-level model is mainly heuristic, and needs more theorization in order to attain stringency. All borders have a spatial element (at the very least), and it is possible to talk about the topography of a text, a symbolic mental landscape, a temporal progression, or a field of knowledge. This means that the borders above tend to be re-complicated at the very point at which they have taken their proper places as elemental denominators in an analysis. A person crossing from one territory into another crosses a topographical but also temporal border; and this temporal border, in being designated a border, figures time as an imaginary topography. Yet the topographies of space and time (and text, and symbolic structure, and knowledge), while overlaid, are not wholly commensurable, causing a sense of slippage when their borders are juxtaposed. This sense of slippage, of the diffusion of the border across larger areas of the text, will form part of the particularity of any individual border reading.

A Border Reading

Crossing the border into – or opening the border to – a short story by Bessie Head, I am awkwardly aware of the richness of Head's writings in general as a field for border studies. Practically all her texts have to do with the formation of community and, as a specific problem within the formation of community, with the way in which communities adapt to strangers.[4] This is perhaps something only to be expected, written as they are by a naturalized Botswanan of South African birth, and indeed, the biographical background for Head's border themes has been thoroughly discussed by Rob Nixon.[5] One obvious place to start would be *A Question of Power* (1974), a novel of borderline states (in the psychological sense). Nancy Topping Bazin writes that the dystopian fantasies and hallucinations in this novel are the product of the barriers between people in Southern Africa.[6] Another potential opening would be those novels of Head's that allow the reader to cross the border of the text in parallel with the main character crossing the border into Botswana. I am here referring to *When Rain Clouds Gather* (1969), a novel of border zones, and addressed as such by Edward O. Ako.[7] This novel is in itself a border zone, with

---

[4] Besides being a theme in many other studies, this is the focus of Maria Olaussen's major monograph on Head's novels, *Forceful Creation in Harsh Terrain: Place and Identity in Three Novels by Bessie Head* (Frankfurt am Main: Peter Lang, 1997).

[5] Rob Nixon, "Border Country: Bessie Head's Frontline States," *Social Text* 36 (1993): 106–37.

[6] Nancy Topping Bazin, "Madness, Mysticism, and Fantasy: Shifting Perspectives in the Novels of Doris Lessing, Bessie Head, and Nadine Gordimer," *Extrapolation* 33.1 (1992): 73–87.

[7] Edward O. Ako, "Crossing Borders: A Study of Bessie Head's *When Rain Clouds Gather* and *Maru*," *Commonwealth: Essays and Studies* 22.2 (2000): 5–11. James M. Garrett's exemplary Jamesonian reading of *When Rain Clouds Gather* also focuses on textual borders or "ruptures" – "Writing Community: Bessie Head and the Politics of Nature," *Research in African Literatures* 30.2 (1999): 124. Bessie Head herself identified the main theme of this novel as "refugeeism" in her essay "Social and Political Pressures that Shape Literature in Southern Africa," in *The Tragic Life: Bessie Head and Literature in Southern Africa*, ed. Cecil Abrahams (Trenton NJ: Africa World Press, 1990): 13–14.

the main character not really crossing the border into the local community before the end of the novel, the reader's point of exit. To quote Kenneth Harrow, "In fact, with Bessie Head boundaries, the forces that maintain and perpetuate them, and those that dissolve them, could be said to be the focus and key to her work."[8]

Here I will be examining a lesser-known text which has received comparatively little critical attention, one of the stories in her collection *The Collector of Treasures and other Botswana Village Tales* (1977): "The Wind and a Boy."[9] This is a text which intimates a great many symbolic, temporal and epistemological borders, but which contains very few and almost imperceptible concrete topographical borders. At the same time, it quite clearly both performs and plays with the textual borders of the short-story genre.

"The Wind and a Boy" is set in a village in post-independence Botswana. It tells the story of a small boy, Friedman, and his grandmother, Sejosenye – two characters who "captivate the imagination and hearts of all the people of their surroundings."[10] But precisely because of this air of enchantment, they may be said to be set apart from the people around them, similar to other strangers and "detribalized" characters in Head's novels.[11] Friedman's mother, who works as a typist in a town a hundred

---

[8] Kenneth W. Harrow, "Bessie Head and Death: Change on the Margins," in *Shades of Empire: In Colonial and Post-Colonial Literatures*, ed. C.C. Barfoot & Theo D'haen (Amsterdam: Rodopi, 1993): 165.

[9] For readings, see Coreen Brown, *The Creative Vision of Bessie Head* (Madison WI: Fairleigh Dickinson UP & London: Associated UP, 2003): 124; Sara Chetin, "Myth, Exile, and the Female Condition: Bessie Head's *The Collector of Treasures*," *Journal of Commonwealth Literature* 24.1 (1989): 132; Ezenwa–Ohaeto, "Windows of Womanhood," in *The Tragic Life*, ed. Abrahams, 127; and Olaussen, *Forceful Creation in Harsh Terrain*, 107–108.

[10] Head, "The Wind and a Boy," in Head, *The Collector of Treasures and Other Botswana Village Tales* (London: Heinemann, 1977): 69. Further page references are in the main text.

[11] For discussion of the function of detribalized characters in Head's novels, see Sophia Obiajulu Ogwude, "Protest and Commitment in Bessie Head's Utopia," *Research in African Literatures* 29.3 (1998): 73; and Ako, "Crossing Borders," 6.

miles away, has entrusted him to his grandmother to be brought up in the village. The narrative covers the story of Friedman's life from his birth in a hospital and his naming after a "friendly foreign doctor" (70), to when it is cut short at the age of fourteen by a speeding car, which hits him and his bicycle. His death is rapidly followed by the death of his grandmother, who has gone mad with grief. The story ends with reflections on the driver of the car and what he represents to the community, ending: "And thus progress, development, and a pre-occupation with status and living-standards first announced themselves to the village. It looked like being an ugly story with many decapitated bodies on the main road" (75).

Friedman, however, is a complex, dynamic and tragic character, and the story also suggests other reasons for his death.[12] The car-driver represents neocolonialism, but so does Friedman's absent mother, and the bicycle on which he rides up the embankment: "His mother, who worked in a town far away, sent him the money to purchase the bicycle. The gift brought the story of his life abruptly to a close" (73–74). Maria Olaussen even suggests[13] that Sejonsenye is complicitous in this, for she sends Friedman to the village to buy typical 'neocolonial' foodstuffs: "sugar, tea, and [powdered] milk" (74). But this journey, ending in his death, is also a product of his sense of duty, in bicycling from his grandmother's land some twenty miles away in order to buy food for her. Another reason for his death is his – contradictory – boyish irresponsibility at the moment of his death: "In the devil-may-care fashion of all the small boys, he cycled right into its path, turned his head and smiled appealingly at the driver" (74).

The narrator explicitly divides the story of Friedman and his grandmother into several phases. The two of them make the villagers "smile, laugh, then cry" (70). "They smiled at his first two phases," as an over-coddled baby and then as "a small dark shadow" toddling silently beside his grandmother (70). "They began to laugh at his third phase" (70), when he becomes the mischievous but attractive leader of the small boys of the

---

[12] In addition to the reasons mentioned here, Chetin points to Friedman's sense of uniqueness, constructed by both the villagers and his grandmother; "Myth, Exile, and the Female Condition," 132.

[13] Olaussen, *Forceful Creation in Harsh Terrain*, 108.

village in their tricks. And the deaths of Friedman and his grandmother make them cry, thus ending their story in a fourth phase. But Friedman's third phase, as an object of amused and admiring laughter, may be further divided by his passage from irresponsible child to responsible adult. The mischievous leader of the village boys realizes he must be of help to other people – especially his grandmother. He has an "awakened compassion," and, on entering the last phase of the text, the narrator observes that "Life and its responsibilities began to weigh down heavily on Friedman as he approached his fourteenth year" (73). Memorably, the change has come about after his grandmother has told him the story of one Robinson Crusoe, loner and great hunter, who has killed an elephant all by himself. In giving the elephant to his people, this Robinson Crusoe becomes accepted by his people.

This story contains many borders of the types I have already outlined. It contains *temporal borders*: a birth, two deaths, and a passage from irresponsibility to responsibility: i.e. from childhood to adulthood. It also refers to the recent passage from a protectorate to an independent Botswana, also allegorically, through the name of Friedman (when read as "freed man").[14] It contains *symbolic borders* or differences: between life and death, irresponsibility and responsibility, tradition and modernity, individuals and community, male and female. The last, gender difference manifests itself both in the love between Friedman and his grandmother Sejosenye, and in the division between the irresponsible boys playing in the bush and the girls, who are "useful attachments" to the household (69). There is also, then, a symbolic border between the wild and the domestic, or the bush and the household, and I thus arrive at a major *topographical border* in the story: that lying between the inside of the village and its outside.

---

[14] Cf. Chetin, "Myth, Exile, and the Female Condition," 132. Compare also with the name of the protagonist in the story "Snapshots of a Wedding," Neo, which Femi Ojo–Ade reads as standing for "neocolonialism" – "Of Human Trials and Triumphs," in *The Tragic Life*, ed. Abrahams, 84. Harrow also focuses on the connection between temporal and topographical borders, and micro- and macrospatial borders, in other stories by Head (esp. 167).

Inside the village we find households, the homes of the people, and an archaic, pastoral life. Outside the village we find the boys and their games, the hunting of small animals – also an archaic activity (and I here use the word 'archaic' in the sense in which it is used by Homi K. Bhabha – calling attention to its complicity in colonialist or developmentalist discourse.[15]) But also outside the village we find the main road and, further away, the town – that is to say, modernity.

However, the opposition between inside and outside is explicitly articulated as a border only twice in the story. The first time this articulation takes place, the border is a window. The boys steal something from a house: "Friedman showed us how to open the window with a knife and string" (71). While this incident belongs to the mischievous and irresponsible phase of his life – he is the "worst thief," a "real nuisance" (71) – it also shows something of his compassionate responsiveness – if not responsibility – in teaching the other boys to open the window. It again marks him out as someone special: "'Friedman isn't as bad as you,' the parents would reply, irrationally. They were hypnotized by a beautiful creature" (71). In the entering of the domestic sphere, the incident presages his later, responsible closeness to his grandmother at the same time as it symbolizes an aggressive, irresponsible encroachment on women's territory.

The second time the topographical border is explicitly articulated, it is as an embankment by the main road:

> He pushed the bicycle through the winding, sandy pathway of the village ward, reached the high embankment of the main road, peddled vigorously up it and out of the corner of his eye, saw a small green truck speeding towards him. (74).

This embankment territorializes temporal borders by dividing the "timeless, sleepy village" from the "progress" and "development" of the main road (75). Its upward slope can be read as the upward curve of development. It also territorializes symbolic borders by dividing a realm of responsibility (the village) from one of irresponsibility (the main road), the

---

[15] Homi K. Bhabha, *The Location of Culture* (London: Routledge, 1994): 130.

latter present both in the irresponsibility of the driver and the irresponsibility of the small boy. But in Friedman's smile to the driver, his responsibility and desire for human contact and compassion are revealed at the heart of this realm of irresponsibility. This sense of bringing the responsibility of the village with him into a territory of irresponsibility, and thus experiencing a state of inner contradiction and splitting, mirrors the doubleness of the earlier window episode. Through this mirroring of episodes, the irresponsible modernity of the road is aligned with the irresponsible archaicness of the bush in a chiasmatic (=ABBA) structure. The splitting of the self is intimately connected with the territorial and symbolic divide created by the embankment, a phenomenon often associated with border-crossing.[16]

The chiasmus is also present in the ironic echoing in the meeting between a car and a boy of the meeting between Robinson Crusoe and an elephant. In the Robinson Crusoe story, the smaller hero meets the larger elephant – "Ah, people, I saw a terrible sight! I was standing at the feet of the elephant. I was just a small ant" (72). He then kills the elephant. The smaller Friedman meets the larger car (a small truck). The car then kills Friedman. Again, in both cases, the antagonist comes from the world outside the village, and thus the archaic and the modern are aligned.

Most strikingly, then, the embankment divides between life and death, and between the story of the boy and what happens afterwards. Its upward slope thus also follows the curve of tension in the story, leading up to its moment of crisis. It announces the beginning of the border zone the reader must negotiate to get out of the text. In this final zone, central events – the death of Friedman, the death of his grandmother Sejosenye – are not directly described, but figured in metonymic absences: the remains of the boy, horrifically described, stand for Friedman's death, as the ellipsis

---

[16] For a provisional guide to the 'logic' of border-crossing, see Johan Schimanski, "Den litterære grensen: Knut Hamsuns 'Dronningen af Saba'," in *Att forska om gränser*, ed. José L. Ramírez (Stockholm: Nordregio, 2001): 67–68. <http://www.nordregio.se/Files/ro103p141.pdf>. For an English version, see Johan Schimanski, "A Poetics of the Border: Nation and Genre in *Wythnos yng Nghymru Fydd* and Other Texts by Islwyn Ffowc Elis" (doctoral dissertation, Oslo University, 1996): 320–21.

delineated by the sentence "Two weeks later, they buried her" (75) stands for Sejonsenye's. In this zone, the narrative focus is shifted to the people and their view of events, to the crossing of the divide between the absence and the presence of knowledge, and the zone ends in a final, framing interpretation. We have thus arrived at the *textual borders* of the story, and here I will be focusing on these as contingent on genre: i.e. as textual territorializations of genre differences. For this final border zone, like the introductory exposition of the story, is *part* and *parcel* of the compression necessary for the text to function generically as a short story, with its accompanying production of a sense of an ending.

The ending of "The Wind and a Boy," with its fable-like moral, has, however, been read as a signal of an element of oral tradition in the story[17] – and indeed, as a re-affirmation that the oral tradition is present in all of the stories in *The Collector of Treasures and other Botswana Village Tales* – with an emphasis on "Village Tales." But I would like to add two qualifications to this sense of orality in the story. The first concerns the ending of "The Wind and a Boy." It is only comparatively recently in the short-story tradition – in the twentieth century – that it has become less common to include a framing interpretation at the end of the story. The second qualification concerns the story and the book as a whole. In using the phrase "and other Botswanan Village Tales" in her title, Bessie Head is most certainly playing on the reader's expectations, in a piece of what Bhabha would call "sly civility."[18] Put on sale in a local Southern African bookshop, it seems designed to land beside similar titles, but different contents. An illustration would be books in a series published by Howard Timmins in Cape Town, one of which, *The Song of the Golden Birds* (1970), I was given as small boy myself, living for shorter periods of my childhood in Botswana and Zambia. This book, written by Phyllis Savory, contains mostly tales of meetings between humans and magical speaking animals from the oral traditions of the Bemba and Tonga peoples of Zambia. But the title, if we are to trust the list of other titles in the series

---

[17] H. Nigel Thomas, "Narrative Strategies in Bessie Head's Stories," in *The Tragic Life*, ed. Abrahams, 97.

[18] See the chapter of that name in Bhabha, *The Location of Culture*, 93–101.

on the back cover, is an anomaly. Most of the other books in the series contain the words "fireside tales" in their titles, *Zulu Fireside Tales*, *Matabele Fireside Tales*, etc. – and also, not so far off "Botswana Village Tales," *Bechuana Fireside Tales* ("Bcchuana" being the earlier English spelling of "Botswana"). But there is a great contrast in the contents of Head's tales and these books: Head's tales mostly address everyday life in contemporary village communities, and thus do not live up to expectations of safely archaic and magical folk-tales from a 'pure' oral tradition.[19]

This subversion of genre expectations is also played out in "The Wind and a Boy," as the text crosses the border into another story, into Sejosenye's story of the hunter Robinson Crusoe. Genre borders are crossed here within the text, switching as it does to what is quite clearly a folk-tale in the oral tradition, and at the same time into an archaic time. However, in the use of the name Robinson Crusoe there is also a sly civility, an uncanny mimicry, and a play with the expectations of those readers familiar with Daniel Defoe's novel about British protocolonialism, moral progress and economic development.

---

[19] Here I agree with Brown when she states that "Even when Head does seem to be drawing directly upon the legacy of oral literature, [...] she does so with the understanding that the reader holds a very different relationship with the dramatized storyteller than the one experienced by the storyteller's immediate audience"; *The Creative Vision of Bessie Head*, 115. However, as my reading here shows, I am not so convinced by her claim that this story or Head's other work must be read in isolation from the postcolonial context (cf. her reading of "The Wind and a Boy," 124). H. Nigel Thomas also points to the way in which the play between oral and short-story tradition undermines the expectations of the reader ("Narrative Strategies in Bessie Head's Stories": 96, 103). For a very clear statement of the narrative structure of the play between different types of audience, see Chetin, "Myth, Exile, and the Female Condition," 114–15. On narrative distance, see also Françoise Lionnet, "Geographies of Pain: Captive Bodies and Violent Acts in the Fictions of Myriam Warner–Vieyra, Gayl Jones, and Bessie Head," *Callaloo* 16.1 (1993): 147. Rob Nixon aligns Head's stories (specifically "The Wind and a Boy") with journalism rather than with the short story; "Border Country," 124.

These plays with a difference between the short story and oral tradition are also clear in those aspects of the story involving questions of knowledge, representation and narrative focus: i.e. questions of the *epistemological border*. Oral tradition is also represented in "The Wind and a Boy" by the figure of the people (or just "people"), who surface all through the exposition as intrusive fragments of pseudo-iterative narrative – for example, "She is like that," people remarked, "because he may be the last child she will ever nurse..." (70). The people also surface in the mixing of focal agents at the end of the narrative and in the conflict of interpretations of whose fault this tragedy is:

> As was village habit, the incident was discussed thoroughly from all sides till it was understood. In this timeless, sleepy village, the goats stood and suckled their young ones on the main road or lay down and took their afternoon naps there. The motorists either stopped for them or gave way. But it appeared that the driver of the truck had neither brakes on his car nor a driving licence. He belonged to the new, rich civil-servant class whose salaries had become fantastically high since independence. They had to have cars in keeping with their new status; they had to have any car, as long as it was a car; they were in such a hurry about everything that they couldn't be bothered to take driving lessons. And thus progress, development, and a pre-occupation with status and living-standards first announced themselves to the village. It looked like being an ugly story with many decapitated bodies on the main road. (75)

Reading through the story, it is possible to trace the project-values of the people as being to maintain the social order, to be entertained or charmed, to understand and to remember. They thus become a figure of storytelling in general and – in their need to understand – of representational discourse. But in this last passage, their focus is intertwined with that of the narrator-figure of the short story and of the "sly civility" of these village tales. Through framing comments, the narrator interprets their interpretation and adds to it. The narrator's initial marker that we are to hear what the villagers made of the tragedy becomes part of the explanation, reaffirming the status of "this timeless, sleepy village" (an outside perspective) as place where by "habit" an incident could be "discussed thoroughly from all sides till it was understood." After giving the reader access to what has become evident to the villagers – the nature of the car-driver – the narrator's perspective returns in the last two sentences, making it ambivalent to what degree the people (be it in contrast to or in agreement with the narrator) see this specific road death as symbolic of national progress, etc.

Some commentators on Head's work set out to analyse her use of the tragic form, reaching the conclusion that this use is subversive, either in its 'African' attitude to community and to conflict within the family, or in its focus on the suffering of people living on the margins – rather than at the centre of the state.[20] I have already invoked the tragic here several times; like many short stories, "The Wind and a Boy" bears more structural similarities to the dramatic form of tragedy than to longer prose works. It utilizes compression, unity of action, and a climactic turning-point, and raises questions of fault and of audience affect. The pseudo-iteratives of the people function in a way similar to that of the chorus in classical tragedy. As in classical tragedies, the turning-point in "The Wind and a Boy" comes near to the ending, and lends the latter a certain finality – in this case, the finality of death. This ending, however, is at the same time a beginning, here clearly announced as the beginning of "an ugly story with many decapitated bodies on the main road."[21] Here, Head's use of the tragic form is subversive in the sense that it makes one aware that this may also be the case in classical tragedy – the prime example being the ending of *King Oedipus*, which marks the end of Oedipus' reign over Thebes, but also the start of a new era for the plague-threatened Thebes, now cleansed of Oedipus.

If the death of Friedman is the main temporal border in the text – the main motif which Sejosenye, the people, the narrator and the reader must

---

[20] Carole Anne Taylor, "Tragedy Reborn(e): *A Question of Power* and the Soul-Journeys of Bessie Head," *Genre* 26.2–3 (1993): 331–51; Earl G. Ingersoll, "The Universality of Tragedy? The Case of Bessie Head," *International Fiction Review* 26.1 (1999): 36–45.

[21] Head, "The Wind and a Boy," 75. This final phrase takes the name symbolism of the story to a new, autobiographical level by evoking Bessie Head's own name – a curiously erased signature at the very edge of the text.

interpret – it is, of course, intimately connected to the birth of a new era of "progress" and "development" (75). Its associated topographical border, the embankment which divides the village from the main road, thus attains the status of being the primary such border in the text. The window violated in the break-in carried out by the boys of the village is a secondary version of this topographical border, and is associated with another temporal border in Friedman's life, that of coming into subjecthood, of ceasing to be an extension of Sejosenye. As this border zone is disseminated back through the text in its various re-complications, it reaches right back to Friedman's birth and naming at the hospital. But already this temporal border is associated with the division between the village and its outside, or home and the foreign: for Friedman is named after "a friendly foreign doctor named Friedman" (70) who took a liking to Sejosenye. Using phonemic and orthographic repetition (*f-r-* repeated three times in association with *ie* or *ei*), the phrase sets up a striking symbolism to the name *Friedman*, bringing it together with both *friendly* (not unconnected to the German *Friedmann*, Peace-man) and *foreign* (uncanny when juxtaposed with the aforementioned word-play on national independence, the *Freed man*).

The implication of this dissemination of the border back through the text is that Friedman is always already a split character – from the moment of his naming, even from the moment of his birth and conception by his town-dwelling mother. He has always carried the border between the village and its outside within him – as has his grandmother, from the moment she learns about Robinson Crusoe at the missionary school she attended as a girl (70). He is akin to the bridge figures Edward O. Ako finds elsewhere in Head's work, and is one of Head's "good" men. But, as Sara Chetin implies, he is an unsuccessful "Friday" (again, a word-play on "Friedman") in comparison to Robinson Crusoe, both in Sejosenye's elephant-killing and in Defoe's colonial version.[22] As I have shown in connection with the two explicit topographical borders of the novel, this

[22] Ako, "Crossing Borders"; Chetin, "Myth, Exile, and the Female Condition," 132. For another failed border figure in Head's fictions, see Harrow's reading of Galethebege in the story "Heaven Is Not Closed"; "Bessie Head and Death," 170–71.

splitting is not only based on a political or social neocolonial border, but also on an tragic fault in Friedman's character, his internal split between irresponsibility and responsibility. The question is whether in Friedman's case responsibility and irresponsibility – and the whole problem of his character 'development', his individual 'progress' towards subjective 'independence' – can avoid an interpretative return to the neocolonial border on a more allegorical level.

The Postcolonial Border

Whether the theme of the story has to do with the specificities of neocolonialism or with the concept of responsibility in general, it does provide an apposite and realist description of a postcolonial situation. While, as Rob Nixon points out, Botswana was only very lightly colonized and precolonial culture there was certainly allowed to survive in different forms, its whole socio-economic structure – especially where gender and work are concerned – is predicated on the heavily colonized South Africa.[23] Parental absence in the story is a social fact as much as it is a matter of morality.

The ending also makes clear that the story must also be read against a neocolonial horizon. Here the placing of the border between the local and the global – an embankment separating the village and its outside – is crucial. Spivak's international division of labour does not, in Head generally and in "The Wind and a Boy" specifically, coincide with national borders, but appears, rather, as an internal border within the nation (and even, of course, within individual subjects). It is the village, and not the ex-colony, that is threatened by modernity. As Nixon notes, "for Head the nation was less an organic community than a set of administered categories that militated against her efforts to cultivate community and ancestry."[24] This is an example of the national uncanny as described by Bhabha, and encapsulated in the association of 'foreign' and 'indepen-

---

[23] Nixon, "Border Country," 124.

[24] "Border Country," 111.

dent' in the name "Friedman" as presented above.[25] The way in which Nixon describes Head's wish to create transnational and local identities suggests that her exilic consciousness rejects organic and pseudo-organic conceptions of identity, giving preference to incomplete and performative affiliations.

The temporal specificity of the postcolonial situation is, however, threatened by the dissemination of the border within the time of the story. The dead boy and the dead grandmother are not victims of a postcolonial situation alone, but victims of a paradoxically postcolonial *and* neocolonial situation. The fact that Friedman and Sejosenye are revealed as always already split implies that we have to do not only with split subjects here, but with split societies as well, and societies that are split *along* the well-ordered historicist precolonial–colonial–postcolonial continuum. As Nixon writes,

> The sense of Head's passage through versions of the precolonial, colonial, and postcolonial eras – though not in that order and decidedly not in any sequence that could be read as synonymous with "progress" – ensures that her later writing offers a rare commentary on the porous, ambiguous frontlines among these historical divides.[26]

The tragic situation in "The Wind and a Boy" makes it impossible to locate or date the exact turning-point: Did Friedman die because he was hit by a car, or because he was sent to buy food, or because his mother gave him money for a bicycle, or because he was told the story of Robinson Crusoe, or because he broke into a house, or because his grandmother named him after a friendly foreign doctor, or because his grandmother was an independent woman, or because she was taught in a missionary school, or because she had had the gift of storytelling passed on to her?

---

[25] See the chapter "DissemiNation: Time, Narrative and the Margins of the Modern Nation," in Bhabha, *The Location of Culture*, 139–70, 266–69.

[26] Nixon, "Border Country," 124–25. He also makes an important point about a certain shifting in Head's writing when he states that it addresses problems common to rural communities in South Africa and to those ostensibly described, in Botswana (123–24).

On the outside of the village, the modern is aligned with the archaic. As Bhabha writes in the introduction to *The Location of Culture*,

> we find ourselves in the moment of transit where space and time cross to produce complex figures of difference and identity, past and present, inside and outside, inclusion and exclusion. For there is a sense of disorientation, a disturbance of direction, in the "beyond": an exploratory, restless movement […]..[27]

The allegory of development, progress, and responsibility in Head's story is an allegory ambivalent to the very concept of development, progress, and (paternal) responsibility.

However, Spivak's global border is not just a violent imposition of power resulting in deaths of the kind described in "The Wind and a Boy." It is also an epistemological border, a divide to be crossed not only by the political representations associated with physical power (*vertreten*), but also by the discursive representations associated with the aesthetic (*darstellen*).[28] In her article "Can the Subaltern Speak," she criticizes the notion that the (neo)colonial divide can be made transparent, for in allowing the appropriation of the Other, such transparency – such uncritical representation – only becomes part of the power-structure. However, in "The Wind and a Boy," as in "Can the Subaltern Speak" (with its analyses of colonial and nationalist appropriations of widow-burning in India), this problem of representation becomes emblematically the problem of representing women's suffering. "The Wind and a Boy" ends apparently in interpretative closure, with the agreement that the kind of death Friedman has succumbed to will happen again and again. But as shown above, his death may be explained in other ways as well, and besides, this is the perspective of the story which begins with the ending of the tragedy. The other perspective, that of the story which ends together with the tragedy and which carries inside it the moment of tragic recognition (as set out by Aristotle in his *Poetics*), is Sejosenye's perspective. The grandmother provides an alternative interpretation,

---

[27] Bhabha, *The Location of Culture*: 1.

[28] For discussion of the two different terms used by Marx, both translatable by 'represent', see Spivak, "Can the Subaltern Speak?" 275–79.

but one that cannot be represented except through the absence of representation.[29] It is an interpretation beyond language: "they [People of Ga-Sefete-Molemo ward] heard the matter-of-fact voice of the policeman announce the death, then they heard Sejosenye say piteously: "Can't you return those words back?" (74) … "The stories brought to them by way of the nurses were too terrible for words. They said the old woman sang and laughed and talked to herself all the time" (75). It is, like death itself, beyond the human: "Then her feet tripped her up and she fell to the ground like a stunned log" (75). And, as shown above, even Sejosenye's death is covered in an ellipsis.[30] Indeed, the whole story is figured by absences of other kinds, especially those of Friedman's mother and father, the latter replaced by Dr. Friedman, Robinson Crusoe, and the car-driver in ways that call attention to the original absence.[31]

Thus, as Sara Chetin writes, "The storyteller's tales end as the old woman lies talking and laughing to herself, her audience [Friedman] having become a victim of its own susceptibility."[32] The story told, presumably like the songs Sejosenye sang "as they sat by the outdoor fire" (71), is replaced by the "ugly story" of car-crashes in the last sentence, and

---

[29] Cf. Lionnet (writing in extension of a reading of the story "The Collector of Treasures"): "This is the contradiction inherent in the relationship between textuality and reality: it emphasizes that the problematics of universalism in the context of women's literatures remains a dead letter so long as women's silences and body languages continue to be ignored or recuperated by the symbolic order, thus becoming 'black holes' (so to speak) within and against which all interpretive discourses can only come to a halting stop"; Lionnet, "Geographies of Pain," 150.

[30] The figure of Sejosenye might be discussed further, including consideration of her connection with the land – she is a successful agriculturalist – and the fact that her lands are also outside the village. Cf. Lionnet's discussion of female heterotopias (utopian female "other spaces") in Head ("Geographies of Pain," 133). Cf. also Nixon's discussion of Head's views on the relationship between women and territory ("Border Country," 125–31).

[31] For a discussion of absent mothers in Head's writing and own life, see Liz Gunner, "Mothers, Daughters and Madness in Works by Four Women Writers: Bessie Head, Jean Rhys, Tsitsi Dangarembga and Ama Ata Aidoo," *Alif: Journal of Comparative Poetics* 14 (1994): 139–41.

[32] Chetin, "Myth, Exile, and the Female Condition," 132.

finds new audiences. For these, the expected representations of oral literature are replaced by something less reassuring. Here, the "sly civilities" of Bhabha's native when interrogated by the colonist are brought together with the horror encountered at the very border of culture in Bhabha's "colonial" literature, situated within "a fine tension between the melancholic homelessness of the modern novelist, and the wisdom of the sage-like storyteller whose craft takes him no further afield than his own people."[33] Appropriately, the ugliness comes at the very end of the story, when the reader is on the verge of understanding what has happened, much like Marlow discovering the "horror" in Joseph Conrad's *Heart of Darkness*, at the point where he has finally made contact with that symbol of modernity, Kurtz, in the middle of the jungle – coincidentally, also the point of contact (or absence of contact, the border he does not cross) with the presumed archaic life of the people who live in this "jungle."

The figure of the postcolonial border (and not purely in its symbolic form) thus informs very clearly the double lesson of the story: that development is not necessarily a good thing, but that it is not necessarily easy to represent its ambivalence. This is ultimately because representations are always part of the situation, and not just representations *of* it. Part *and* parcel.[34]

❧

---

[33] Bhabha, *The Location of Culture*, 123. Bhabha, as his footnote makes clear, refers in this tension to Walter Benjamin's essay on the storyteller.

[34] Many thanks to Ulrike Spring for her incisive comments and suggestions during the writing process, and to those students in Tromsø and conference delegates in Bergen who have also given me many helpful hints.

WORKS CITED

Abrahams, Cecil, ed. *The Tragic Life: Bessie Head and Literature in Southern Africa (*Trenton NJ: Africa World Press, 1990).

Ako, Edward O. "Crossing Borders: A Study of Bessie Head's *When Rain Clouds Gather* and *Maru.*" *Commonwealth: Essays and Studies* 22.2 (2000): 5–11.

Bazin, Nancy Topping. "Madness, Mysticism, and Fantasy: Shifting Perspectives in the Novels of Doris Lessing, Bessie Head, and Nadine Gordimer," *Extrapolation* 33.1 (1992): 73–87

Bhabha, Homi K. *The Location of Culture* (London: Routledge, 1994).

Brown, Coreen. *The Creative Vision of Bessie Head* (Madison WI: Fairleigh Dickinson UP & London: Associated UP, 2003).

Chetin, Sara. "Myth, Exile, and the Female Condition: Bessie Head's *The Collector of Treasures.*" *Journal of Commonwealth Literature* 24.1 (1989): 114–37.

Derrida, Jacques. "La loi du genre" (1980), in *Parages* (Paris: Galilée, 1986): 249–287; tr. by Avital Ronell as "The Law of Genre," in *Acts of Literature*, ed. Derek Attridge (New York: Routledge, 1992): 211–52.

Ezenwa–Ohaeto, "Windows of Womanhood" (1990), in *The Tragic Life*, ed. Abrahams, 123–31.

Garrett, James M. "Writing Community: Bessie Head and the Politics of Nature," *Research in African Literatures* 30.2 (1999): 122–35.

Gunner, Liz. "Mothers, Daughters and Madness in Works by Four Women Writers: Bessie Head, Jean Rhys, Tsitsi Dangarembga and Ama Ata Aidoo," *Alif: Journal of Comparative Poetics* 14 (1994): 136–51.

Harrow, Kenneth W. "Bessie Head and Death: Change on the Margins." *Shades of Empire: In Colonial and Post-Colonial Literatures*, ed. C.C. Barfoot & Theo D'haen (Amsterdam: Rodopi, 1993): 165–78.

Head, Bessie. "The Wind and a Boy," in Head, *The Collector of Treasures and Other Botswana Village Tales* (London: Heinemann, 1977).

——. "Social and Political Pressures that Shape Literature in Southern Africa" (1990), in *The Tragic Life*, ed. Abrahams, 11–17.

Ingersoll, Earl G. "The Universality of Tragedy? The Case of Bessie Head," *International Fiction Review* 26.1 (1999): 36–45.

Lionnet, Françoise. "Geographies of Pain: Captive Bodies and Violent Acts in the Fictions of Myriam Warner–Vieyra, Gayl Jones, and Bessie Head," *Callaloo* 16.1 (1993): 132–52.

Nixon, Rob. "Border Country: Bessie Head's Frontline States," *Social Text* 36 (1993): 106–37.

Ogwude, Sophia Obiajulu. "Protest and Commitment in Bessie Head's Utopia," *Research in African Literatures* 29.3 (1998): 70–81.

Ojo–Ade, Femi. "Of Human Trials and Triumphs" (1990), in *The Tragic Life*, ed. Abrahams, 79–92.

Olaussen, Maria. *Forceful Creation in Harsh Terrain: Place and Identity in Three Novels by Bessie Head* (New York: Peter Lang, 1997).

Schimanski, Johan. "Genre Borders in a Border Novel: Nadine Gordimer's *My Son's Story*," in *Genrer och genreproblem: teoretiska och historiska perspektiv / Genres and Their Problems: Theoretical and Historical Perspectives*. ed. Beata Agrell & Ingela Nilsson (Göteborg: Daidalos, 2003): 505–13.

——. "Den litterære grensen: Knut Hamsuns 'Dronningen af Saba'," in *Att forska om gränser*. ed. José L. Ramírez (Stockholm: Nordregio, 2001): 141–70. <http://www.nordregio.se/Files/ro103p141.pdf>. For an English version, see Johan Schimanski, "A Poetics of the Border: Nation and Genre in *Wythnos yng Nghymru Fydd* and Other Texts by Islwyn Ffowc Elis" (doctoral dissertation, Oslo University, 1996).

Spivak, Gayatri Chakravorty. "Can the Subaltern Speak?" in *Marxism and the Interpretation of Culture*, ed. Cary Nelson & Lawrence Grossberg (Urbana: U of Illinois P, 1988): 271–313.

Taylor, Carole Anne. "Tragedy Reborn(e): *A Question of Power* and the Soul-Journeys of Bessie Head," *Genre* 26.2–3 (1993): 331–51.

Thomas, H. Nigel. "Narrative Strategies in Bessie Head's Stories" (1990), in *The Tragic Life*, ed. Abrahams, 93–103.

❧

The Intimate Presence of Death in the Novels of Zakes Mda

❧ Necrophilic Worlds and Traditional Belief

DAVID BELL

THE FIRST NOVEL by the South African author and playwright Zakes Mda, *Ways of Dying* (1995), is set mainly in the period of extreme internecine strife that followed the release of Mandela in 1990, but prior to the first democratic elections in 1994. It does, however, through flashbacks and memory, include the last years of the apartheid regime. As a comment on both apartheid and the 1990–94 period, with its horrific violence, the novel contains the memorable phrase "our ways of dying are our ways of living."[1] Although death and dying are significant features of all Mda's work, not just in the novel mentioned above, I would argue that death has wider implications than being simply a reflection of the violence that has characterized the history of Southern Africa. The seemingly simple expression quoted above draws attention to the dual meaning of death in life and non-life. My purpose here is to explore the ways in which death acts as a metaphor applicable to two separate conditions in Mda's novels. First, it functions ideologically as a means of depicting oppressive societies, and is thereby an implicit critique of those societies. Secondly, it functions as a mode of expression for, and exploration of the role of, traditional belief in South Africa. In this study I

---

[1] Zakes Mda, *Ways of Dying* (Cape Town: Oxford UP, 1995): 98.

will focus on Zakes Mda's first three novels, *Ways of Dying* (1995), *She Plays with the Darkness* (1995), and *The Heart of Redness* (2000).

The starting-point for my discussion of death as a political metaphor in these novels is Paulo Freire's term 'necrophilic worlds'. Freire applies the term to societies discernible in a class analysis of the specific historical conditions obtaining in Latin America during the 1960s and 1970s. Though basing his observations on Latin America, Freire considered these conditions to be equally applicable to other Third-World countries, which would include those of the Africa continent.[2] On the basis of his Marxist analysis, Freire postulates two contrasting types of societies, the anti-dialogic and the dialogic, which constitute dehumanizing and humanizing societies. In Freire's view, anti-dialogic behaviour occurs in societies that are sectarian: i.e. engage in "myth making" and "false reality," and in which the distinguishing behavioural characteristics are conquest, divide and rule, manipulation, and cultural invasion.[3] This description applies to societies he labels 'metropolitan' and 'director', of which the former are imperial and colonial and the latter national and neocolonial.[4] Characteristically, the ruling elites in these societies oppress their citizens (with whom they operate in a relationship of interdependence), generate a culture of silence, and have the propensity to attempt to domesticate/determine the future. Within themselves they generate an object-society of the oppressed and thereby constitute what Freire terms 'necrophilic worlds'.[5] Even from this brief survey of the salient points in Freire's argument, it should be clear that this type of left-wing critique of society applies equally well to apartheid South Africa and to the countries of Latin America. It is also clear that the work of liberation in which both Freire and Augusto Boal were involved has echoes in the struggle against apartheid.

---

[2] Paulo Freire, *Cultural Action for Freedom 2000 Edition* (Cambridge MA: Harvard Educational Review, 2000): 44.

[3] Paulo Freire, *Pedagogy of the Oppressed*, tr. Myra Bergman Ramos (1972; Harmondsworth: Penguin, 1990): 17, 108–22.

[4] Freire, *Cultural Action for Freedom:* 8–9, 45–46.

[5] *Cultural Action for Freedom*, 56.

The link between Freire to Mda is not, however, fortuitous. Mda has already expressed his debt to Freire and Boal, among others, in his scholarly study of theatre for development, *When People Play People* (1993),[6] and his early novels have been seen by one critic as an extension of this interest in creating a "new kind of text with a humanistic ethos," and as indicating "new ways of living which are able to free the social imagination of the oppressed from the mind-set induced by the conditions of apartheid."[7] More importantly, Freire's concepts of the dialogic and anti-dialogic society[8] function as integral and determining features of Mda's narratives, thereby enabling a critical analysis of both the historical development of and the current situation in Southern Africa. From this perspective, I would argue that the critique of past and present social structures in Southern Africa contained in Mda's novels can be seen in terms of a denunciation of these societies as anti-dialogic and is thus in keeping with Freire's dynamics of revolution.[9] The latter model has the dual function of both identifying the true conditions of anti-dialogic societies and of initiating the process of change that will bring into being a dialogic society – one that frees people from their currently oppressed state. In applying Freire's ideas to Mda's novels, my focus is on the anti-dialogic nature of the societies he depicts, and represents one aspect (the negative) of the revolutionary process.

In Mda's novels, this anti-dialogic and sectarian world is explored as the site of the exercise of power by an entrenched elite, whether this power be exercised by imperialist Europeans, the neocolonial rulers of African states, or the leaders of the revolution in the new South Africa – all of whom exhibit, to varying degrees, conquest, manipulation and cultural invasion. The inability of this elite to engage in dialogue ensures the continuation of the silence of the oppressed and the perpetuation of the, in

---

[6] Zakes Mda, *When People Play People: Development Communication Through Theatre* (Johannesburg: Witwatersrand UP; London & New York: Zed, 1993).

[7] Margaret Mervis, "Fiction for Development: Zakes Mda's *Ways of Dying*," *Current Writing* 10.1 (1998): 41, 42.

[8] Freire, *Pedagogy of the Oppressed*, 135–46, 108–16.

[9] Freire, *Cultural Action for Freedom:* 30.

Freire's terms, 'unauthentic' society.[10] From this perspective, death and dying in the worlds Mda creates is not simply the result of an oppressive rule, but is a metaphor for these necrophilic worlds.

The three novels discussed here cover various periods in the history of Southern Africa, but in order to foreground the historical consistency of the metaphor the following periodization will be followed: a period of colonization; the apartheid period; the interregnum of 1990–94; neocolonialism in Lesotho; and the democratic period in South Africa.

The premeditated destruction and barbarism of the British imperial project in South Africa is most closely explored in *The Heart of Redness*, where Mda intertwines an historical narrative, which deals with the 1850–53 Mlanjeni War and the Nongqawuse episode and its attendant Cattle-Killing of 1856–57, with a story of contemporary South Africa set in the Eastern Cape. At a number of points in the historical narrative, Xhosa and British perceptions and beliefs are set in opposition. This contrast is singularly apparent in a gruesome scene in which British troops are observed boiling the head of a dead amaXhosa warrior. The amaXhosa guerrillas who witness this incident believe that the British soldiers are engaging in the practice of removing *iqungu*, the vengeful force of war medicine, which the amaXhosa do by mutilating the bodies of dead soldiers.[11] However, the process is explained to them, quite unconcernedly, by one of the British soldiers/interpreters who is captured by the guerrillas as one carried out by "civilized men" who will use the heads as "souvenirs" or for "scientific enquiry."[12] In a situation of insular rationalizations that replace dialogue, the amaXhosa mutilation of the dead enemy to prevent *iqungu* is considered by the British as "savagery of the worst kind" and the collection of boiled heads for souvenirs or for scientific enquiry becomes, in the minds of the amaXhosa, the "witchcraft of the white man."[13] Within the context of belief held by the amaXhosa guerrillas whose father has been beheaded, the death of the headless ancestor, who

---

[10] Freire, *Pedagogy of the Oppressed*, 60.

[11] Zakes Mda, *The Heart of Redness* (Cape Town: Oxford UP, 2000): 20.

[12] Mda, *The Heart of Redness*, 21.

[13] *The Heart of Redness*, 20, 21.

may thereby not mediate with the dead, is believed to have significant consequences for the future of the family and the clan, which the contemporary narrative confirms.[14]

The British determination to win the Mlanjeni war and subjugate the amaXhosa ensures that atrocities to individual Xhosa warriors are compounded by other practices that go beyond the expected conventions of normal warfare as seen by Europeans and far exceed the normal boundaries of military behaviour that the amaXhosa could expect from an enemy.[15] In Mda's fictive account, which closely follows Peires' definitive history, *The Dead Will Arise* (1989), Sir George Cathcart, the Governor, orders his soldiers "to go on a rampage and burn amaXhosa fields and kill amaXhosa cattle," and, as Mda expresses it, when the troops find "unarmed women in the fields they [kill] them too."[16] For the soldiers, this becomes merely an extension of the official imperial policy as expressed by the previous Governor, Sir Harry Smith: that of wishing to "exterminate the beasts."[17]

Although Mda's depiction of British aggression is faithful to the available historical accounts, the historical narrative in *The Heart of Redness* is not concerned simply with the oppression of imperialism, but equally with the failure of Xhosa society to cope with the external pressure of British colonial expansion and the internal dissension brought about by the prophecies of Nongqawuse. As a result of the cattle-killing and the burning of the crops in expectation of the return of the dead, many thousands of the amaXhosa starved to death. The denouement of the cattle-killing episode of 1856–57 is most poignantly expressed in the description of widespread starvation that ensues and in the death of Twin, who epitomizes the fate of the believers, the followers of Nongqawuse. Images of death and destitution are seen through the eyes of Twin and his family as they travel the country in search of nourishment:

---

[14] Mda, *The Heart of Redness*, 22.

[15] J.B. Peires, *The House of Phalo: A History of the Xhosa People in the Days of Their Independence* (1981; Berkeley: U of California P, 1982): 66.

[16] Mda, *The Heart of Redness*, 25.

[17] *The Heart of Redness*, 19.

> On the way they came across many dead bodies lying on the road. Some of the bodies had not finished dying yet. [...] Their cracked skin looked like land that had been thoroughly punished by drought.[18]

The British response to this tragedy is to take the remaining able-bodied people into the colony as cheap labour and to take over the abandoned farms. The amaXhosa who are not able-bodied are left to be cared for by charity, but even this is eventually prohibited. Twin is one of the more unfortunate:

> Twin was too weak to attract the interest of anyone at the labour market. He ended up as an inmate of the Kaffir Relief House, and there he lived with people who had been made raving mad by starvation until he went raving mad himself.[19]

Twin finally dies a lonely, undignified death.

While *The Heart of Redness* focuses on the early-nineteenth-century expansion of the British into the amaXhosa lands, and also on the contemporary Eastern Cape (an aspect to which I will return), his other two novels, *Ways of Dying* and *She Plays with the Darkness*, bring into focus the later apartheid years, the interregnum of 1990–94, and neocolonialism in Lesotho.

Again the images of death serve to define the nature of these societies and the options available. Toloki's progress in *Ways of Dying* from rural deprivation to an urban slum is primarily a story of insight into the realities of apartheid and a decline into silence. "Toloki's odyssey to a wondrous world of freedom and riches" finds him walking "day and night, passing through farmlands and through small towns that reeked of discrimination against people of his colour."[20] This discrimination is reinforced by the burning to death of the man who befriended him in a joyless game played between black servant and white master – the latter described as "a big white baas [who] is very friendly and likes to play with

[18] Mda, *The Heart of Redness*, 294.

[19] *The Heart of Redness*, 298.

[20] Mda, *Ways of Dying*, 51, 52.

black workers," though his idea of fun is to douse them with petrol, set them alight, and laugh at their antics.[21] Perhaps more disconcertingly, Toloki is only able to make a living from the one activity that embraces all society – the burial of the dead. His creativc invention of the occupation of a professional mourner keeps him alive, but it is an alienated life-style and generates a 'thought-language', the language used to refer to reality,[22] which is so ingrained that after only a day's absence from his profession "his body needs to mourn."[23] Despite Toloki's much-appreciated performances, it is also a profession that effectively silences him. Thus Toloki's odyssey is a pilgrim's progress through the valley of the shadow of death.

Being deliberately set alight by a white "baas" constitutes a key image for the inhuman nature of apartheid, but death by fire is also a significant metonym for the violence of the interregnum, the 1990–94, period. In a particularly horrifying scene, the Young Tigers of an unofficial settlement force a young girl to set light to the petrol-filled tyre hung around her five-year-old friend Vutha (which means 'fire'):

> Danisa's match fell into Vutha's tyre. It suddenly burst into flames. His screams were swallowed by the raging flames, the crackle of burning flesh, and the blowing wind.[24]

The necklacing of Vutha and his friend is meant as a punishment for their consorting with the enemy, who consists of the nearby migrant-worker hostel-dweller and the reactionary elements in the police and armed forces. These groups have already made a vicious attack on the settlement indiscriminately killing women, children and even a new-born baby.[25] As both Freire and Boal would express it, it is a world that lacks dialogue and is one that removes all options excepting the terminal.[26]

---

[21] Mda, *Ways of Dying*, 56.

[22] Freire, *Pedagogy of the Oppressed*, 69.

[23] Mda, *Ways of Dying*, 141.

[24] *Ways of Dying*, 177.

[25] *Ways of Dying*, 170.

[26] Cf. Augusto Boal, *Theater of the Oppressed*, tr. Charles A. McBride, Maria–Odilia Leal McBride & Emily Fryer (1979; London: Pluto, 2000): 254; Freire, *Oppressed*, 61.

In *She Plays with the Darkness*, Mda offers two contrasting responses, in the lives of Radisene and Dikosha, to a neocolonial society and the development of alienated thought-language. Here, death offers a means of making money in a free-market economy or a retreat from the 'real' world through contact with the ancestors. Radisene's success is built around the corrupt and macabre occupation of a claimant of third-party insurance from motor-vehicle accidents. His job is to claim bodies and sign up the relatives of the deceased to help them gain their insurance. Radisene exploits the ignorance and illiteracy of the relatives to cheat them of much of their money, and this makes him a rich man who is able to embrace and imitate a Western life-style. However, having lost his wealth and in desperate need of re-making his life-style, Radisene finds himself in a situation in which he transgress against the rituals and respect of a family in mourning. He is no longer able to continue his 'profession' and is thereby forced to accept his fate as bankrupt and failure.

Dikosha, by contrast, seeks self-fulfilment by making contact with the spirits of the ancestors who are realized in the prehistoric paintings in the Cave of Barwa. These are paintings which spell-bind and overwhelm her.[27] By communicating with the dead, Dikosha lives an estranged life from her community and is able to survive almost without ageing until the graffiti of the tourists finally conceal and smother the figures, thus preventing their continued communication with her.[28] Lacking support from her primordial ancestors, Dikosha seeks solace in the traditional music of a young boy,[29] Shana, and, after his death in the mist, in darkness.[30]

The responses of both Radisene and Dikosha to a neocolonial society represent Freire's "ineffective, false words" in which "the reality as thought does not correspond to the reality being lived objectively."[31] In the penultimate scene of the novel, the brother and sister are brought together; the final lines indicate their transformation into doves, a transcendence into the symbolic world of the dead but not forgotten.

---

[27] Mda, *She Plays with the Darkness* (Florida Hills, SA: Vivlia, 1995): 16.

[28] Mda, *She Plays with the Darkness*, 102.

[29] *She Plays with the Darkness*, 103.

[30] *She Plays with the Darkness*, 169.

[31] Freire, *Cultural Action for Freedom*, 8.

My final example of death as a metaphor for necrophilic worlds is that of post-apartheid South Africa, the nature of which is foregrounded at the beginning of *The Heart of Redness*. Camagu, the protagonist of the contemporary narrative in this novel, finds himself at Giggles, a nightclub in Hillbrow, Johannesburg, an area where "every morning a number of dead bodies adorn the streets."[32] Dispirited by the company and "the out-of-tune piano [which] murdered Abdullah Ibrahim with every clunk," he decides to go for a walk. Rather than walk the unsafe streets, he follows some people who are climbing to the top of a high-rise building where "a vigil is in progress in a tattered tent," and here "he joins the mourners and mourns the dead."[33] At this vigil, neither the music nor the deceased man has been murdered. He has "waned away, until he was a bag of bones" and his departure is mourned by a "'home-girl' with a beautiful voice."[34] The deceased is the modern-day Twin who has suffered the same fate as his nineteenth-century namesake, with clear implications for the interpretation of the contemporary and historical narratives of the novel, the link between past and present.

❧

The intimate presence of death in Mda's novels lends itself, I would argue, to the kind of interpretation I have engaged in so far. The lesson is, in the sense that Mda's work is didactic and allegoric, that Southern Africa, both historically and in the present, can be seen as a depressingly necrophilic world. In this second part, I wish to extend the discussion and explore the way in which beliefs arising out of death and the rituals associated with death constitute an area of critical awareness within the debate on tradition versus modernity with reference to the authenticity of cultural renewal. In this respect, my discussion shifts from the negative qualities of death as envisaged in my first part to an understanding of death as a means to understanding the rituals of life and thereby initiating a process

---

[32] Mda, *The Heart of Redness*, 29.

[33] *The Heart of Redness*, 29.

[34] *The Heart of Redness*, 4.

of identity and critical awareness that enables the radical transformation of societies that Freire sees as necrophilic.

Implicit in my discussion of the rituals of death is the recognition of synthesis that is a feature of Mda's exposition of beliefs in Southern Africa, but it also pays attention to his recognition of the complexities of the synthesis of cultures. I will focus on two episodes in *The Heart of Redness* that illustrate my argument. *The Heart of Redness* is apt for this purpose, as it deals specifically with the nature of Xhosa belief both historically and in the present, yet does not condemn or condone a particular set of beliefs. As David Lloyd comments on this novel, Mda displays "a belief in the spirituality of the people without necessary embracing belief."[35]

The two episodes in *The Heart of Redness* I will examine are the initial voicing of Nongqawuse's prophecies to the amaXhosa in the historical narrative and the lingering death of Zim in the contemporary one. In the first, Mda draws attention to the syncretic nature of traditional belief as represented by the Nongqawuse prophecies and problematizes the dynamics of change. In the second, he draws attention to the nature and role of belief in the modern world.

In the historical narrative, Mhlakaza's announcement of the appearance of strangers to his niece Nongqawuse and his account of their message is clearly received with some scepticism by the Xhosa people. Mhlakaza claims that Nongqawuse has been instructed by "messengers of Naphakade, He-Who-Is-Forever, the descendant of Sifuba–Sibanzi, the Broad-Chested-One."[36] This is problematic for the amaXhosa present – as the narrator explains, "People were confused. They had not heard of He-Who-Is-Forever, nor of the Broad-Chested-One." Thus, to be accepted these deities have to be incorporated into a known frame of reference which is given as "the name of the god of the amaXhosa people ... the one who is known by everyone as Qamata or Mvelingqangi ... the one who was called Mdalidephu by Nxele."[37]

---

[35] David Lloyd, "The Modernization of Redness," review of *The Heart of Redness*, by Zakes Mda, *Scrutiny 2* 6.2 (2001): 35.

[36] Mda, *The Heart of Redness*, 59.

[37] Mda, *The Heart of Redness*, 59.

It is clear that Mda is focusing here on the realignment of belief that, Peires argues, takes place among the Xhosa in the early nineteenth century. As Peires points out in his account of the Xhosa, *The House of Phalo*, Xhosa beliefs prior to the appearance of the prophets Nxele and Ntsikana encompassed a world in which "health and fertility were accepted as the natural condition of things and any deficiency was attributed to dereliction of duty or to the unseen influence of malevolent persons."[38] These beliefs accompanied a practical exercise of religion that included ancestor-worship. With the appearance of the Europeans and their new gods and ideas, an explanation was needed. Peires' thesis is that the Xhosa embraced the Christian ideas of the Last Judgement and the Resurrection to fill a gap in their belief-system. In particular, he argues that

> There had been no satisfactory explanation for death, which was regarded as a product of witchcraft and as the ultimate impurity. [....] The missionary message that the dead did not really die but would rise up again was thus received with joyful misunderstanding.[39]

Mda's narrative draws on this perception and the historical account of the period by ensuring that Nongqawuse's reference to new gods is supplemented by her statement that "The Strangers say that the whole community of the dead will arise."[40] By drawing attention to the internal debate within the amaXhosa following Nongqawuse's revelations, Mda is able to explore the processes involved in a change in belief that causes dissension within the nation and ultimately its self-destruction. In Mda's world, the Believers extend their understanding of "the unseen world [as] active in this one and exercis[ing] an important causal influence" to incorporate a Xhosa vision of the Christian ideas of redemption and resurrection.[41] The vital element in Nongqawuse's prophecies is the idea that, following the killing of cattle, the dead will arise and help to drive the white invaders to

---

[38] Peires, *The House of Phalo*, 67.

[39] *The House of Phalo*, 68.

[40] Mda, *The Heart of Redness*, 60.

[41] Peires, *The House of Phalo*, 68.

the sea. The subsequent narrative of internecine strife and enslavement and the expropriation of land raises the issue of the validity of the Nongqawuse legend and its relevance to the present – which provides the *raison d'être* for the contemporary narrative.

The second episode illustrating my point occurs in the contemporary narrative and is the long-drawn-out death of Zim, descendant of Twin and father of the Twin who died in Hillbrow. Having seen his daughter Qukezwa, the embodiment of Nature, marry Camagu, the Western-educated newcomer to the village, Zim declares "that he could now go in peace, for his work was done."[42] As occurs in both *Ways of Dying* and *She Plays with the Darkness*, the dying person is transfixed in a world between life and death until released into the world of the ancestors: "Then he sat there staring at nothing."[43] Zim's limbo status, in which he remains for many weeks, is explained by the *igqirha*, the diviners, as a battle between Qukezwa, who is nursing Zim, and No England, his deceased wife, who is calling him from the land of the ancestors. Zim's hovering between life and death is compounded by the appearance of his former mistress NomaRussia outside his home. The tussle between the ancestors and the living for the soul of Zim is played out in a macabre tapestry of encroaching death for both Zim and NomaRussia. It is only with NomaRussia's disclosure that Zim's son Twin is dead that the struggle ends: "Zim is told of Twin's demise. For the first time he gives a wan smile. And dies. [...] When people wake up the next morning they find NomaRussia has also died."[44] Thus death becomes a ritual of traditional belief in which the living and the long-dead struggle for the 'soul' of the dying. Although Zim's family is seen as a family of death within the context of the believer/unbeliever struggle, "Zim is now venerated as an ancestor," and can be seen as a victor avenging the failure of the past.[45]

While the demise of Zim is couched in terms of traditional beliefs surrounding dying, death, and ancestors, his descendants, Qukezwa and

---

[42] Mda, *The Heart of Redness*, 288.

[43] *The Heart of Redness*, 288.

[44] *The Heart of Redness*, 308, 309.

[45] *The Heart of Redness*, 309, 314.

Heitsi, embody the synthesis of tradition and modernity. Qukezwa's marriage to Camagu unites her traditional knowledge with Western learning, and the product of their relationship is the unity of these worlds. In the final scene of the novel, Heitsi is seen to reject the sea, from which the believers thought the dead would arise with the cry that "This boy does not belong in the sea! This boy belongs in the man village!"[46]

To my mind, throughout this novel Mda uses traditional beliefs surrounding death and images of dying to explore the dynamic processes of belief-formation within the Xhosa people. In this respect, his representation questions a static concept of an African past and instead suggests a flexible African culture that absorbs, adapts and converts other beliefs into its own practices in a steady process of synthesis.

My purpose has been to develop a twofold approach to death and dying in the novels of Zakes Mda. First, I have argued that Mda's images of death are a metaphor for the necrophilic world described by Freire in his analysis of oppressive societies. Secondly, I have sought to explore the use of ritual and belief as a contribution to the complexities involved in a discussion of tradition versus modernity. It is a discussion that raises pertinent questions about the nature of colonial and postcolonial societies and about the role and relevance of a renewal of African culture and spirituality.

❧

---

[46] *The Heart of Redness*, 320.

WORKS CITED

Boal, Augusto. *Theater of the Oppressed*, tr. Charles A. McBride, Maria–Odilia Leal McBride & Emily Fryer (1979; London: Pluto, 2000).

Freire, Paulo. *Cultural Action for Freedom: 2000 Edition* (Cambridge MA :: Harvard Educational Review, 2000).

——. *Pedagogy of the Oppressed*, tr. Myra Bergman Ramos (1972; Harmondsworth: Penguin, 1990).

Lloyd, David. "The Modernization of Redness," review of *The Heart of Redness*, by Zakes Mda, *Scrutiny 2* 6.2 (2001): 34–39.

Makgoba, M.W., ed. *African Renaissance: The New Struggle* (Cape Town: Tafelberg & Sandton: Mafube, 1999).

Mervis, Margaret. "Fiction for Development: Zakes Mda's *Ways of Dying*," *Current Writing* 10.1 (1998): 39–56.

Mda, Zakes. *The Heart of Redness* (Cape Town: Oxford UP, 2000).

——. *She Plays with the Darkness* (Florida Hills, SA: Vivlia, 1995).

——. *Ways of Dying* (Cape Town. Oxford UP, 1995).

——. *When People Play People: Development Communication Through Theatre* (Johannesburg: Witwatersrand UP & London:: Zed, 1993).

Peires, J.B. *The House of Phalo: A History of the Xhosa People in the Days of Their Independence* (1981. Berkeley: U of California P, 1982).

——. *The Dead Will Arise: Nongqawuse and the Great Cattle-Killing Movement of 1856–7* (Johannesburg: Ravan & Bloomington: Indiana UP, 1989).

❧

Controlling Jean Rhys's Story "On Not Shooting Sitting Birds"[1]

ULLA RAHBEK

WHENEVER I READ Jean Rhys's short story "On Not Shooting Sitting Birds," I always feel compelled to ponder the issue of control. It is there from the very beginning: "There is no control over memory," are the first words of the story.[2] And since the tale is structured around several episodes of intertwined memory we may thus say that, by extension, the structure as such is uncontrollable. But it is not only the issue of time and memory that is hard to pin down, for reader and characters alike. The same is also true on the level of characterization and character communication: the female protagonist and the shadowy male character struggle to control themselves and each other as they don masks to hide their identities. Finally, the issue of control also affects the readers and their attempts at interpretation. If we consider the dictionary definitions of control – to command, check, regulate, limit – might we not say that the act of interpretation is an attempt at controlling the text? In this essay, I try to control "On Not Shooting Sitting Birds," by focusing on these three textual levels: memory, in Jean Rhys's fiction and structure, character, and interpretation. I begin in a circumlocutory

---

[1] Thanks to Annabelle Despard for discussing some of the most uncontrollable aspects of this story.

[2] Jean Rhys, "On Not Shooting Sitting Birds," in *Sleep It Off Lady: Stories by Jean Rhys* (1976; Harmondsworth: Penguin, 1979): 89–92. Further page references are in the main text.

manner, via another person who tried to control Jean Rhys, her one-time rival, Stella Bowen.

In her memoirs, the Australian painter Stella Bowen devotes a couple of pages to her partner Ford Madox Ford's infatuation with the young and beautiful expatriate Jean Rhys. In terms of the issue of control, it is interesting to note how Bowen describes Rhys without ever mentioning her name: she is "Ford's girl," "a really tragic person" who shows Bowen and Ford "an underworld of darkness and disorder" and who, through her poverty and cynicism, teaches the rather prim Australian that "you can't have self-respect without money. You can't even have the luxury of a personality."[3] These comments, I feel, resonate with the story under discussion. We might say that in "On Not Shooting Sitting Birds" Rhys gives us a glimpse of that underworld of darkness and disorder. In the story, the reader is presented with some acts of remembrance that the first-person narrator, the unnamed female protagonist, admits she cannot control. There is a specific piece of memory, though, which sets the wheels in motion: the buying of "pink Milanese silk underclothes" (89). This is a strikingly vivid and detailed concrete object, metonymically hinting at the sensual, even sexual, things about to happen. However, like "the bedroom very obvious in the background" (90) later in the story, when the woman (wearing her new underwear) is taken out to dinner, it remains only an object of unfulfilment and frustration, the effects of which the narrator cannot control.

Structurally, the notion of lack of control, of being unable to restrain and regulate something, is also apparent in the way that specific piece of remembrance (buying the silk underwear) is immediately interrupted by, first, some general reflections on the protagonist's loneliness and outsider status, which give rise to what Bowen called cynicism: "I had started out in life trusting everyone and now I trusted no one" (89). Such feelings make the protagonist embark on bold adventures (no doubt taking place in what Bowen would term an underworld of darkness and disorder), and one of those adventures is what the story centres on. But as she remem-

---

[3] See Stella Bowen, *Drawn From Life: A Memoir* (1941; Sydney: Picador, 1999): 195–96.

bers being on the potentially bold dinner-date with the young man, in a restaurant with a *chambre séparée*, the narrator is unable to control what she remembers, how she remembers it, and the manner in which she expresses her memories.

This lack of control is frustrating for the reader, as it plays havoc with linear structure; for the male character, as he is wholly incapable of grasping what the narrator is talking about; and for the narrator herself, as she experiences this lack of control yet is unable to do anything about it. She remembers that she was sitting there in the restaurant – "on and on I went, almost believing what I was saying" (91) – telling the nearly silent man a story about a shooting party from her Caribbean childhood while at the same time remembering the real party, or at least remembering the childhood memories of the real party. So, just as the story pitches the specific and concrete – the underwear, the bedroom – against the unspecific and general – the unnamed man in some restaurant sometime in the past – so also does it pitch what is expressed against what is unexpressed, the vividly remembered against the, to use the narrator's term, "vague" (89). Affecting it all is the issue of control.

When she comes home from her unsuccessful date, the bedroom unused, the silk underwear still in its pristine state, the narrator again attempts to control the situation: "Some other night perhaps, another sort of man. I slept at once" (92). This conclusion to the story is offered as closure, at least to the recalled event and its effects. The protagonist seems to be in control: she has limited, regulated and curbed the memories which instigated the episode the story centres on. The fact that she immediately falls asleep underlines this. But the fact that the ending also points forward to another, potentially similar story, at the same time suggests that there is no control – just as she cannot control memory, she cannot control the future.

The issue of control is developed further on the level of characterization. There are two characters in the story: the first-person narrator, a young woman, and a shadowy man whom the narrator met somewhere sometime. From the female protagonist–narrator we learn that the man is young and nice enough, but stiff and seemingly confused. "He kept eying me in such a wary puzzled way" (90), we are told. The man is allowed to voice two sentences, both of which illuminate this essay's focus on the question of control. As they are sitting in the restaurant, awkwardly aware of the strategically placed bedroom, the man abruptly says, "But you're a lady, aren't you?" (90). What exactly does he mean? He is clearly judging her both socially and sexually. This blunt and rather extraordinary remark seems to show how confused he his, yet it also provides us with an explanation of why he is so out of place. It is because he cannot control her: her lady-like mask seems to hide a different identity, an identity that the man seems to find threatening and ambiguous. It is also important here to remember that the reader knows about the silk underwear, and the importance of it to the protagonist. We may thus also ask ourselves, in the terms of this story, whether the emphasis on the underwear is a sign that she is, indeed, not a lady at all? The few hints we get of the female protagonist's background may help us understand why the man should feel so unsettled.

We learn in a somewhat roundabout manner that the woman grew up in the Caribbean and that her knowledge of things English is thus received in a manner twice removed, through books. In an attempt to win the man over, she tells him of a shooting party, embroidering on the truth so that, while the man learns about the fictitious party, the narrator also lets the reader know what she remembers of the real event. The man is silent during this tale, clearly still increasingly uneasy. Perhaps he is initially fooled by the narrator, since, to appropriate a phrase by Homi Bhabha, she is almost the same, but not quite. Almost a lady, but not quite. There are no visible signs of difference. She looks like a lady, but by the standards of the young Englishman, she is not. Face to face with her, he is out of control. To draw on Bhabhaian insight once more, might we not say that the young woman is burdened with what he calls a colonial identity, a sort of half-way house between colonizer and colonized, a neurotic, erotic and ambiguous identification with both (the narrator, like Rhys herself, is a white Creole).[4] This double identification accounts for the ambiguity the young man finds disturbing.

---

[4] Homi Bhabha discusses colonial identity primarily in connection with Frantz Fanon. See, for example, his "Foreword: Remembering Frantz Fanon: Self, Psyche and the Colonial Condition," foreword to Frantz Fanon, *Black Skin, White Masks* (1952; London: Pluto, 1986). See also virtually the same essay, entitled

The narrator interrupts her own flow of words by a side remark on the old Dominican parrot in Regent Park Zoo – "a sulky bird, very old" (90). This bird, which the young man evidently does not care about nor has ever paid any attention to, clearly provides the woman with some sort of communal fellowship. Like her, the bird is a Caribbean exotic, alone and out of place, yet on display for those visitors who notice. And, more generally, of course, parrots are the perfect symbol of what we may here call "mimic women." Mimicry, we remember Bhabha suggests, is constructed around ambivalence, difference and excess, the very elements that make it problematic for the young man to stay in control, as he sits there in the restaurant, growing increasingly uncomfortable.[5] Perhaps this is what he gradually understands: instead of being the lady he thought she was, she is to him an uncontrollable and ambiguous mimic woman.

The woman's somewhat neurotic and incessant talk is interrupted by the second sentence the man voices in this story: "Do you mean to say that your brothers shot sitting birds?" (91) The "cold and shocked" (91) voice silences the woman narrator. This question, like his early one about being a lady, concerns class, social status, and proper behaviour: she is clearly no lady and her brothers do not act like gentlemen. To the young man, the woman's looks, like her brother's shooting party, are just pale imitations of the real English thing. To him, they are literally out of control: neither the woman nor her brothers behave as real English people do.

However, we also learn from the woman that she, too, is puzzled and frustrated. Her story about the shooting party, most of it fictitious anyway, had just been an attempt at small talk. She is not able to control her own story, her memories of it, nor the reception of the story. The whole shooting-party story is thus much more evasive and vague than the much more

---

"Interrogating Identity: Frantz Fanon and the postcolonial prerogative" in Bhabha's *The Location of Culture* (London: Routledge, 1994). Although the rest of Bhabha's phrase "almost the same, but not quite" is "almost the same but, not white," I still feel that this idea, together with his notion of colonial identity, works really well in illuminating the portrayal of white Creoles, at least in the fiction of Jean Rhys.

[5] See his "Of mimicry and man: The ambivalence of colonial discourse" in *The Location of Culture* (London: Routledge, 1994).

concrete and controllable recollections of the pink silk underwear. It is as if two worlds are contrasted here: the half-mysterious male world of shooting parties and guns, and the half-intimate female world of silk underwear. We may almost say that in a way, the 'real' English world, which the protagonist only knows after a fashion, is symbolized through the notion of the shooting party. And for the protagonist, as we have seen, it is vague, unknowable and not that fascinating. It is clear from this story that it is in the latter sphere that the woman is in control. By extension, we may say that she thus controls her own body. The ending of the story seems to illustrate this point. She will be able to use her underwear, but with another man on another night.

Reading the ending of the story thus, we are brought to the final section of this essay, where I reflect upon the nature of interpretation as a manner of controlling a text. As has already been pointed out, "On Not Shooting Sitting Birds" is an annoyingly vague text when it comes to time, setting, characterization etc. Since it is also extremely short – just a little over three pages – there is much that has been left unsaid. We have also already seen that the first-person narrator is highly selective and creative in what she chooses to focus on and how she goes about it.

I now want to discuss briefly how Rhys's story has been received by some of her critics, and how she seems to evade their attempts at controlling "On Not Shooting Sitting Birds." The critic Judith Kegan Gardiner reads the story as confirming female self-realization and validating the special nature of female creativity.[6] Gardiner suggests that we may see a specifically female creativity in the protagonist's use of her "uncontrollable female memory."[7] It seems to me that Gardiner is trying to control the story in the sense of limiting and checking it so that it fits her feminist project where she sees the story as describing the fall from female innocence to male experience as envisaged in the male attempt at controlling uncontrollable female memory. And, by extension, this female memory is by her seen as a kind of female creativity in embryo. Rhys, however,

---

[6] See Judith Kegan Gardiner's article "'The Grave', 'On Not Shooting Sitting Birds,' and the Female Aesthetic" in *Studies in Short Fiction* 20 (1983): 265.

[7] Gardiner, "'The Grave'," 270.

seems to evade this attempt at control by deliberately setting the story in an intimate female world of silk underwear, seduction and dinner-dates that does not permit any self-realization on the part of the female protagonist. Rather, in the light of the closing sentence of the story, the repetitive element hinted at seems to point forward to a cycle of experiences that similarly frustrate the protagonist. This again may be seen as the very opposite of female self-realization and creativity. Rhys's protagonist seems to be stuck in a world from which it is hard to escape, recycling her precious underwear and hoping for better luck next time. Gardiner's suggestion of female innocence is again countered by Rhys, since "On Not Shooting Sitting Birds" is very much about a woman who knows how to use her body, a woman who is experienced – indeed, much more experienced, it seems, than the foolish man she accompanies in the story. It is quite obvious that it is the woman who is trying to seduce the man and that this is one of the reasons why he is so bewildered and put out. The woman is indeed very adept at playing the seduction game, as we see at the end of the story when she is busy imagining her next opportunities. Thus Rhys also reveals how cleverly she avoids critics' attempts at casting her as a feminist writer.

There is another point in Gardiner's article where the problem of interpretative control surfaces. Concerning the narrative time of the story, Gardiner suggests that since its subject-matter resembles that of another story ("Till September Petronella"), which takes place in 1914, then the events in "On Not Shooting Sitting Birds" also have to take place about 1914. In the story, then, she continues, the protagonist remembers the date of an event perhaps ten years earlier. What we do know is that there is draft of this story from October 1974, and that the story was eventually published in 1976.[8] Clearly, however, the events of the story take place at a much earlier date than the 1970s, but Gardiner's suggestions seem too early. Whatever the specific narrative time, the reader has to accept the fact that Rhys has deliberately left open such elements as time and place, character names and situations. This vagueness seems part of Rhys's endeavour to fashion a story about an ongoing process, a repetitive pattern

---

[8] See www.lib.utulsa.edu/Speccoll/rhysjOI.htm

of failure and frustration in the seduction game, a game which again, according to Rhys, is beyond time and place. This openness, however, surely also lures the controlling readers into making statements that are not as cogent as they might have hoped.

Whereas Gardiner reads the story as a parable of female creativity, Cheryl Alexander Malcolm and David Malcolm choose to focus on the colonial aspect of the story. They are interested in the contrast between the protagonist's identity and her masks, and see the confusion the story centres on as cultural in nature. They discuss the protagonist as a portrayal of someone who is in control, as calm and in command of herself and her body. To them, it is the man who has lost control over the situation: he cannot comprehend, they argue, that the protagonist is "at once a lady *and* a tramp."[9] Their focus on the colonial aspect of the protagonist is very useful, since this is surely one of the reasons for the lack of success at the dinner-date described in the story. But they seem to me to invest the protagonist with too much control. Might we not also see the outward calm of the protagonist as a mask that hides frustration and confusion as she struggles to accommodate the conflicting roles of both lady and tramp? She faces the English class system as well as a set of gender stereotypes that go beyond the colonial aspect of the tale. The confusion at the heart of the story is a cultural one, but it is also a result of different gender expectations, class associations and attitudes to life in general. Indeed, Rhys again seems to be suggesting that the colonial aspect of the story is just one aspect of the protagonist and her tale. This is too narrow, too reductive a way of reading this story. Thus Rhys also seems to evade attempts at limiting her to the role of (post)colonial writer.

It is interesting to compare the above feminist reading with the (post) colonial reading of the story. Both reflect the more general reception of Jean Rhys that Coral Ann Howells helpfully sums up as three ways of reading her work: within the critical framework of feminism; within that of colonialism and postcolonialism; and, since Rhys was active in the

---

[9] See Cheryl Alexander Malcolm & David Malcolm, *Jean Rhys: A Study of the Short Fiction* (NY: Macmillan, 1996): 92.

1920s, that of modernism.[10] The labels 'feminist', 'colonialist' and 'modernist' that have been placed on the reluctant and label-resistant author are, of course, also a means of controlling both the author and her texts. And it seems to me interesting that in the story "On Not Shooting Sitting Birds" Rhys explores the issue of control, of both successful and unsuccessful attempts at control. At the same time, she also reveals how she, the author, evades being controlled. The focus in the story is both on how characters try to exercise control over themselves and others, and, by extension, on how the reader attempts to control text, characters and author.

By way of conclusion, we might return to Stella Bowen and her attempt at controlling Jean Rhys and her memories of that other woman, who, according to Bowen, had "written an unpublishably sordid novel of great sensitivity" but who still suffered "bad health, destitution, shattered nerves, an undesirable husband, lack of nationality, and a complete absence of any desire for independence."[11] If we untangle these comments, we see that, like more contemporary critics, Bowen, too, tried to control Rhys with the help of the same labels – only, some of them in reverse: Rhys as a failed modernist of poor literature, an anti-feminist who is stuck with a rotten husband yet shows no sign of wanting freedom, and, lastly, an expatriate, lost and without a nation. However, Rhys knew how to answer back: in a letter from 1964 we read a dismissive comment about the "well-washed Stella hovering about Ford."[12] The impulse to control – to limit, check and restrain – runs deep indeed. And, to end" (Rhys) - END on a note of speculation: is it not almost as if Rhys caricatured the fastidious Stella Bowen and her attitudes in her portrait of the shocked Englishman who is unable to cope with a woman whose ambiguity completely upsets his equilibrium?

---

[10] Coral Ann Howells, *Jean Rhys* (Key Woman Writers; Hemel Hempstead: Harvester Wheatsheaf, 1991).

[11] Bowen, *Drawn From Life*, 195.

[12] See Jean Rhys, *Letters 1931–1966*, sel. & ed. Francis Wyndham & Diana Melly (Harmondsworth: Penguin, 1985): 280.

WORKS CITED

Bhabha, Homi. "Foreword: Remembering Fanon," in Frantz Fanon, *Black Skin, White Masks*, tr. Charles Lam Markmann (1952; London: Pluto, 1986).

——. *The Location of Culture* (London: Routledge, 1994).

Bowen, Stella. *Drawn from Life: A Memoir* (1941; Sydney: Picador, 1999).

Gardiner, Judith Kegan. "'The Grave', 'On Not Shooting Sitting Birds', and the Female Aesthetic," *Studies in Short Fiction* 20 (1983): 265–70.

Howells, Coral Ann. *Jean Rhys* (Key Woman Writers; Hemel Hempstead: Harvester Wheatsheaf, 1991).

Malcolm, Cheryl Alexander, & David Malcolm. *Jean Rhys: A Study of the Short Fiction* (NY: Macmillan, 1996).

Rhys, Jean. *Sleep It Off Lady: Stories by Jean Rhys* (1976; Harmondsworth: Penguin, 1979).

——. *Letters 1931–1966*, sel. & ed. Francis Wyndham & Diana Melly (Harmondsworth: Penguin, 1985).

❧

II

❧ Performing Possibilities

Isaac Julien's *Looking For Langston* and the Limits of the Visible World

Asbjørn Grønstad

Many films are in fact declarations of love, if we could but see it
— David MacDougall

IN ONE SCENE in the Taiwanese filmmaker Edward Yang's stunning family saga *Yi Yi* (2000), the main protagonist NJ Jian's eight-year-old son is shown assiduously at work photographing other people's backs.[1] When confronted about his eccentric interest in capturing dorsality, the boy usefully explains that he would like to help people see what they cannot ordinarily see, to help them obtain – or at least get a brief glimpse of – that perpetually receding view that always eludes them. What the boy proposes to do, essentially, is to offer up for spectation a fraction of the invisible world. As long as people only see what is given to be seen in front of them, the boy reasons, they only have access to "half the truth," as he puts it.

However innocuous or insignificant the endeavours of Yang-Yang (the little boy) may appear, his pursuits in the field of photography establish an unexpected metaphor for that signifying practice which Laura Marks terms 'interstitial cinema'.[2] The expression denotes a type of filmmaking

---

[1] In English, the film is known as *A One and a Two*.

[2] Laura U. Marks, *The Skin of the Film: Intercultural Cinema, Embodiment, and the Senses* (Durham NC: Duke UP, 2000): 6.

which takes place in the spaces and gaps between the ubiquitous images manufactured by the so-called Institutional Modes of Representation.[3] Like Yang-Yang's project, interstitial cinema – which Marks sees as a distinctively intercultural phenomenon – seeks to overcome a state of oppressive invisibility, seeks to bring the previously hidden into view.[4] This

---

[3] For the Noël Burch of *Life to Those Shadows* (1990), the phrase refers to the hegemonic language of film as it developed in the imperialist West between 1892 and 1929. According to Burch, there is "nothing natural about the route taken by the constitution of the IMR"; Burch, *Life to Those Shadows*, tr. Ben Brewster (London: BFI, 1990): 267. The IMR n3, obviously, is intimately related to the concept of Classical Hollywood Cinema, which, needless to say, has itself spawned an entire industry of academic studies. Key formal functions usually associated with this aesthetic and ideological paradigm are, to cite Peter Wollen, narrative transitivity, identification, transparency, single diegesis, closure, pleasure, and fiction; Wollen, "Godard and Counter-Cinema: *Vent d'Est*," in *Narrative, Apparatus, Ideology*, ed. Philip Rosen (New York: Columbia UP, 1986): 120. For now canonized theories exploring the interrelation between the aesthetics of this institutional mode of representation and the spectator, see Jean–Louis Baudry's "Ideological Effects of the Basic Cinematographic Apparatus" and "The Apparatus: Metapsychological Approaches to the Impression of Reality in Cinema," both in *Narrative, Apparatus, Ideology*, ed. Rosen, 299–318; 286–98; John Berger's *Ways of Seeing* (London: BBC, 1972); Stephen Heath's *Questions of Cinema* (Bloomington: Indiana UP, 1981); Christian Metz's *The Imaginary Signifier: Psychoanalysis and the Cinema*, tr. Celia Britton, Annwyl Williams, Ben Brewster & Alfred Guzzetti (Bloomington: Indiana UP, 1982); and Kaja Silverman's *The Subject of Semiosis* (New York: Oxford UP, 1983).

[4] A central precedent for an intercultural cinema, according to Marks, is the work of, among others, Chris Marker, Jean Rouch, and Trinh T. Minh-ha. The latter is also one of the leading critics of filmic interculturality, along with Hamid Naficy, Julio García Espinosa, Coco Fusco, Fernando Solanas, Teshome Gabriel, and Kobena Mercer. It should be pointed out that intercultural cinema is more than a purely general moniker for the diverse manifestations of diasporic film-making. Significantly, intercultural film movements herald new aesthetic practices by necessity, as they seek to render visible experience which the Institutional Mode of Representation has traditionally overlooked. Particular to intercultural cinemas, for example, is the concern with modes of visuality other than the strictly optical. I shall return to this toward the end of the essay. It is through reinventions of film form that intercultural cinema "takes part in a global current that flows against the wave of economic neocolonialism, by making explicit the cultural and

is also to some extent Isaac Julien's objective in his award-winning biographical film poem about Langston Hughes, *Looking For Langston* (1988). In this short essay I shall be mainly concerned with the film-theoretical ramifications of the kind of interstitial or intercultural cinematic methodology that Julien's movie embodies. More particularly, in a very tentative manner this article will indicate ways in which the nature of the film image as well as the nature of the relation between that image, the look, and processes of vision may be productively reconceptualized, or re-imagined, if you like.

Isaac Julien, one of the architects of the London-based Sankofa collective,[5] made *Looking For Langston* under the aegis of the Black Audio Film Collective in 1988.[6] A film presently regarded as a foundational text of the New Queer Cinema, *Looking For Langston* is "a polyglossic re-contextualization of the many-voicedness of Black and White gay culture, both that which is lost and absent, and that which is reclaimed."[7] Perhaps chiefly known to a wider audience as the director of the black gay drama *Young Soul Rebels* (1991), Julien has also made the experimental documentary *Frantz Fanon: Black Skin, White Mask* (1996) and *Baadasssss Cinema* (2002), a documentary on 1970s blaxploitation films.

---

economic links between people that capital erases," to quote Marks (*The Skin of the Film*, 9). By exploring what Marks calls 'haptic' forms of visuality, and by filming in the gaps of cultural experience, so to speak, intercultual films may be seen as an antidote to the aesthetic colonialism that Clyde Taylor critiques in his *The Mask of Art: Breaking the Aesthetic Contract – Film and Literature* (Bloomington: Indiana UP, 1998).

[5] The Sankofa collective was a group of young black British filmmakers whose work explores issues such as masculinity, desire, the gaze, and racial/sexual difference.

[6] Black Audio's first feature, *Handsworth Songs* (John Akomfrah 1986), is exemplary for the group's concern with "the search for the language with which to express cultural memory," a search which ultimately leads to a confrontation with "silence and absence" (Marks, *The Skin of the Film*, 21). A film like *Looking For Langston* "approached the visual archive warily and interrogated it for what it could not tell" (*The Skin of the Film*, 134).

[7] Gwendolyn Audrey Foster, *Captive Bodies: Postcolonial Subjectivity in the Cinema* (Albany: State U of New York P, 1999): 130.

Looking For Langston is a black-and-white fantasy depicting gay masculinity during the Harlem Renaissance. A lyrical and dreamy meditation on the logistic of desire and the homoerotic gaze, the film is a fictionalized account of Harlem's jazz and dance-club scene, interspersed with archival footage and photographs of Langston Hughes, and accompanied by a voice-over who reads from the poetry of Hughes, Bruce Nugent, and Essex Hemphill among others. Combining in one single mode elements of both documentary realism and stylized enactments of imagined scenes from Hughes's work, Julien's film is an elusive and tantalizing examination not of its eponymous subject but, rather, of the fundamental inaccessibility of that subject. As Kaja Silverman notes, the film is "about" Hughes, but then again not really, presenting the audience with figures that "both offer themselves up to visual scrutiny, and turn that scrutiny back on itself."[8]

Neither fiction nor documentary, *Looking For Langston* is that rare film which eschews the narrative conventions of art cinema and the avant-garde alike. It is a discursively charged text, as much a theoretical essay on filmicity and vision as a poetic homage to Langston Hughes. The prevailing mode of the film is ceremonial and elegiac; the images dramatize the appearance (in the sense of coming into being) of a performative kind of looking whose spatial parameters converge at the site of remembrance and mourning: sight as insight. Beginning with a series of documentary shots of a train moving across a Manhattan bridge at night, we are next taken to Hughes's funeral and then to a nightclub in which a wake celebration is unfolding. These images of dancers petrified like statues will recur later in the film. Curiously, the effect of this graceful immobility is redolent of that created by the freeze-frame, though depleted of the intrinsic theatricality of the latter technique. The freeze-frame, as Garrett Stewart, among others, has noted,[9] tends simultaneously to signify mortality and preservation, but the images of Julien's statuesque dancers invite no less of a paradox. There is a rupture in the temporality of these images,

[8] Kaja Silverman, *The Threshold of the Visible World* (New York: Routledge, 1996): 106.

[9] Garrett Stewart, "Photo-Gravure: Death, Photography, and Film Narrative," *Wide Angle* 9.1 (1987): 13.

a crack caused by the fact that filmic or narrative time continues to elapse while the temporality of the diegetic characters has stagnated. Such a temporal rupture also has spatial implications, in the sense that the visual field fragments and consequently sets up two separate spaces: that of the characters, which remains in the past, and that of the setting itself, which belongs to a continuously evolving present. In turn, this spatial di-vision entails a corresponding fracture of the gaze of the spectator, whose act of envisaging will struggle to unify the two separate spatio-temporalities. What Julien essentially achieves by this poetic of disjuncture is to foreground the materiality of the image and the consequences that awareness of this materiality has for the process of vision through which the viewer phenomenologically and psychically captures and comprehends the image. As Silverman argues, Julien's images address themselves to the spectator's look,[10] reciprocating that look in a strategy designed to forestall appropriation and containment by the viewer. It is precisely this strategy that Vivian Sobchack theorizes in her *The Address of the Eye* (1992), in which she conceives of the film as a viewing subject whose solicitation of the spectator's look encourages a dialectic of vision where the interface of the visual act and the visual object breaks down.[11] Not only does the viewer internalize what she sees, the film in turn sutures the viewer into the text in an act that the Italian film theorist Francesco Casetti calls 'figurativization', the process whereby "an abstract instance (a film's implicit *you*) becomes manifest within the visual field."[12]

Following the images of the frozen dancers is a series of sequences starting with some documentary footage shot during Riverside Radio's tribute to Hughes after his death; two shots of a Manhattan street; a close-up of a record player; a close-up of Alex (the Hughes persona within the film); a montage of neon signs, black musicians, and some photographs of the "real" Hughes (all set to the song "Blues For Langston"); and, finally,

---

[10] Silverman, *The Threshold of the Visible World*, 106.

[11] Vivian Sobchack, *The Address of the Eye: A Phenomenology of Film Experience* (Princeton NJ: Princeton UP, 1992): 23.

[12] Francesco Casetti, *Inside the Gaze: The Fiction Film and its Spectator*, tr. Neill Andrew with Charles O'Brien, intro. Christian Metz (1996; Bloomington: Indiana UP, 1998): 125 (emphasis in original).

an image of a black angel standing in a cemetery while exhibiting two large photographs, the first of Hughes, the second of James Baldwin. The angel also reappears later in the film. What is remarkable about this tableau is not only its celebratory sensuousness, its hypergraphic commemorativeness, or its meta-representational framing, but also its complex orchestration of multiple trajectories of looking. The angel is looking at us looking back at him and the photographs of Hughes and Baldwin, the poets who in turn are looking at us. In the context of this particular composition, to look "for" Langston implies, as Silverman argues, "to transfer to the bodily coordinates of another the luster which in the Lacanian account of the mirror stage attaches only to one's own visual imago."[13] There is, furthermore, an overwhelming sense of openness, or lack of closure, in the way in which the film configures this multilayered interaction of affirmative sight-lines. For me, as both a viewer and a critic, this sequence takes place just on that threshold of the visible world which Silverman explores in her book. As I watch this sequence again, I am reminded of one of that text's concluding passages, which I take the liberty of quoting at length here:

> no look ever takes place once and for all. Rather, each act of spectation is subject to a complex series of "vicissitudes," which can completely transform the value of what is originally seen, and which cannot be easily predicted in advance. Subsequently, the eye may invest libidinally in the given-to-be-seen, or pursue a radically other itinerary, one which works to derealize rather than to affirm the visual standard.[14]

For Silverman, *Looking For Langston* comes to epitomize what she dubs a "cinema of rapture,"[15] a film aesthetic immersed in the business of decolonializing the gaze (according to Silverman, "the look is under cultural pressure to apprehend the world from a preassigned viewing position"[16]). Going beyond the limits of the visible world implies transcending these

---

[13] Silverman, *The Threshold of the Visible World*, 120.

[14] *The Threshold of the Visible World*, 223.

[15] *The Threshold of the Visible World*, 104.

[16] *The Threshold of the Visible World*, 3.

viewing positions generated and maintained by the scopic regime of the Institutional Mode of Representation. Evidently, this process requires that we discard (however painfully and slowly) not only the colonial look that Hollywood has taught us but also the myopic look that Maurice Merleau–Ponty describes in the following statement: "Since the seer is caught up in what he sees, it is still himself he sees: there is a fundamental narcissism of all vision."[17]

It seems that, for Silverman, our capability for seeing differently, for decolonializing the look as it were, hinges on a process of ideality, or idealization. Some images, like those of "socially devalued bodies," solicit from the viewer what Silverman calls an "investitory" look.[18] In *World Spectators* (2000), a later monograph, she introduces the notion of desire as the operational condition for the work of ideality. "It is through speaking our particular language of desire," she writes, "that we facilitate the appearance of other creatures and things."[19] This language of desire, as Silverman conceives it, is predominantly visual in nature; "the look has chronological as well as affective priority over the word," she claims.[20] Importantly, Silverman acknowledges the primacy of the aesthetic in the formation of this desire:

> When we look [...] we are always responding to a prior solicitation from other creatures and things. This solicitation is aesthetic in nature: the world addresses us through its formal parameters. However, in displaying their colors, shapes, patterns and movements to us, things do not merely request us to turn our eyes toward them, or even to answer in kind. What the world of phenomenal forms solicits from us is our desire.[21]

The kind of investitory, idealizing look favoured by Silverman is also a palpably libidinal look, and her theory of desire inevitably begs the ques-

---

[17] Maurice Merleau–Ponty, *The Visible and the Invisible*, tr. Alphonso Lingis (Evanston IL: Northwestern UP, 1968): 139.

[18] Silverman, *The Threshold of the Visible World*, 4, 111.

[19] Kaja Silverman, *World Spectators* (Stanford CA: Stanford UP, 2000): 75.

[20] Silverman, *World Spectators*, 101.

[21] Silverman, *World Spectators*, 144.

tion whether such an insistently idealizing process of vision can actually take place without also positing an equally ideal spectator. A negative answer would, in fact, challenge the foundations of Silverman's argument, since nowadays it has become largely uncontroversial to question the existence of such a spectator.[22] Sobchack's concept of 'embodied vision' is a timely reminder that each act of spectation originates in a concrete and unique, individual corporeality and that the dream of the ideal spectator exists only as a theoretical construct. How, then, is it possible to salvage Silverman's notion of ideality and desire without at the same time resurrecting the impossible look of an ideal viewer? First of all, it should be pointed out that, for Silverman, vision, or visibility, is more than just a physical act; it is constituted, rather, by "a confluence of the phenomenal, the psychic, the specular, and the social."[23] This makes seeing without really seeing a manifest prospect. I would then suggest that we could start by re-routing the address of the eye and its libidinal mode from the object in the image to the image itself, in all its splendid texturality. As André Bazin once so evocatively and movingly reminded us, the cinematographic lens, "stripping its object of all those ways of seeing it, those piled-up preconceptions, that spiritual dust and grime with which my eyes have covered it, is able to present it in all its virginal purity to my attention *and consequently to my love*."[24] Embedded in the phrase "and consequently to my love" is the kernel of a different kind of cinephilia, not the cinephilia of those cineastes who know by heart every film that Rita Hayworth appeared in, from the short musical *La Fiesta* in 1926 to Ralph Nelson's *The Wrath of God* (1972) half a century later, but the cinephilia of those who see in Silverman's quest for the idealizing and libidinal look the extension of Bazin's very own and indestructible love of the film image.

As far as the ambition of decolonializing the gaze goes, however, this is only the beginning. Problems remain. How do our acts of looking faci-

---

[22] See, for instance, Linda Williams in *Viewing Positions: Ways of Seeing Film*, ed. Williams (New Brunswick NJ: Rutgers UP, 1995): 3.

[23] Silverman, *World Spectators*, 3.

[24] André Bazin, "The Ontology of the Photographic Image," in Bazin, *What Is Cinema?* vol. 1, tr. Hugh Gray (Berkeley: U of California P, 1967): 15 (my emphasis).

litate what Marks describes as "the double movement of tearing away old, oppressive representations and making room for new ones to emerge"?[25] Furthermore, if the Institutional Mode of Representation, as Burch maintains, "implicitly constitutes the spectator as a voyeur,"[26] how can we surpass the limitations of this possessive gaze? As Gwendolyn Audrey Foster contends in her *Captive Bodies* (1999), the film-viewer dialectic promulgated by the IMR runs the risk of imprisoning the body in the image in a process of subjugation that structurally and rhetorically is comparable to a kind of semiotic slavery: "Capturing an/other is the project of narrative films, just as much as the 'ethnographic' film and image making is an extension of the ethnographic practice of denial of subjectivity, and the privileging of the gaze of the captor."[27] Foster, in fact, employs the phrase "the Plantocracy of Hollywood."[28]

If we are to resolve this conundrum, it may be that we have to move beyond the idealistic proclamations of a Bazin or a Silverman. We have to return once more to the ontology of the film image to redefine it, and we have to return slightly estranged. More theory is not necessarily always the answer to problems whose nature is chiefly ideological or experiential, yet it appears that it is the image itself that has to be retheorized if we are to overturn the hegemony of the institutional or colonial look. In film theory it has long been a commonplace to explain the historically variable perceptions of the essential modality of the film image in terms of a succession of metaphors. Thus, in the formalist register that dominated classical film theory (this is the time of Rudolf Arnheim and Sergei Eisenstein) the screen came to be thought of as frame, a canvas upon which were configured the expressive visions of the filmmaker. Later, realist theories came to prominence (theories of which Bazin himself was a champion) and the screen now became a window through which the viewer could discern the world as it really was. Where the frame metaphor had promoted expression, the window metaphor promoted perception. Post-

---

[25] Marks, *The Skin of the Film*, 11.

[26] Burch, *Life to Those Shadows*, 213.

[27] Foster, *Captive Bodies*, 3.

[28] *Captive Bodies*, 2.

structuralism, finally, apprehended the screen as a mirror in which expression and perception got confused.[29] The problem with all these models is that they presuppose, however implicitly, that the screen is a transparent entity, that its spectacles are transparent, that filmicity is in fact a trans-spectacle. What these conceptions neglect is the materiality of the image. In order to make a case for the non-transparency of the film image, therefore, I want to introduce a fourth metaphor for the screen: namely, that of the image as a mask, or veil.[30]

The non-transparent, visual density which the notion of the image as a mask incites is theoretically contiguous with Marks's idea of 'haptic visuality', "the way vision itself can be tactile, as though one were touching a film with one's eyes."[31] Marks's term "the skin of the film" (which is also the title of her book on intercultural cinema) denotes "the way film signifies through its materiality."[32] Intercultural cinema, she writes,

> has quite specific reasons for appealing to the knowledge of the senses, insofar as it aims to represent configurations of sense perception different from those of modern Euro-American societies, where optical visuality has been accorded a unique supremacy.[33]

What Marks problematizes is the paradox of working in a visual medium in order to stir up memories and moods that are mostly non-visual. However, because the point of departure for an intercultural or interstitial cinema is the inability to speak, it is also characterized by "a suspicion of visuality, a lack of faith in the visual archive's ability to represent cultural memory."[34]

The awareness that the screen is not something that we can see straight through but is, rather, something material – an impenetrable texture, a

---

[29] Williams, *Viewing Positions*, 9.

[30] Casetti inadvertently moves toward an understanding of the image as mask when he discusses the film-viewer interface in terms of "an array of costumings" (*Inside the Gaze*, 126).

[31] Marks, *The Skin of the Film*, xi.

[32] *The Skin of the Film*, xi.

[33] *The Skin of the Film*, xiii.

[34] *The Skin of the Film*, 21.

mask – changes our relationship to the image and the objects it shows. This new phenomenology has at least a potential for surmounting that inescapable voyeurism that has remained a contingency in the cinema since the days of Lumière and Méliès. Discussing thc tablcaux vivants in *Looking For Langston*, Foster finds evidence of a non-voyeuristic poetics in the exchange of erotically charged glances between and among men of all colours:

> These gazes stage the ethnographic third eye in a strikingly post-modern sensibility. Here everyone is Other, so the look back of the Other is at once dangerous and inviting, comforting and acknowledging.[35]

Julien's narrative is immersed in moments that highlight the materiality of the image—the scene of the frozen dancers and the scene of the angel with the photographs of Hughes and Baldwin previously discussed, and the numerous intertextual quotations that make up what Marie–Claire Ropars–Wuilleumier calls *cinécriture*:[36] Nugent's "Smoke Lilies and Jade," Hughes's "Stars, " Hemphill's "If His Name Were Mandingo," "The Brass Rail" and "The Edge, Third Movement," Robert Mapple-thorpe's *Black Book*, the documentary footage, and Julien the filmmaker inserting himself into his own narrative as the dead Hughes in the coffin. Neither a frame, nor a window or a mirror, the image here may be conceived of as a self-conscious mask that displays and validates a kind of visuality that is haptic rather than merely optical. The "Looking" in *Looking For Langston* is the process of recognizing the skin of the film as a "membrane that brings its audience into contact with the material forms or memory,"[37] that Other of optical visuality that is found beyond the limits of that which is merely institutionally visible.

---

[35] Foster, *Captive Bodies*, 129.

[36] Marie–Claire Ropars–Wuilleumier, "The Graphic in Film Writing: *À bout de soufflé*, or the Erratic Alphabet," *Enclitic* 5.2–6.1 (1982): 143.

[37] Marks, *The Skin of the Film*, 242.

WORKS CITED

Barthes, Roland. *Camera Lucida: Reflections on Photography*, tr. Richard Howard (1980; New York: Hill & Wang, 1981).

Baudry, Jean–Louis. "The Apparatus: Metapsychological Approaches to the Impression of Reality in Cinema," in *Narrative, Apparatus, Ideology*, ed. Rosen, 299–318.

——. "Ideological Effects of the Basic Cinematographic Apparatus," in *Narrative, Apparatus, Ideology*, ed. Rosen, 286–98.

Bazin, André. "The Ontology of the Photographic Image," in Bazin, *What is Cinema?* vol. 1, tr. Hugh Gray (Berkeley. U of California P, 1967): 9–16.

Burch, Noël. *Life to Those Shadows*, tr. Ben Brewster (London: BFI, 1990).

Casetti, Francesco. *Inside the Gaze: The Fiction Film and Its Spectator*, tr. Neill Andrew with Charles O'Brien, intro. Christian Metz (1996; Bloomington: Indiana UP, 1998).

Foster, Gwendolyn Audrey. *Captive Bodies: Postcolonial Subjectivity in the Cinema* (Albany: State U of New York P, 1999).

Heath, Stephen. *Questions of Cinema* (Bloomington: Indiana UP, 1981).

Hughes, Langston. "Movies," in *The Collected Poems of Langston Hughes*, ed. Arnold Rampersad & David Roessel (New York: Alfred A. Knopf, 1994): 395.

MacDougall, David. "The Fate of the Cinema Subject," in MacDougall, *Transcultural Cinema*, 25–60.

——. "The Subjective Voice in Ethnographic Film," in MacDougall, *Transcultural Cinema*, 93–122.

——. *Transcultural Cinema*, ed. Lucien Taylor (Princeton NJ: Princeton UP, 1998).

——. "Visual Anthropology and the Ways of Knowing," in MacDougall, *Transcultural Cinema*, 61–92.

Marks, Laura U. *The Skin of the Film: Intercultural Cinema, Embodiment, and the Senses* (Durham NC: Duke UP, 2000).

Merleau–Ponty, Maurice. *The Visible and the Invisible*, tr. Alphonso Lingis (Evanston IL: Northwestern UP, 1968).

Metz, Christian. *The Imaginary Signifier: Psychoanalysis and the Cinema*, tr. Celia Britton, Annwyl Williams, Ben Brewster & Alfred Guzzetti (Bloomington: Indiana UP, 1982).

Ropars–Wuilleumier, Marie–Claire. "The Graphic in Filmic Writing: *À bout de souffle*, or The Erratic Alphabet," *Enclitic* 5.2–6.1 (1982): 147–61.

Rosen, Philip, ed. *Narrative, Apparatus, Ideology* (New York: Columbia UP, 1986).

Silverman, Kaja. *The Subject of Semiotics* (New York: Oxford UP, 1983).

——. *The Threshold of the Visible World* (New York: Routledge, 1996).

——. *World Spectators* (Stanford CA: Stanford UP, 2000).

Sobchack, Vivian. *The Address of the Eye: A Phenomenology of Film Experience* (Princeton NJ: Princeton UP, 1992).

Stewart, Garrett. "Photo-Gravure: Death, Photography, and Film Narrative," *Wide Angle* 9.1 (1987): 11–31.

Stewart, Jacqueline. "Negroes Laughing at Themselves? Black Spectatorship and the Performance of Urban Modernity," *Critical Inquiry* 29.4 (2003): 650–77.

Taylor, Clyde R. *The Mask of Art: Breaking the Aesthetic Contract – Film and Literature* (Bloomington: Indiana UP, 1998).

Willemen, Paul. "The National," in *Fields of Vision: Essays in Film Studies, Visual Anthropology, and Photography*, ed. Leslie Devereaux & Roger Hillman (Berkeley: U of California P, 1995): 21–34.

Williams, Linda, ed. *Viewing Positions: Ways of Seeing Film* (New Brunswick NJ: Rutgers UP, 1995).

Wollen, Peter. "Godard and Counter-Cinema: *Vent d'Est*," in *Narrative, Apparatus, Ideology*, ed. Rosen, 120–29.

❧

Western Theatrical Performance in Africa and Gender Implications

EVELYN LUTWAMA

THE EUROPEAN COLONIZATION OF AFRICA introduced many cultural changes to the indigenous people and these peoples' theatrical practices. This discussion will take up several elements of these changes. Although, justifiably, Africans cannot be viewed as one and the same, there are certain shared features that mark them as a people with a similar background. These shared experiences are my main focus here. However, although this essay discusses African theatrical practices and the changes experienced, it will bear in mind the fact that, beyond shared characteristics, each society is unique.

Certain limitations of this discussion become apparent, such as the use of a few communities to represent a wider whole. Thus, although some West African, East African and Southern African communities are cited as examples, several other communities within the same regions are left out. This concentration on the above regions also leaves out a large area of North and Central Africa. Since it is impossible here to go into an in-depth discussion, this essay will highlight areas with potential for deeper discussion. All the above limitations, however, raise the question of the relevance of discussing the similarities, rather than the differences, between various African performances.

> If Western theatre, from which we draw the didactic model, revolves around real-life social experience presented in the form of discursive reasoning subdivided into dialogue, scenes and acts,

> African theatre, in contrast, normally revolves around a mythological, legendary, collective social experience, presented in the form of a ritual, collective drama. In this regard it is thus much closer to the origins of early Greek Theatre.[1]

Precolonial African Indigenous Performances

Despite the neat packaging of the above definition of African theatre, the use of the term 'theatre' for indigenous African performances has on several occasions been contested. The argument advanced is that rituals, myths and the like cannot as separate entities constitute theatre; at most, they can serve as elements of theatre. Some scholars have attempted to counter these arguments by addressing these forms of entertainment in several broader terms, such as 'popular entertainment' or sometimes 'popular performance'. For this essay, we shall use a less controversial term, 'indigenous African performances'. As David Kerr points out in *African Popular Theatre*, fathoming indigenous African performances is limited by the fact that "pre-colonial theatre has not been very thoroughly researched."[2]

Some scholars have questioned the authenticity of documented indigenous performances. It has been pointed out that 'indigenous' theatre has been viewed through the eyes of researchers aware of the colonial impact in the area. There is, therefore, no guarantee that the material researched is free from colonial influence. Consequently, this suggests a looming presence of Western influence even in apparently documented precolonial indigenous African performances. This essay thus limits itself to certain general tendencies in these precolonial performances rather than actual definitions. It goes without saying that each of Africa's numerous ethnic groups possesses its own history, language and indigenous performances. Within this diversity, however, certain unifying performance features can

---

[1] Article 19 African Programme, *Women's Voices and African Theatre: Case Studies from Kenya, Mali, the Democratic Republic of Congo and Zimbabwe* (Braamfontein 2017, 23 Jorissen Street, South Africa, 2003): 35. (found on www.article19.org)

[2] David Kerr, *African Popular Theatre* (London: James Currey, 1995): 2.

be traced: namely, communal participation, ritualism, improvisation, and spontaneity.

West African societies stand out as having been highly inclined to religious performance. This is depicted in the *Egungun*[3] practised by the Yoruba (and thought to have been imported from the Nupe people in the sixteenth century). There were, however, other forms of performance, such as *Koteba* in Mali, which "began in the fourteenth century in the Bamana Kingdom [...] a secular drama performed without masks, which consists of improvised satire about antisocial elements in the community, such as lazy or wicked farmers";[4] secular myths and rituals of the Ekpo (from Benin), which celebrated a culture-hero, Agboghidi;[5] and rituals such as the "Sande" and "Poro" of Sierra Leone, which are theatrical initiations of girls and boys into womanhood and manhood respectively.

East African performances were more secular than religious, though religious activities in the region could also be seen as theatrical endeavours in their own right. In Kenya, for instance, "activities such as 'blessing the spear' and the warriors before they embarked on defending the community had many elements of ritual and ceremony but were a form of participatory drama."[6]

In the Democratic Republic of Congo, it was "more than a simple requirement to celebrate events such as a birth, a death, a marriage or the enthroning of a chief, all of which were associated with special rites which ended in local festivals." Numerous rites of this nature can be listed in Congo, including the Nkanda, practised by the Yaka, and Masoba, practised by the Luba of Katanga.[7] The ceremonies practised in Uganda – the *Okwalula abalongo* ritual performed at the birth of twins, practised by

---

[3] "*Egungun* was almost certainly connected with a widespread and much older tradition of Masquerades found all over West Africa and derived from communalistic ancestral cults [...] it was out of such specialized *Egungun* groups that professional semi-secular Yoruba theatre emerged, variously called *oloje*, *oje*, Alarinjo and *Apidan*" (Kerr, *African Popular Theatre,* 11–12).

[4] Article 19: 23.

[5] Kerr, *African Popular Theatre*, 9.

[6] Article 19: 10.

[7] Article 19: 35.

the Baganda, and the *Imbalu* circumcision ritual initiating young boys into manhood, practised by the Bagishu – are loaded with intense theatrical activity. In Tanzania, the Chagga people also displayed theatrical behaviour during the circumcision ceremonies of both boys and girls called *Rina*.

Southern African communities also practised similar indigenous performances as depicted in the *Nkolola* ritual – a preparatory counselling and theatrical session for a young girl entering womanhood,[8] practised mainly by the Tongas in southern Zambia but also shared by the Lozis in western Zambia, as well as the Chewas and Sengas in eastern Zambia. A similar preparatory ritual, *Ntonjane*, is found among the Xhosa of South Africa. In central Malawi, the Chewas also theatrically initiate girls into adulthood in a ritual called *chinamwali*,[9] while the Yao of southern Malawi ritually and theatrically circumcise young boys into manhood in a ceremony bearing the same name.

Indigenous African performances were thus largely contextual, and differences in context inevitably resulted in differences in subject-matter and meaning. Despite this, however, the unifying features of dramatic improvisation, ritualism, spontaneity and communal participation always seemed to be present in all aspects of African life. Thus most "ceremonies, festivals, religious rites, storytelling, and various kinds of celebrations, all interwoven into the daily life of the various African cultures,"[10] continue to be recognized as forms of Indigenous African performance.

Colonial Theatre

Faced with a problem of unifying diverging and rebellious ethnic groups, colonial powers sought to rid the groups of much of their culture. Similar stories of the European suppression of indigenous African performances

[8] This ritual takes place at the onset of menstruation.

[9] *Chinamwali* is performed for a woman when she becomes pregnant, in which case the girl's relations are informed and a counselling session is held. She is instructed both theatrically and through counselling about what to expect – hygiene, traditional treatment of morning-sickness etc.

[10] Oscar Brockett, *History of the Theatre* (New York: Simon & Schuster, 7th ed. 1995): 665.

are echoed in different parts of Africa. Whereas some colonial powers, such as the French, attempted to erase all forms of indigenous expression through a policy of assimilation, others, such as the British, realized the rallying power of the performances for the masses and attempted to replace the performances' indigenous values with eurocentric ones. For instance, in 1944 many Congolese indigenous performances were replaced by cinema shows in large cities such as Leopoldville (Kinshasa) and Elizabethville (Lubumbashi). These were based on no specific topic; their aim, rather, was to entertain, and occasionally educate, the masses.[11] *Koteba* performances in Mali were in the "nineteenth and twentieth centuries [...] often used by the colonial power to advance its ideology, and its policy of economic and cultural domination."[12] In Kenya, the colonial regime often imposed draconian bans on traditional forms of theatre, terming them primitive and un-Christian.[13] Hence, in several ways indigenous performances were either completely outlawed or exploited by Europeans for purposes of assimilation. The forms of indigenous performances that were encouraged during the colonial era were evidently highly controlled by Europeans and used to convey and emphasize eurocentric views.

To ensure even greater control over African theatrical expression, the European powers introduced, along with formal education, the Western theatre tradition. High schools soon taught "the classics of European drama, and sometimes encouraged performances of the plays on proscenium-arch stages, which were built as part of many schools [...]. Those Africans who aspired to be writers usually chose the language of their colonial rulers."[14] The playscript, introduced from Europe, was a strategically effective harnessing of African creative power, easily monitored.

To date, the vast majority of the recorded/documented theatre in Africa consists of plays designed in accordance with Western structures and languages. This does not mean, however, that indigenous African per-

---

[11] Article 19: 36.

[12] Article 19: 23.

[13] Article 19: 10.

[14] Brockett, *History of the Theatre*, 637.

formances were wiped off the continent. It simply suggests that, for a certain period in history, these forms were forced underground and operated illegally. The undying force of the unifying features identified earlier remained significant to the indigenous people, and, when opportunity arose, some of these performances emerged into the open again. Some reappeared in their original form with very slight alterations, such as a number of contemporary community theatres, while some were modified more extensively through incorporation of European theatrical elements. The 'Yoruba opera' or 'concert party' in West Africa and many "Theatres for Development" projects prominent in the rest of Africa are examples of this.

Gender in African Theatre

It would be deceptive to claim that present-day African gender relations were shaped only by Western colonialism and the Western theatre, though both played a recognizable part in the shaping process of modern gender relations in many parts of Africa.

Gender relations in Africa had for many centuries been male-biased, an aspect shared with many other parts of the world. But, as elsewhere still, there was no uniformly prescribed patriarchal behaviour in Africa. For most African societies, strong male dominance was the order of the day, while for others a sense of egalitarianism in gender relations existed.

Theatrical patterns followed suit. In some parts of Africa, the theatre gave women an opportunity to present freely issues concerning them in the form of drama, songs and sometimes dances, such as the aforementioned initiation theatre for young girls. In other cases, powerful female figures provided the basis of some indigenous religious and sacred performances. One theory suggests that *Egungun* is the story of a union between a monkey and a woman, and that the twin ceremonies in Uganda exalt the importance of the mother of the twins as a special, almost supernatural being. Other performances were based on females with special powers, such as the royal princesses of Buganda (Uganda), who were addressed by male titles and held powerful offices in the political system; or the women who attained the status of men, such as the 'male' daughters and 'female' husbands among the Nnobi in Nigeria; the queen mothers who possessed certain political powers among the Akan-speaking groups of Ghana; and also, on a more general level, other performances that exalted priestesses, goddesses and "mothers of societies." From the advent of colonialism up to the present, women have used songs, especially during secular performances in West Africa and social functions in East and Southern Africa, to ridicule male chauvinism.

But generally, most indigenous African performances were male-dominated and women's issues were rarely 'centre-stage' unless they affected male interests like prostitution or 'deviant' wives (in the form of adulteresses, witches, etc). Surprisingly, women, too, sometimes used theatre to knit a tighter web of female submissiveness to males, as in some *Kiganda* musical performances in Uganda. In Mali, "female griottes could only raise their voices in front of men to sing their praises, songs which were handed down from one generation to another in order to pass on the history of the country"[15] while, according to Kerr, among the Afikpo in Nigeria,

> [w]omen were not allowed to have any contact with Okumkpa[16] and so could not vent their grievances against a male-dominated society, but young men could express their resentment against elders, despite the respect given to elders in the theatrical mode of production. (7)

Hence, there are examples that range from the liberal use of theatre by women to cases of the complete exclusion of women from theatrical participation in different parts of Africa. This discussion does not propose that Western intervention caused remarkable changes in gender relations, but points to the role intervention played in accentuating imbalances in gender relations in many parts of Africa. And, as Femi Euba has pointed out in his lecture on "Forms of Black Drama," there is no uniform description of its effect.[17]

---

[15] Article 19: 27.

[16] These were ancestral cults by males who performed satirical drama under the possession of the spirit Mma.

[17] http://www.alexanderstreetpress.com/articles/article.femi.euba.htm 14.08.2003

According to Euba's analysis, colonialism in West Africa had less of an impact on the cultures of the people there than it did in East and Southern Africa. He cites the tropical conditions of West Africa as a hindrance to the prolonged settlement of colonial powers, as opposed to the more equable climates of East and Southern Africa. Thus, a longer stay had greater impact on the cultures of the latter than on those of the former. While West Africa had more contact with its original culture and performances, as is evident in later postcolonial plays like Wole Soyinka's *Death and the King's Horseman*, East and Southern African theatre replaced its social role with a more political one. It became a theatre of "struggle over recognition, definition, and control."[18]

Despite the difference in the degree of Western influence, some traits of influence seemed cross-regional. For instance, several writings in West, East or Southern Africa, dating from 1900 to the early 1930s, clearly replicate the missionaries' and colonist's ideals of gendered roles from their European background. The suggested roles entrenched the place of the female more deeply in the domestic sphere of cooking, sewing, child-bearing and other domestic duties, while the male's place was in economically empowering activities such as (given the opportunity) being school-teachers, clerks, administrators, or commercial farmers.

European colonialism did not stop at replicating these roles in writing, but fully implemented them in practice. Economically, men were favoured in more ways than women. In Kenya, Tanzania, and Zimbabwe a shared impact was the emphasis that the colonial system laid on 'individual' gain versus the traditional 'communal' benefit. This, as the opening principle, introduced paid labour vs material pay for community work. Men went out to work on the white settlers' farms for a small wage, and women stayed home to raise a family without much of a financial base in a new monetary economic system. Thus, a distinct sexual division of labour (similar to the one that existed in Europe at the beginning of industrialization) became apparent. When education replaced manual labour on the farms as a means of survival, men were the immediate benefactors.

---

[18] http://athena.english.vt.edu/~carlisle/postcolonial/popular_theatre.html 14.08.2003:2

This setting gave greater power to men in already patriarchal societies, accentuated sexual differences, and paved the way for the current intolerable gender imbalance in the economic sectors of those regions.

When Africans took to writing for theatre in the mid-twentieth century, gender differences were hardly among the immediate priorities. In East and Southern Africa, theatre was preoccupied with seeking political independence from colonial rule. It had become a political weapon. The woman was thus disadvantaged in two ways.

One was that the colonial system had mainly empowered literary men as playwrights and as such, during this period, it became even more difficult for women to contribute to the subject-matter. Secondly, the subject-matter of the theatre was a man's affair – war – and focused on issues of nationalism and treason. This did not, historically, pay much heed to the role women played in it. Men therefore became the main characters fighting for freedom, as in Ngugi wa Thiong'o and Micere Mugo's *Trial of Dedan Kimathi*. Even in cases of participatory theatre such as the all-night entertainment *Pungwe*, made up of songs and dances called *nziyo dzechimurenga*, and which was practised in the guerrilla camps of Botswana, Mozambique, Zambia and in the liberated zones of Zimbabwe, it was men who mobilized the community members in the resistance struggle against the white oppressors. Colonialism in this sense further consolidated theatre as the mouthpiece and weapon of men, rarely women, and least of all as something contributing to bridging the ever-widening gap between the two sexes.

The decolonizing struggle was also a force in West Africa; playwrights advocated a change from eurocentric to afrocentric systems, yet the correction of skewed gender relations seemed the issue given least attention. In fact, in many cases the gender stereotypes that Western theatre had left behind were simply perpetuated in the new postcolonial theatre, as Wole Soyinka's *The Lion and the Jewel* demonstrates.

When gender issues have been chanced upon in the writings, they have been portrayed in most cases from a male point of view. Micere Mugo, in her article "The Woman Artist in Africa Today,"[19] highlights a number of views on the matter by strong female African theatre practitioners. The Malawian Jessie Sagawa argues that "discussion of African Literature usually centres on the male writer and character."[20] The Tanzanian Penina Mlama says:

> I think there are very good women artists. If you look at the traditional performances the women are some of the best performers. But when it comes to writing it is men who are given prominence.[21]

And she quotes the Ghanaian writer Ama Ata Aidoo:

> In fact, the whole question of what attention has been paid or not paid to African women is so tragic, sometimes one wonders what desperation keeps us writing. Because for sure, no one cares.[22]

The exclusion of females from the world of playwriting has made it difficult for them to use theatre to convey an independent view of what they consider desirable gender relations. Patriarchal tendencies in culture, together with colonialism, have effectively handicapped female participation not only as playwrights but also as actresses, directors, stage managers, scenic designers and other theatrical professions.

Actresses have continued to be stigmatized as women of "loose morals," as depicted in the experiences recounted in *Women's Voices and African Theatre*,[23] while those women who have attempted to acquire other theatrical skills such as directing or scenic designing have been discouraged; creating an impression of a lack of equal creativity between male and female artists.

---

[19] Mugo Micere, "The Woman Artist in Africa Today: A Critical Commentary," *Africa Development* 19.1 (1994), repr. in *Challenging Hierarchies: Issues and Themes in Colonial and Postcolonial Literature*, ed. Leonard A. Podis & Yakubu Saaka (New York: Peter Lang, 1998): 37–61.

[20] Mugo, "The Woman Artist in Africa Today: A Critical Commentary," 50.

[21] "The Woman Artist in Africa Today," 51.

[22] "The Woman Artist in Africa Today," 51.

[23] See Article 19.

Participation in African theatre today is still largely male-dominated. This fact notwithstanding, a number of female artists have fought their way into being recognized as participants in African theatre and have contributed persistently to the struggle against gender inequality in several ways. In literary theatre, names such as Ama Ata Aidoo (Ghana; playwright and fiction-writer), Stella Oyedepo (Nigeria), Rose Mbowa (Uganda), Micere Mugo (Kenya; playwright and poet), Fatima Dike (South Africa), Tsitsi Dangarembga (Zimbabwe, mainly film and novels), to mention but a few, can be cited. In the more grassroots participatory community theatre, other less renowned women are also contributing to the struggle, and examples can be found in *African Theatre: Women.*[24]

Although a large number of women and gender-sensitive men are presently trying to correct the existing gender imbalance, they are waging a battle against societies built doubly on male bias, first by themselves and secondly by colonialism. Currently, a postcolonial feminist struggle for gender equality is gradually overtaking the earlier postcolonial political struggle for the independence of the African theatre. African theatre is once again in a "Struggle over portrayal: What is portrayed? By whom? With whom? Where? And How?"

❧

[24] Martin Banham, James Gibbs, Femi Osofisa & Jane Plastow, ed. *African Theatre: Women* (Oxford: James Currey, 2002).

WORKS CITED

Article 19 African Programme. *Women's Voices and African Theatre: Case Studies from Kenya, Mali, The Democratic Republic of Congo and Zimbabwe* (Braamfontein 2017, 23 Jorissen Street, South Africa, 2003). Accessed at www. article19.org

Banham, Martin, James Gibbs, Fem Osofisan & Jane Plastow, ed. *African Theatre: Women* (Oxford: James Currey, 2002).

Breitinger, Eckhard. *Theatre and Performance in Africa* (Bayreuth African Studies, 1993).

Brockett, Oscar. *History of the Theatre* (New York: Simon & Schuster, 7th ed. 1995).

Euba, Femi. "Forms of Black Drama," 14 August 2003, http://www.alexanderstreetpress.com/articles/article.femi.euba.htm

Kerr, David. *African Popular Theatre* (London: James Currey, 1995).

Mugo, Micere. "The Woman Artist in Africa Today: A Critical Commentary." *Africa Development* 19.1 (1994), repr. in *Challenging Hierarchies: Issues and Themes in Colonial and Postcolonial Literature*, ed. Leonard A Podis & Yakubu Saaka (New York: Peter Lang, 1998): 37–61.

"Popular Theatre in Africa" (lecture notes), 14 August 2004 <http://athena.english.vt.edu/~carlisle/postcolonial/popular_theatre.html >

Schiller, D, Laurence. "The Royal Women of Buganda," *International Journal of Historical Studies* 23.3 (1992): 455–74.

Ngugi wa Thiong'o, & Micere Mugo. *The Trial of Dedan Kimathi* (African Writers Series; London: Heinemann. 1977).

Soyinka, Wole. *Death and The King's Horseman* (Methuen Modern Plays; London: Eyre Methuen, 1975).

——. *The Lion and the Jewel* (Three Crowns; Oxford: Oxford UP, 1963).

❧

Imagining a Nation

❧ The Necessity of Producing Canadian Drama

ANNE NOTHOF

POSTMODERN CANADIAN DRAMA participates in the imaginative construction and revision of a nation as a "semiotic field."[1] It creates the history, places, people, images, and ideologies as participatory experiences – recognized or contested – that interact in the formation of the diverse national character of a country of immigrants. Although it assumes a political nationalism as the right to self-government and self-determination, it typically has a profound mistrust of social and political processes, and enacts the alienation and isolation of individuals.[2] Although it assumes the importance of a sense of belonging and a sense of place, it may construct "imaginary homelands" that comprise a hybridization of cultures. As Graeme Turner has pointed out,

> Settler/postcolonial societies face enormous problems in articulating a common identity across competing forms of ethnicity and against a history of occupation and dispossession of the original inhabitants. The more we become aware of these internal differences and ambiguities, the more problematic becomes any simple affirmation of collective identity.[3]

---

[1] Frank Davey, *Post-National Arguments: The Politics of the Anglo-Canadian Novel since 1967* (Toronto: U of Toronto P, 1993): 5.

[2] Davey, *Post-National Arguments*, 265.

[3] Graeme Turner, *Making it National* (Sydney: Allen & Unwin, 1994): 123.

A Canadian national "identity" is ambivalent and shifting. It wears the masks of immigrants from some 210 countries. According to *Canadian Issues* editor Robert Israel, "No other developed country comes anywhere close to Canada's per capita intake of immigrants, nor by extension, to the pace of Canada's social and cultural transformation."[4] Multiculturalism, assuming racial and religious tolerance, is an embedded political ideology. But multiculturalism may also be a locus of tension, confusion, and anxiety – constructing a hyphenated identity of divided loyalties and beliefs. Richard Gwyn contends, for example, that "by treating differences of race, ethnicity, colour, as integral to identity rather than manifestations of heritage, official multiculturalism encourages apartheid."[5]

"Canada" derives from the Iroquois word 'kanata', meaning a cluster of huts. In many respects, the country is a collection of dispersed, regional habitations, linked by common laws and government, and by communication and transportation systems. Perhaps, as the playwright John Gray suggests in his self-reflexive consideration of the "imaginary Canadian," the "global village" as envisaged by Marshall McLuhan is Canadian society and culture writ large.[6]

Increasingly, Canadian theatres are staging diversity. The mandate of Cahoots Theatre in Toronto since the 1990s has been to present theatrical works that reflect and represent Canada's diverse cultural mosaic. Productions have included *Big Buck City* (1991) by the Native playwright Daniel David Moses and *Mom, Dad, I'm Living with a White Girl* (1995) by Marty Chan. Factory Theatre, also in Toronto, annually produces "Crosscurrents: a new play festival of Cultural Ideas" – featuring plays by "writers of colour" with themes involving the intersection of different cultures and questioning "old ideas of culture in light of the dynamic changes around us today; for stories in which cultures clash, cross, or

---

[4] Robert Israel, "A Nation of Immigrants," *Canadian Issues* (April 2003): 3.

[5] Richard Gwyn, *Nationalism Without Walls: The Unbearable Lightness of Being Canadian* (Toronto: McClelland & Stewart, 1995): 274.

[6] John Gray, *Lost in North America: The Imaginary Canadian in the American Dream* (Vancouver: Talonbooks, 1994): 197.

come together."[7] The Factory Theatre season for 2003–2004 included *Tiger of Malaya* by Hiro Kanagawa, a coproduction with the National Arts Centre in Ottawa, based on the Manila war-crimes trial of a Japanese general. Ironically, the scheduled production of *The Refugee Hotel* by Carmen Aguirre, about a group of Chilean refugees struggling to adapt to an unfamiliar life in Canada after fleeing Pinochet's military regime in 1974, was cancelled because of a difference of opinion between the artistic director, Ken Gass, and the playwright over the casting of minority-group actors as Chileans.

Factory Theatre, established in 1970 by current and founding artistic director Ken Gass, was the first company in Canada to devote itself exclusively to producing Canadian plays, and advertises itself as having been at the "forefront of the national theatre scene" for over three decades. Plays developed and premiered at Factory Theatre have been produced across the country and abroad. In 1976, in Factory Theatre Lab, the playwright John Palmer, adopting the persona of Henrik Ibsen, articulated the necessity of producing Canadian drama, implicitly comparing Ibsen's promotion and management of a national theatre in Bergen for six years in the 1850s to a fledgling Canadian indigenous theatre in the 1970s. In Palmer's play, entitled *Henrik Ibsen on the Necessity of Producing Norwegian Drama*, Ibsen expounds on the cultural and social need for a national theatre that articulates a sense of place, belonging, and identity. He interrogates the idea of nation and the ways in which nations and individuals define themselves through boundaries, politics, economics, and culture:

> The much touted 'identity crisis' which we in Norway are said to suffer is a foul and inane lie propagated by those who stand to profit by it. It does not exist. I certainly know who I am. If you do not know who you are, according to the laws of psychiatry and the state, you are insane and have no rights in the affairs of Norway.
>
> Norwegian art is abundant and at this very moment is clearly defining Norwegian existence for those who choose to see; to

---

[7] Brian Quirt, "Call for Submissions for Crosscurrents 2004," Candrama@listserv.unb.ca

> remain deaf to it is the prerogative of any citizen: to claim its non-existence is either to be blind or wicked, but to oppose its legitimate growth and establishment is a criminal act against the people of Norway.[8]

Canadian playwrights and critics have continued to reconfigure a 'national drama' as inclusive, diverse, multi-ethnic, and indigenous. It is a constantly changing syncretic performance, which challenges the ideological implications of Canada's historical narratives. Canadian dramatic texts often suggest internally conflicted understandings of the formation and importance of 'nation'. Playwrights such as Sharon Pollock have revisited Canadian history to interrogate the construction of a national myth of "peace, order, and good government," and to revisit sites of national trauma. As the critic Sherrill Grace has pointed out,

> history and identity in Pollock's hands, are a matter of performance and [...] Pollock always sees a chance to change the story by not blindly performing the accepted roles or repeating the dominant scripts.[9]

In *Walsh* (1973), Pollock deconstructs the heroic image of the Royal Canadian Mounted Police, and shows its complicity with the Canadian government in forcing Sitting Bull's Sioux nation to leave the sanctuary of Canadian soil and to return to genocidal annihilation in the USA. In *The Komagata Maru Incident* (1978), she dramatizes the consequences of a racist government policy to keep Canada a "white man's country," when 376 immigrants from the Punjab were held in quarantine for three months on a Japanese freighter in Vancouver harbour. In *Fair Liberty's Call* (1993), she replays the struggle between independence and authority that tore apart families in the American colonies on the soil of what would

---

[8] John Palmer, "Henrik Ibsen on the Necessity of Producing Norwegian Drama" (CBC 1978), in *The CTR Anthology: Fifteen Plays from Canadian Theatre Review*, ed. Alan Filewod (Toronto: U of Toronto P, 1993): 43.

[9] Sherrill Grace & Albert–Reiner Glaap, "Texts and Contexts: An Introduction," in *Performing National Identities: International Perspectives on Contemporary Canadian Theatre*, ed. Grace & Glaap (Vancouver: Talonbooks, 2003): 16.

become the Canadian province of New Brunswick. Like Ibsen, Pollock dramatizes the beginnings of a nation as complicated by divided loyalties, personal tragedies, and failed myths. In a 1984 "Review" of her plays, the critic Robert Nunn presaged Pollock's importance in the creation of a "national drama," with "her steady attention to the impact of public issues, and public myths, on individual lives":

> John Palmer's marvellous tirade, "Henrik Ibsen on the Necessity of Producing Norwegian Drama" implied that there was no reason why Canada could not produce a playwright of Ibsen's stature, as long as it undertook not actively to prevent such an occurrence. When Canada's answer to Ibsen emerges, it will be someone like Sharon Pollock, with her long-haul commitment to the discipline, with her experimentation, and expansion of the boundaries of her dramatic universe.[10]

Yet Pollock herself does not consider her plays distinctively 'Canadian': she "has the gall to believe that if they're good plays anybody ought to be able to get something from them."[11]

John Gray has also been engaged in interrogating the construction of Canadian nationalism in his essays and plays. In *Lost in North America: The Imaginary Canadian in the North American Dream* (1994), he contends that Canada is "an electronic magazine stand, an accumulation of arbitrarily juxtaposed images and random details, both fact and fiction, some local but most imported from other parts of Canada, from America, and from no place at all."[12] In his play *Billy Bishop Goes to War*, he challenges the historical narrative of Canada's 'coming of age' as an independent nation through the trauma of the First World War, by demythologizing the flying ace Billy Bishop, showing him to be focused primarily

---

[10] Robert Nunn, "Sharon Pollock's Plays: A Review Article," in *Sharon Pollock: Essays on Her Works*, ed. Anne Nothof (Toronto: Guernica, 2000): 42. Originally published in *Theatre History in Canada* 5.1 (1984): 72–83.

[11] Sherrill Grace, "How Passionate Are You? An Interview with Sharon Pollock," *Canadian Theatre Review* 114 (Spring 2003): 27.

[12] John Gray, *Lost in North America: The Imaginary Canadian in the American Dream* (Vancouver: Talon, 1994): 38.

on winning in his deadly contests with German pilots, and on survival. Billy Bishop is a problematic hero, used by the British imperialists to serve their own propagandist ends. As Lady St. Helier, who has been instrumental in this construction of a national symbol, points out,

> Bishop, I'm only going to say this once. It is not for you to be interested, amused or entertained. You are no longer a rather short Canadian with bad taste and a poor service record. You are a figurehead, unlikely as that may seem. A dignitary. The people of Canada, England, the Empire, indeed, the world, look to you as a symbol of victory and you will act the part.[13]

The play asks the ironic question which John Gray considers to be quintessentially Canadian: "Who do you think you are?"

Native playwrights have also challenged the construction of a national identity in terms of a transplanted European culture. In Marie Clements' *Burning Vision*, Canada is envisaged as a hybridization of cultures, languages, and peoples – Japanese, Dene, Métis, Irish – and, in her scenario, all are connected by the dropping of the atomic bombs on Japan. The protagonist, Rose, a young Métis woman, learns how her grandfather died of radiation sickness from mining uranium in northern Canada for the manufacture of the atomic bomb in the USA. Rose is a bread-maker and a dreamer, and finds in the dough that she kneads an image of herself and the country:

> This perfect loaf of bread is plump with a rounded body and straight sides. I have a tender, golden brown crust which can be crisp, or delicate. This grain is fine and even, with slightly elongated cells; the flesh of this bread is multi-grained. You never know what you're going to look like. Some say it's in the current. Others say, if you're mixed and from Canada, it's in the currency of blood.[14]

---

[13] John Gray, *Billy Bishop Goes to War*, in *Modern Canadian Plays*, vol. 1, ed. Jerry Wasserman (Vancouver: Talon, 4th ed. 2000): 315.

[14] Marie Clements, *Burning Vision* (Vancouver: Talonbooks, 2003): 58.

Imagining a postmodern nation is necessarily iconoclastic – the deconstruction of imperialistic ‘national’ symbols, such as the Canadian Pacific Railway, which has functioned as an image of Canadian unity and cohesiveness. The completion of the CPR in 1885 to ensure that British Columbia would be brought into Confederation and not lost to the USA opened the prairies to European immigration, and to the political and legal authority of the federal government. It also resulted in a collision between European colonization of land and resources, and the indigenous First Nations. It is no accident that in *The Ecstasy of Rita Joe* by George Ryga, Rita’s Native lover, Jamie Paul, dies under the wheels of a train, as does the French-Canadian philosophy student François in *Polygraph* by Robert Lepage. The route to the west coast was blasted through the mountains by Chinese immigrant labourers, many of whom died in the construction of the “National Dream.” The Edmonton playwright Marty Chan disinters these fragments of history in *The Forbidden Phoenix*, a fable that uses Chinese characters to enact a political allegory about Chinese immigrant experience in the late-nineteenth century. Deluded by the myth of the Gold Mountain – the riches that awaited them in Canada – Chinese men toiled on the railways and in the mines, forbidden to bring their families with them, and denied citizenship.

In Chan’s play, the hero/protagonist is the Monkey King, the archetypal Chinese trickster-figure, who leaves the starving Kingdom of the East and the repressive regime of the Empress Dowager to find hope for his people in the Western land of plenty. He also leaves behind his beloved adopted son, a starving young peasant. In the West, however, he is co-opted by Tiger (the forces of the establishment and government) to dig a tunnel through Gold Mountain so that Tiger can join his lover, the fearsome Iron Dragon. His only hope for a new life in the West is in the Phoenix (an imagined creature), and together they defeat the Tiger and the Iron Dragon. Once this is accomplished, Monkey King can rescue his peasant son from the Empress, and “lead his people” into the West. As a tamed Tiger explains, “Home is not a place. It is a state of mind. As long as the curtain of water flows, [the Monkey King's] home is both kingdoms."[15]

In Chan's revisioning of the East/West binary, then, the forces of the industrialized West are destructive of environment, culture, and social harmony. They are violent and exploitative, and only defeated by intellect and imagination. Chan casts his fable in the form of a Chinese opera, with some modifications to accommodate the martial arts and singing skills of local actors, only one of whom was Chinese (Elyne Quan, who played the Monkey King). Chan believes that in order to tell his story of Chinese immigrants from a Chinese point of view, it is important to use the conventions of Chinese theatre. His main purpose, however, is to introduce this tradition to Canadian audiences, since there has been little infiltration of Chinese mythology into the Canadian cultural scene; nor is it in the public consciousness. But the mythology is inflected to show the exploitation of the Chinese in Canada: it tells a Canadian 'nation-building' story from the point of view of the builders.

Canadian drama also appropriates and satirizes American popular culture, both resisting and exploiting its forms and images. Despite the strong economic and cultural presence of the USA in Canada, the "surrealistic collage" of images from television, film, and advertising, Canadians' perception of their distinctiveness remains clear: they are not Americans. The Edmonton playwright Stewart Lemoine typically places his ingenuous characters in the USA or in exotic foreign locales to show their response to seductive but dangerous social and cultural systems, and to explore their potential for independent self-realization. In *The Margin of the Sky* (2003), set in Los Angeles, he places the different cultural perspectives in the USA and Canada in ironic juxtaposition. A young Canadian playwright named Leo has been commissioned by his American brother-in-law, Spence, star of the soap opera *The Lives We Borrow*, to write a screenplay for a movie in which Spence will star as an action-hero. Leo has written some plays, which he modestly describes as "Short ones.

[15] Marty Chan, "The Forbidden Phoenix" (unpublished MS, 2003): 74.

Medium sized ones. ... People liked them. Canadian people."[16] However, he is capable only of writing plots with ironic conclusions, even if they reference American films he has seen. In fact, his perspective on life is pervasively ironic, as his opinion of his sister, who is about to become Spence's latest "ex," demonstrates: "If she can see the irony in a sad situation, that means she's got a good idea of finding her sense of humour at some point in the future."[17] En route to a meeting with Spence, he rescues a young woman eating a sandwich on a park bench from certain death by dislodging a chicken bone on which she is choking. In his consideration and compassion, he enacts the stereotype of the polite Canadian:

LEO:	Your body's had a shock. I think it needs fluids and companionship. I can provide those things.
ALICE:	What a good citizen you are!
LEO:	Why thank you. I appreciate that. Amusingly, I'm actually a Canadian employed in a kind of questionable employment set-up, so for you to say that is –
ALICE:	It's ironic?
LEO:	Exactly. Like crying for joy. Like laughing at death.[18]

In the meantime, Spence has met a woman in the reception room of his chiropractor, who introduces him to the extraordinary passionate world of the Schönberg opera *Gurrelieder*, to which she has been listening on headphones. Over drinks together, the two couples watch the sunset through newly purchased sunglasses, the women wearing elegant gowns from Sheila's tony dress store. They have become stars in their own movie, reinventing and celebrating their lives, unrestricted by more mun-

---

[16] Stewart Lemoine, "The Margin of the Sky," in *A Teatro Trilogy: Selected Plays by Stewart Lemoine*, ed. Anne Nothof (Edmonton, Alberta: NeWest, 2004): 172.

[17] Lemoine, "The Margin of the Sky," 150.

[18] "The Margin of the Sky," 162.

dane realities. During their conversation, they speculate on the meaning of the words from an English translation of the first aria from *Gurrelieder*, sung by the doomed hero Waldemar as he rides to meet his loved one, Tove:

> Now dusk mutes every sound
> on land and sea.
> the scudding clouds have gathered close
> against the margin of the sky.

Leo is disinclined to interpret the image of "the margin of the sky" at this point. When the women exit, Spence counsels Leo to write the truth about others, and Leo responds to himself that that would be the worst thing he could do. Humankind cannot bear too much reality. The sunset scene then segues into the earlier scene with Alice choking on the park bench. Reality is revisited. This time she declines Leo's offer of help and leaves. Leo returns to his office, and later informs Spence that he will not write his film-script. He immerses himself in the imagined world of Schönberg's opera, until he notices "something extremely obvious on his notepad," and the scene segues back to the scene with Spence and the women contemplating the sunset and the meaning of the words "the margin of the sky." Leo now can see the ambivalence in the image, but also the positive possibilities:

> A margin is an edge. And on a piece of paper, it's a line that *marks* an edge, but it really only has meaning because it denotes a point of entry. You put your pen where the margin tells you to and that's it. [...]. You're in. So the margin of the sky would have to be the point of entry for everything above. That's why you can never say it's the least significant part... The sky is huge. You can't pick a place to get into it just by looking up. But if you look straight on [...] you can let yourself think that there really is a part of the sky that touches this same earth on which we're all standing. You can let yourself think that if you traveled the distance between here and there you would actually get to it.[19]

[19] Lemoine, "The Margin of the Sky," 211.

Leo, the Canadian playwright, finds a way of entering an imagined space through language. To quote Homi Bhabha (citing Heidegger), "a boundary is not just a line at which something stops but a line from which something begins its presencing." Margins, like borders and boundaries, give rise to alternative sites of meaning:

> The 'locality' of national culture is neither unified nor unitary in relation to itself, nor must it be seen simply as 'other' in relation to what is outside or beyond it. The boundary is Janus-faced and the problem of outside/inside must always itself be a process of hybridity, incorporating new 'people' in relation to the body politic, generating other sites of meaning.[20]

Nations, like theatre, are imagined spaces, created from a diversity of shared perspectives and experiences, which articulates who we think we are.

Works Cited

Anderson, Benedict. *Imagined Communities: Reflections on the Origin and Spread of Nationalism* (London: Verso, 1983.

Anderson, Erin, & Michael Valpy. "Face the Nation: Canada Remade," *Globe & Mail* (7 June 2003): A8–A9.

Bhabha, Homi K. "Introduction: Narrating the Nation," in *Nation and Narration*, ed. Bhabha (London: Routledge, 1990): 1–7.

Chan, Marty. "The Forbidden Phoenix" (unpublished MS, 2003).

Clements, Marie. *Burning Vision* (Vancouver: Talonbooks, 2003).

Davey, Frank. *Post-National Arguments: The Politics of the Anglo-Canadian Novel since 1967* (Toronto: U of Toronto P, 1993).

Grace, Sherrill. "How Passionate Are You? An Interview with Sharon Pollock," *Canadian Theatre Review* 114 (Spring 2003): 26–32.

——, & Albert–Reiner Glaap, ed. *Performing National Identities: International Perspectives on Contemporary Canadian Theatre* (Vancouver: Talonbooks, 2003).

[20] Homi Bhabha, "Introduction: Narrating the Nation," in *Nation and Narration*, ed. Bhabha (London: Routledge, 1990): 4.

Gray, John. "Billy Bishop Goes to War," in *Modern Canadian Plays*, vol. 1, ed. Jerry Wasserman (Vancouver: Talon, 4th ed. 2000).

——. *Lost in North America: The Imaginary Canadian in the American Dream* (Vancouver: Talon, 1994).

Gwyn, Richard. *Nationalism Without Walls: The Unbearable Lightness of Being Canadian* (Toronto: McClelland & Stewart, 1995).

Ignatieff, Michael. *Blood and Belonging: Journeys into the New Nationalism* (Toronto: Penguin, 1993).

Israel, Robert. "A Nation of Immigrants," *Canadian Issues* (April 2003): 3.

Lemoine, Stewart. "The Margin of the Sky," in *A Teatro Trilogy: Selected Plays by Stewart Lemoine*, ed. Anne Nothof (Edmonton, Alberta: NeWest, 2004).

Nunn, Robert. "Sharon Pollock's Plays: A Review Article," *Theatre History in Canada* 5.1 (1984): 72–83. Repr. in *Sharon Pollock: Essays on Her Works*, ed. Anne Nothof (Toronto: Guernica, 2000).

Palmer, John. "Henrik Ibsen on the Necessity of Producing Norwegian Drama" (CBC 1978), in *The CTR Anthology: Fifteen Plays from Canadian Theatre Review*, ed. Alan Filewod (Toronto: U of Toronto P, 1993): 35–46.

Turner, Graeme. *Making it National* (Sydney: Allen & Unwin, 1994).

Quirt, Brian. "Call for Submissions for Crosscurrents 2004," Candrama@listserv.unb.ca

❧

The Mask of Aaron

❧ "Tall screams reared out of Three Mile Plains": Shakespeare's *Titus Andronicus* and George Elliott Clarke's Black Acadian Tragedy, *Execution Poems*

SUSAN KNUTSON

THIS STUDY of George Elliott Clarke's award-winning *Execution Poems* in relation to Shakespeare's *Titus Andronicus* is part of a larger research project that explores Canadian writers' use of Shakespeare. The project aims to sound the layered meanings of Shakespearean passages once they have found their way into Canadian poetry and fiction.[1] In *Execution Poems*, several of those layers have to do with Canada's colonial history, and with the ways that Shakespeare has been a key building-block of the British Empire.[2] Others have to do with the par-

---

[1] George Elliott Clarke, *Execution Poems: The Black Acadian Tragedy of "George and Rue"* (Wolfville, Nova Scotia: Gaspereau, 2001). *Execution Poems* was awarded the Governor-General's Literary Award for Poetry in English.

[2] Michael Neill writes: "Shakespeare's writing was entangled from the beginning with the projects of nation-building, Empire and colonization; [...] Shakespeare was simultaneously invented as the 'National Bard' and promoted as a repository of 'universal' human values [... and] the canon became an instrument of imperial authority as important and powerful in its way as the Bible and the gun"; Neill, "Post-Colonial Shakespeare? Writing Away from the Centre," in *Post-Colonial Shakespeares*, ed. Ania Loomba & Martin Orkin (London: Routledge, 1998): 168–69. For a recent discussion of Canada's postcolonial status, see *Is*

ticular resonance of Shakespeare, and history, for generations of African Nova Scotians, or, as Clarke has named them (and himself), the Africadians. At the end of the eighteenth century and the beginning of the nineteenth they came to Canada from the USA to escape slavery and the Fugitive Slave Laws, only to experience generations of economic, social and educational discrimination.[3]

One such resonance traced by Clarke's poetic suite is the deep and spontaneous identification between his character, Rufus Hamilton, and Shakespeare's dramatic villain, Aaron the Moor – an identification that has an historical counterpart in the enthusiastic reception of Aaron by black audiences in South Africa, as reported by Anthony Sher and Gregory Doran, and discussed by Ania Loomba, in *Shakespeare, Race and Colonialism*.[4] In *Execution Poems*, Clarke's Africadian character identifies with Aaron and speaks in the rhetorical tropes of Shakespeare's *Titus Andronicus*. The rhetorical excess and violent action place *Execution Poems* in the tradition of the revenge tragedy, of Marlowe and Seneca and also of the African American literary tradition that followed on the heels of Nat Turner's bloody revolt in Southampton County, Virginia, in 1831.[5] The mask of Aaron is worn in the pursuit of revenge

---

Canada Postcolonial? Unsettling Canadian Literature, ed. Laura Moss (Waterloo, Ontario: Wilfrid Laurier UP, 2003).

[3] Most Africadians trace their arrival in Canada to one of the two waves of immigration following the American Revolution and the war of 1812, when the "Black Loyalists" supported the British against the Americans, but, as Clarke points out, there have been persons of African origin in the Atlantic region since the early seventeenth century – *Odysseys Home: Mapping African-Canadian Literature* (Toronto: U of Toronto P, 2002): 18n3. The Africadians' history in Canada thus begins at the same time as that of the French Acadians; in other words, at the beginning of the European colonization of North America. See esp. "The Birth and Rebirth of Africadian Literature" in *Odysseys Home*, 107–25.

[4] Ania Loomba, *Shakespeare, Race, and Colonialism* (London: Oxford UP, 2002): 75.

[5] See *The Confessions of Nat Turner, and Related Documents*, ed. & intro. Kenneth S. Greenberg (Boston MA Bedford & New York: St. Martin's, 1996); Frank Lambert, "'I Saw the Book Talk': Slave Readings of the First Great Awakening," *Journal of Negro History* 77.4 (1992): 185–98; Jeffery Ogbonna

and social justice. In tracing the intertextual labyrinth that binds Clarke's *Execution Poems* to Shakespeare's *Titus Andronicus*, I glimpse an Africadian Shakespeare and a Shakespearean George Elliott Clarke, and so understand something of thc Classical and European patrimony to which George Elliott Clarke and his black, African Nova Scotian speakers are the legitimate heirs. I align my efforts here with the work of the African-Canadian scholar David Sealy, who notes the "diverse ways in which Black diasporic subjects have selectively appropriated, incorporated, European ideologies, culture, and institutions, alongside an 'African' heritage."[6]

The poems narrate the short and bitter lives of Clarke's first cousins, Rufus and George Hamilton, who were hanged for the murder of a Fredericton taxi driver in New Brunswick, in 1949. The crucial intertext linking the poems to Shakespeare's *Titus Andronicus* both supports and complicates Clarke's social-justice argument, which is articulated rhetorically in his poetry as the chiasmatic linking of the brothers' act of violent murder and their subjection to acts of murderous violence carried out by the society in which they lived. Such a structured and rhetorical performance of violence is as typical of *Titus Andronicus* as it is fundamental to *Execution Poems,* which in this way announce their poetic genealogy, reaching from Shakespeare through Christopher Marlowe's *Jew of Malta* to the "heightened rhetoric" of Seneca's typically gruesome tragedies.[7] Textual kinship is further attested to by the cheerfully brutal style shared by the Clarke and the Shakespeare texts – for example, in this well-known alliteration from *Andronicus*:

Green Ogbar, "Prophet Nat and God's Children of Darkness: Black Religious Nationalism," *Journal of Religious Thought* 53–54 (1997): 51–71.

[6] David Sealy, "'Canadianizing' Blackness: Resisting the Political," in *Rude: Contemporary Black Canadian Cultural Criticism*, ed. Rinaldo Walcott (Toronto: Insomniac, 2000): 91.

[7] Harold Bloom, *Shakespeare: The Invention of the Human* (New York: Riverhead, 1998): 80. See also Jonathan Bate's discussion of the structured violence in *Titus Andronicus*, in "Introduction" to William Shakespeare, *Titus Andronicus*, ed. Bate (Arden Shakespeare; London: Methuen, 2002): 4–21.

> Alarbus' limbs are lopp'd[8]

or this cheery antanaclasis (the repetition of a word in two different senses) from *Execution Poems*:

> I'll draw blood the way Picasso draws nudes, voluptuously.[9]

The excessive literariness of this language opens up a field of dense signification that is both glorious and brutal, celebratory and indeterminate, morally and ethically deferred. As Bart Moore–Gilbert writes in his discussion of Dennis Porter's "*Orientalism* and its Problems," "the excess of the signifier over the signified at such moments produces a complex of meanings which cannot be stabilized [...] in any easy or straightforward way."[10]

The characterization of the brothers articulates two distinct responses to questions of language and of ethical or political action as they are framed in the postcolonial situation, urgently counterposing creole or patois to Shakespearean English, and violence to counter-violence, moral righteousness, and revenge. Clarke invokes paradox and oxymoron even as he introduces "George & Rue: Pure, Virtuous Killers," and summarizes their shared story:

> They sprouted in Newport Station, Hants County, Nova Scotia, in 1925 and 1926.
> They smacked a white taxi driver, Silver, with a hammer, to lift his silver.
> [...]
> They had face-to-face trials in May 1949 and backed each other's guilt.
> [...]
> They were dandled from a gallows in the third hour of July 27, 1949, A.D.[11]

---

[8] *Titus Andronicus*, I.ii.143.

[9] *Execution Poems*, 32.

[10] Bart Moore–Gilbert, *Postcolonial Theory: Contexts, Practices, Politics* (London: Verso, 1997): 55.

[11] *Execution Poems*, 12.

The young men's contrasting characters and contrapuntal confessions help to structure the story and ground the multiple voicing of the poems as a whole:

> George Albert Hamilton confessed – to theft – and mated the Sally Anne.
> Rufus James Hamilton polished his refined, mint, silver-bright English.[12]

George Hamilton is both less guilty and less interesting than his brother. He is the good victim of racism and discriminatory violence. His story, that he only *robbed* the taxi driver, and that, because he was hungry and in need, is elaborated in the following poem, "Ballad of a Hanged Man":

> … See, as a wed man,
> I don't care if I wear uglified overalls.
> But I ain't going to hear my child starve.
> ….
> I had the intention to ruck some money.
> In my own heart, I had that, to rape money,
> because I was fucked, in my own heart.
> ….
> Have you ever gone in your life, going
> two days without eating …?
>
> I ain't dressed this story up. I am enough
> disgraced. I swear to the truths I know.
> I wanted to uphold my wife and child.
> Hang me and I'll not hold them again.[13]

George "mated the Sally Anne" in the sense that he regained the moral high ground in relation to the Salvation Army, by claiming that he only wanted to be able to eat and to support his wife and children. George Hamilton makes this appeal to liberal-humanist values using the non-standard variety of English known to linguists as African Nova Scotian

---

[12] *Execution Poems*, 12.

[13] *Execution Poems*, 13–14.

English, or simply Black English ("I ain't dressed this story up ..."), which is characterized by the use of the subjunctive and by retentions from nineteenth-century, or older, English, and discussed in a groundbreaking essay by George Elliott Clarke.[14] Throughout *Execution Poems*, George Hamilton speaks in this popular language variety, and, fittingly, he states his case here using the popular literary form of the ballad. This does not mean, however, that his language is unsophisticated, for George Hamilton's speech – like the language of the book as a whole – displays a very wide range of classical rhetorical tropes and figures. Two examples here would be anthimeria, the substitution of one part of speech for another, as in the phrase, "But I ain't going to hear my child starve," and paronomasia, words alike in sound but different in meaning, as in "I wanted to uphold my wife and child. / Hang me and I'll not hold them again."[15]

It is Rufus James Hamilton, on the other hand, who identifies most deeply with Aaron. Rufus does not deny his responsibility for the murder. Instead, this bi-dialectal linguistic virtuoso celebrates his crime and spits out his rage and anger in varieties of English ranging from the Shakespearean to the rural Black Nova Scotian, as he pleases. George asks for forgiveness, but his brother sees the act of murder as righteous revenge:[16]

> *Rue:* Here's how I justify my error:
> The blow that slew Silver came from two centuries back.
> It took that much time and agony to turn a white man's whip
> into a black man's hammer.[17]

Rufus denounces the bloody history of African slavery and looks for vengeance against the society that abused him. His character is based on the historical Rufus Hamilton, who, as George Elliott Clarke explains, spoke so articulately during his trial that his prosecutor, unable to "shake" or

---

[14] "The Career of Black English in Nova Scotia: A Literary Sketch," in *Odysseys Home*, 86–106.

[15] *Execution Poems*, 14.

[16] *Execution Poems*, 41.

[17] "The Killing," *Execution Poems*, 35.

"flap" him, commented on his excellent command of English.[18] The character of Rufus is also Shakespearean. In "Reading *Titus Andronicus* in Three Mile Plains, N.S.," Rufus tells how he came to identify with one of Shakespeare's most unredeemed villains, Aaron the Moor:

> *Rue:* When Witnesses sat before Bibles open like plates
> And spat sour sermons of interposition and nullification,
> While burr-orchards vomited bushels of thorns, and leaves
> Rattled like uprooted skull-teeth across rough highways,
> And stars ejected brutal, serrated, heart-shredding light,
> And dark brothers lied down, quiet, in government graves,
> Their white skulls jabbering amid farmer's dead flowers –
> The junked geraniums and broken truths of car engines,
> And *History* snapped its whip and bankrupted scholars,
> School was violent improvement. I opened Shakespeare
> And discovered a scarepriest, shaking in violent winds,
> Some hallowed, heartless man, his brain boiling blood,
> Aaron, seething, demanding, "Is black so base a hue?"
> And shouting, "Coal-black refutes and foils any other hue
> In that it scorns to bear another hue." O! Listen at that![19]

---

[18] George Elliott Clarke comments: "To turn to Rufus in *Execution Poems* [...] his English is 'concocted' BUT it is also meant to correspond deliberately to a beautiful 'oddity' in both his and general Afro-North American experience: the tendency of black autodidacts to compose/speak either an extremely 'correct'/ poised English, or to deconstruct the hell out of it! The 'real' Rufus spoke well enough that his prosecutor, unable to 'shake' or 'flap' him, commented, during the trial, on his excellent command of English. (My poem, 'Malignant English,' is based on this episode.) At the same time, chronicles of black settlers on the Prairies a hundred years ago gave me ideas about how to fashion Rufus's English, and I should also mention that my own father, who achieved only Grade 10, as a relatively self-taught adult, possesses the lexicon of a lawyer and the confident ease in utilizing standard English that one could expect of a politician or a professor. To sum up, Rufus's English is partly invented, and he probably never read Shakespeare, BUT I did/do see his character as exemplifying the tendency among 'out-group' speakers of a more powerful group's language to treat it practically as putty – to use it for ornamentation. (See also 'Haligonian Market Cry' in this regard.)"; email interview with Susan Knutson, 20 March 2002.

[19] *Execution Poems*, 25.

The intertextuality linking *Execution Poems* and *Titus Andronicus* rests here on the bedrock of an explicit identification between Rufus and Aaron, founded on Aaron's defence of blackness as he turns on the nurse to protect his newborn son. His baby is described as a "devil",[20] "A joyless, dismal, black and sorrowful issue /…as loathsome as a toad / Amongst the fair-faced breeders of our clime."[21] Aaron responds with rhetorical argument – "Is black so base a hue?"[22] – and with his sword.

Clarke also quotes, a few lines later, and in the epigraphs to the poems as a whole, a passage from Seneca's *Hippolytus* which Shakespeare wove into *Titus Andronicus*, where the lines are spoken by Demetrius as he readies himself to assault Lavinia:

> *Sit fas aut nefas*, till I find the stream
> To cool this heat, a charm to calm these fits,
> *Per Stygia, per manes vehor.*[23]

The Latin translates into English as: "Be it right or wrong / I am borne through the Stygian regions among shades." Clarke writes, in Rue's voice:

> *Sit fat aut nefas,* I am become
> Aaron, desiring poisoned lilies and burning, staggered air,
> A King James God, spitting fire, brimstone, leprosy, cancers,
> Dreaming of tearing down stars and letting grass incinerate
> Pale citizen's prized bones. What should they mean to me?
> A plough rots, returns to ore; weeds snatch it back to earth;
> The stones of the sanctuaries pour out onto every street.
> Like drastic Aaron's heir, Nat Turner, I's natural homicidal:
> My pages blaze, my lines pall, crying fratricidal damnation.[24]

Locating both hell and apocalyptic vengeance in the human world, these lines may remind us of Marlowe's Mephistopheles, who famously turns

---

[20] *Titus Andronicus*, IV.ii.66.

[21] *Titus Andronicus*, IV.ii.68–70.

[22] *Titus Andronicus*, IV.ii.71.

[23] *Titus Andronicus*, II.i.133–135.

[24] *Execution Poems*, 25.

up in Gutenberg to declare, "Why this is hell, nor am I out of it."[25] Damnation, Marlowe taught, is a state of mind, and the bloody violence of Clarke's "Original Pain" elaborates on Rufus's life as one of the living damned, and further underpins the Old Testament referents of fratricidal murder and original sin. Rue's final speech, which claims, "We'll hang like Christ hanged,"[26] goes one better than Aaron's last words, pronounced as he is literally being buried alive for his sins:

> If one good deed in all my life I did
> I do repent it from my very soul.[27]

At the least, both characters are in unqualified rebellion against the imperial power which would negate them.

While Aaron's calligraphy of social vengeance is acted out as murder and rape within the play itself, at the level of the literary text Aaron models the counter-discourse of the postcolonial writer, as Clarke suggests:

> The smartest, wiliest character in TA is black Aaron, and his malice toward Titus and the whole Roman power structure is driven in part by his lust for revenge against a civilization that considers him barbarous. Aaron is the model of the frustrated and embittered black (minority) intellectual who uses his mastery of the codes of the opposing civilization to wreak endless havoc within it – with a smile… He is Othello as if played by Iago. [28]

In keeping with this interpretation, we should note that literary experience is signified as such both in Shakespeare's play and in *Execution Poems*. For, just as Rufus, for better or for worse, discovers a way to navigate through the violence of his childhood world via an identification with Shakespeare's Aaron, so Lavinia's rape and mutilation is communicated to her father, nephew and uncle through their reading of Ovid's account of the story of Tereus, Philomena, Procne and Itys. When Titus communi-

---

[25] Christopher Marlowe, *Christopher Marlowe's Dr. Faustus: Text and Major Criticism*, ed. Irving Ribner (New York: Odyssey, 1966): I.iii.76.

[26] "Famous Last," *Execution Poems*, 41.

[27] *Titus Andronicus*, V.iii.189–90.

[28] Email interview, 2 May 2002.

cates with Tamara's sons by sending them a quotation from Horace, it is Aaron who is able to decode this literary sign and who understands and acts on the message of the text. *Titus Andronicus* and *Execution Poems* are both concerned with poetry and the place of poetry in relation to the struggle for social justice. It is no accident, then, that in his prefatory poem "Negation" Clarke introduces himself in terms that appear to deliberately recall Aaron's determination to act, early on in *Titus Andronicus*:

> Away with slavish weeds and servile thoughts!
> I will be bright, and shine in pearl and gold[29]

Clarke writes:

> I mean
> To go out shining instead of tarnished,
> To take apart poetry like a heart[30]

Aaron's determination to voice "the venomous malice of his swelling heart"[31] is expressed appropriately, as a rhetorical question – "Ah, why should wrath be mute and fury dumb?"[32] His sentiments could easily be those of Rufus Hamilton, or even those of Rufus's poet cousin, George Elliott Clarke, who like Shakespeare has employed both his voice and his rhetorical virtuosity in the service of wrath and fury.

Titus Andronicus himself is also a writer, whose response to the bloodbath in this family is to retire to his study to compose "crimson lines"[33]:

> Who doth molest my contemplation?
> Is it your trick to make me ope the door,
> That so my sad decrees may fly away
> And all my study be to no effect?
> You are deceived; for what I mean to do
> See here in bloody lines I have set down;
> And what is written shall be executed.[34]

---

29 *Titus Andronicus*, II.i.18–19.

30 *Execution Poems*, 11.

31 *Titus Andronicus*, V.iii.13.

32 *Titus Andronicus*, V.iii.183.

33 *Titus Andronicus*, V.ii.22.

It is Titus, too, who articulates the topographical boundaries of his world that conform to the traditional three levels of the Heavens, the Earth (made up of Rome and of the Country of the Goths) and Hell. When Lavinia writes in the sand the names of Chiron and Demetrius, identifying them as her tormenters, Titus cites Seneca to accuse the heavens of looking passively on as crimes are committed: "*Magni dominator poli, / Tam lentus audis scelera, tam lentus vides?*" [Ruler of the great heavens, dost thou so calmly hear crimes, so calmly look upon them?].[35] The heavens are disengaged and passive. Later, as he plots to cast the net of vengeance for Tamora and her sons, Titus comments that Justice has fled the earth, so that he and the remnant of his family must turn to hell for help in their distress:

> *Terras Astraea reliquit* [Justice has fled the Earth]:
> Be you remembered, Marcus, She's gone, she's fled.
> Sirs, take you to your tools. You, cousins, shall
> Go sound the ocean, and cast your nets;
> Happily you may catch her in the sea.
> Yet there's as little justice as at land.
> No, Publius and Sempronius, you must do it.
> 'Tis you must dig with mattock and with spade
> And pierce the inmost centre of the earth;
> Then, when you come to Pluto's region,
> I pray you deliver him this petition.
> Tell him it is for justice and for aid,
> And that it comes from old Andronicus,
> Shaken with sorrows in ungrateful Rome.[36]

When hell responds, through Publius, that Revenge is in Hell but that Justice must be hiding in the heavens, Titus' thoughts again turn skyward, and he does a remarkable thing: he initiates a new dynamism within his topographical field through the comedic device of firing many arrows,

---

[34] *Titus Andronicus*, V.ii.9–15.

[35] *Titus Andronicus*, IV.i.80. Seneca, *Hippolytus*, ll. 671–72.

[36] *Titus Andronicus*, IV.iii.4–17.

burdened with writing and appealing for justice to Jove, Apollo, Mars and Pallas, to the end that "There's not a god left unsolicited"[37]:

> And sith there's no justice in earth nor hell,
> We will solicit heaven and move the gods
> To send down justice for us to wreak our wrongs.[38]

His solicitation, his attempt to move another through the power of language, is, of course, the province of rhetoric.

Clarke's *Execution Poems* likewise voices a rhetorical appeal for justice, overlaying Canadian Maritime geography onto the three-tiered world of the Elizabethan stage. A very specific sense of Maritime places accentuates the dynamic address of "Tall screams reared out of Three Mile Plains," from the poem "Original Pain," creating the striking figure of the suffering boys' cries rising to the heavens.[39] The geography is specific and the relationship is dynamic, as the appeal – not one but many "tall screams" – is one that demands to be heard. In this, we may choose to see a parallel to Titus's soliciting scream "to move the gods to send down justice for us to wreak our wrongs."[40] But in the Canadian Maritimes the heavens are equally indifferent, it seems, as the lofty overview of "Haligonian Market Cry" moves indifferently from the "hallelujah watermelons! – virginal pears! – virtuous corn!" to "sluttish watermelons! – sinful cucumbers! – jail bait pears! – / Planted by Big-Mouth Chaucer and picked by Evil Shakespeare!"[41]

To conclude, the Shakespearean intertext, based on the identification between Rufus Hamilton and Shakespeare's Aaron the Moor, extends further to engender both the rhetorical language and dynamic address of Clarke's poems, which, like Titus's arrows, are fired into the heavens as an appeal for justice. They are addressed to the Gods but reach only as far as another bloody act of human retribution. They are fired out of the

---

[37] *Titus Andronicus*, IV.iii.60.

[38] *Titus Andronicus*, IV.iii.50–53.

[39] *Execution Poems*, "Original Pain," 15.

[40] *Titus Andronicus*, IV.iii.53.

[41] *Execution Poems*, 18.

depths of hellish human cruelty towards a heaven mistakenly imagined as the site of transcendent and absolute justice. The arc of the arrows' trajectory transcribes the boundaries of the human universe within which the characters in these stories must act, and in this way, Clarke's *Execution Poems* brings home the message of the ongoing struggle for social justice.

Works Cited

Bate, Jonathan. "Introduction" to William Shakespeare, *Titus Andronicus*, ed. Bate (London: Arden Shakespeare, 2002).

Bloom, Harold. *Shakespeare: The Invention of the Human* (New York: Riverhead, 1998).

Clarke, George Elliott. *Execution Poems: The Black Acadian Tragedy of "George and Rue"* (Wolfville, Nova Scotia: Gaspereau, 2001).

——. *Odysseys Home: Mapping African-Canadian Literature* (Toronto: U of Toronto P, 2002).

——. Email interview with Susan Knutson, conducted between 12 January and 3 May 2002.

Corbett, Edward P.J. *Classical Rhetoric for the Modern Student* (New York: Oxford UP, 3rd ed. 1990).

Greenberg, Kenneth S., ed. *The Confessions of Nat Turner, and Related Documents*, intro. Kenneth Greenberg (Boston MA Bedford & New York: St. Martin's, 1996).

Lambert, Frank. "'I Saw the Book Talk': Slave Readings of the First Great Awakening," *Journal of Negro History* 77.4 (1992): 185–98.

Loomba, Ania. *Shakespeare, Race, and Colonialism* (London: Oxford UP, 2002).

Marlowe, Christopher. *Christopher Marlowe's Dr. Faustus: Text and Major Criticism*, ed. Irving Ribner (New York: Odyssey, 1966).

Moore–Gilbert, Bart. *Postcolonial Theory: Contexts, Practices, Politics* (London: Verso, 1997).

Moss, Laura, ed. *Is Canada Postcolonial? Unsettling Canadian Literature* (Waterloo, Ontario: Wilfrid Laurier UP, 2003).

Neill, Michael. "Post-Colonial Shakespeare? Writing Away from the Centre," in *Post-Colonial Shakespeares*, ed. Ania Loomba & Martin Orkin (London: Routledge, 1998): 164–85.

Ogbar, Jeffery Ogbonna Green. "Prophet Nat and God's Children of Darkness: Black Religious Nationalism," *Journal of Religious Thought* 53–54 (1997): 51–71.

Sealy, David. "'Canadianizing' Blackness: Resisting the Political," in *Rude: Contemporary Black Canadian Cultural Criticism*, ed. Rinaldo Walcott (Toronto: Insomniac, 2000): 87–108.

Shakespeare, William. *Titus Andronicus*, ed. Jonathan Bate (London: Arden Shakespeare, 2002).

Sher, Anthony, & Gregory Doran. *Woza Shakespeare! Titus Andronicus in South Africa* (London: Methuen, 1996).

❧

Crossing the Boundary, Donning a Mask

❧ Spatial Rules and Identity in Daniel David Moses' and Tomson Highway's Plays

KRISTINA AURYLAITĖ

"YOU BEEN HERE BEFORE. I see the city in your eyes," says an Indian prostitute in Daniel David Moses' play *Coyote City* (the first in his city trilogy, published in 1988).[1] Her statement is about Thomas, a middle-aged Indian priest from a remote reserve, who spent a long period of time in Toronto. Years later, the imprint of the city is still with him, even though Thomas repeatedly refers to the place as a realm of darkness and great perils (35–36, 42). As such, the city is to be avoided:

> The city? No, she must not go there. The city is full of emptiness. It's got to be the Dark One tempting her. We must not allow that to happen, Martha, we must restrain her somehow. (32)

These are the words that Thomas addresses to Martha, the mother of a young Native girl, Lena, from the same reserve, who is determined to go to Toronto. He does not know yet that Lena is leaving to meet her dead beloved Johnny, ignoring the fact that he was killed in the city during a drunken fight half a year earlier. Consequently, Thomas's wish to

[1] Daniel David Moses, *Coyote City and The City of Shadows: Two Plays by Daniel David Moses* (Toronto: Imago, 2000): 44. Further page references are in the main text.

"restrain" Lena is motivated primarily by his negative experience and the ensuing negative perception of the city.

"Philomena. I wanna go to Toronto," says Pelajia Patchnose, in the opening of Tomson Highway's play *The Rez Sisters* of the same year.[2] Having spent all her life on the "plain, dusty, boring Wasayichigan Hill" reserve (2), or Wasy, as she and other characters of the play call it, Pelajia, in contrast to the characters in *Coyote City*, obviously fantasizes the city as its opposite: clean, exciting and sophisticated. It is the space of "shiny roads," education, and the fulfilment of all hopes: "Only place educated Indian boys can find decent jobs these days" (7), she says. Incarnating everything that is not of or from the reserve, Toronto becomes a quality mark, as exemplified in the following dialogue between Pelajia and her half-sister Annie:

> ANNIE: Emily Dictionary and I went to Little Current to listen to Fritz the Katz.
>
> PELAJIA: What in God's name kind of band might that be?
>
> ANNIE: Country rock. My favourite. Fritz the Katz is from Toronto. (10–11)

No other explanation or qualification is necessary. No counterargument to challenge the singer's standing is available. Pelajia is only able to utter contemptuously "Fritzy… ritzy…" and turns to her sister Philomena for support, but in vain: "My record player is in Espanola getting fixed" (11), says Philomena, trying to stay neutral and dispute neither her sister, nor Toronto's authority.

Toronto's excellence, according to these characters, lies primarily in the fact that it is big. Indeed, if the city is a quality mark in itself, its size in *The Rez Sisters* is the main determining feature that equals its quality. For instance, Annie says: "the bingo in Espanola is bigger. And it's better. And I'll win. And then I'll go to Sudbury, where the bingos are even bigger and better. And then I can visit my daughter, Ellen…" (13). By contrast, bingos "here in Wasy are getting smaller and smaller all the

[2] Tomson Highway, *The Rez Sisters* (Calgary, Alberta: Fifth House, 1988): 2. Further page references are in the main text.

time" (16). The bingo in Toronto is, undoubtedly, the biggest of all. Indeed, the characters learn that "THE BIGGEST BINGO IN THE WORLD is coming to Toronto" (27, 32, 35; capitals in the original). and from this moment on, this city becomes the site onto which the women project their most precious dreams. Of course, Highway plays on the popular stereotype about Toronto's size – the size that equals money, power and centrality; indeed, a popular Canadian joke says that if Vancouver has raw physical beauty and Montreal has a soul, Toronto has, well, its size. Thus Pelajia does not crave just any escape from the reserve. Toronto is the desired destination and the place of incarnating the wildest dreams. Consequently, the characters' fantasies about winning in the Toronto bingo overshadow even their cancer-struck sister Marie–Adele's fear for medical tests. Moreover, the monologues in which the women enumerate their wishes that the bingo prize could fulfil sound like determinations: no "if" is ever added, even though the jackpot will only be one, and the hypothetical mood that one would expect when talking about winning in the lottery or bingo is replaced by the non-conditional "when":

ANNIE: When I go to the BIGGEST BINGO IN THE WORLD, in Toronto, I will win. For sure, I will win. [...]

MARIE–ADELE: When I win THE BIGGEST BINGO IN THE WORLD, I'm gonna buy me an island. [...]

VERONIQUE: Well, when I win THE BIGGEST BINGO IN THE WORLD. No! after I win THE BIGGEST BINGO IN THE WORLD, I will go shopping for a brand-new stove. In Toronto. At the Eaton Centre. (36)

Thus the two plays open by presenting two different but very familiar sets of ideas about the city. In *Coyote City*, the city is a hostile space of the dominant white Other, full of emptiness and threat, whereas in *The Rez Sisters* the city becomes an incarnation of the rhetoric of "life is elsewhere," full of promises of plenty. However, in either case it is still an alien space for Native people. For instance, after her visit to Toronto,

Pelajia, who was so eager to leave her home reserve for the city, suddenly declares: "I'm not so sure I would get along with him if I were to live down there. I mean my son Tom. He was telling me not to play so much bingo" (117). If space is theorized as relational, in other words, composed of social interrelations that gradually establish a specific set of socializing rules, moving to a particular space would mean adjusting to both the relations and the rules of that space.[3] Having realized this, Pelajia suggests her unwillingness to adjust to a different space, because this would mean change.

Nevertheless, Native people do go to the city. Their own space is already 'contaminated' by it in the form of expectations and fantasies, or simply material products. Indeed, such 'white' objects as cars and record players are part of the everyday reality on the reserve in both plays. Take, for instance, Philomena's lady-like city outfit, including a tight skirt, nylons, and high heels, referred to as "completely impractical" (2) in the dusty rural place with dirt roads. Furthermore, Pelajia's dreams of "jet black," "shiny," paved roads explicitly celebrate and in this way betray the hybridization of the reserve space in terms of values as well as practical comforts. Still, the two spaces do not merge into one. The characters of *Coyote City* dash to Toronto in order to reunite with the lost beloved or to save a family member in order to come back to the reserve together. However, the planned homecoming never takes place; the characters

---

[3] On this point, see Henri Lefebvre's influential analysis of social space, conceptualized as a set of relations between things, of "everything that there is *in space*, everything that is produced either by nature or by society, either through their co-operation or through their conflicts. Everything: living beings, things, objects, works, signs and symbols"; *The Production of Space*, tr. Donald Nicholson-Smith (Oxford: Blackwell, 1991): 101. This suggests process, change and action and thus potential and power for space to influence and affect, i.e. to play a "socialising role" (191). He says: "space commands bodies, prescribing and proscribing gestures, routes and distances to be covered. It is produced with this purpose in mind; this is its raison d'etre" (143).

Lefebvre has influenced a number of theorists of human geography. For instance, Doreen Massey, in a parallel way, proposes to consider space as taking the form of the "simultaneous coexistence of social interrelations at all geographical scales"; *Space, Place and Gender* (Cambridge: Polity, 1994): 168.

remain in the city and perish there. The insatiable seven rez sisters of Highway's play struggle to get to Toronto, but only to bring *back* still more of what it has to offer after they win in the bingo, so that afterwards, back in Wasy, Philomena can say, referring to her nephew, who lives in the city: "His upstairs washroom. Mine looks just like it now" (117).

Philomena strives to mimic the way people in the city live by imitating it on the reserve. Unlike Pelajia, she has no desire to leave: "this place is too much inside your blood. You can't get rid of it" (4), she says to her restless sister, and goes on to dream about her citified bathroom. If "habitation is a strategy," as Bill Ashcroft suggests in his recent book *Post-Colonial Transformations*,[4] the urbanization fantasies of both Philomena and Pelajia demonstrate how one can use and exploit or, taking it one step further, even appropriate what the white space of the colonizer has to offer. Indeed, it is the seven Native women who are going to Toronto to win the biggest jackpot in the world. In this context, the world of the dominant white Other is not perceived as ominous. The 'contamination' of the reserve space vs preservation of its 'purity' and 'authenticity' is desired because it is under the control of the reserve people, who choose what to allow in and how, even in terms of rather trivial details. As W.H. New suggests, "borders, as sites of contestation [...] neither require nor guarantee fixed differences, or inevitably commit to the erasure of difference. The presence of margins [...] gives a culture choices" and "epitomizes differing cultural preoccupations."[5]

However, the city is not just an instrument to be used for improving or beautifying the reserve space, but also a powerful influence that changes both it and its inhabitants. Yi-Fu Tuan says of residents of small isolated communities that they

> do not recognize the extent and uniqueness of their area unless they have experience of [other] areas; but the more they know and experience the outside world the less involved they will be with the

---

[4] Ashcroft, *Post-Colonial Transformation* (London: Routledge, 2001): 157.

[5] W.H. New, *Borderlands: How We Talk about Canada* (Vancouver: U of British Columbia P, 1998): 27.

> life of their own world, their neighbourhood, and hence the less in fact it will be a neighbourhood.[6]

Perceived in different ways by Native people, how does the city change them and their space? How does their experience of the city affect the way they relate to the space of their origin? Are they able to retain control of how much white space will affect their own space? What becomes of a person who crosses the boundary of an alien space?

When the characters of *Coyote City* cross this boundary, they are aware of having entered the alien and hostile space of the city. A reason for this is the fact that the rules that govern city space are not always familiar or understandable to the reserve Native. For instance, when Lena and Thomas leave for the city to look for Lena's dead beloved, her mother and her sister Boo, worried, hurriedly set off after them. The following conversation takes place:

> BOO: We'll lose them, Ma.
>
> MARTHA: We know where they'll be tonight. She should be all right till then.
>
> BOO: But Ma, who knows what will happen if they get to the city? (41)

Boo is competent at, and at ease with, navigating through the rules of the city, having spent enough time in Toronto, where she successfully attends school. Nevertheless, even Boo believes that if anything bad should happen to her sister, this will take place in the city and not on the way there. The journey itself does not seem to be as menacing, although it is emphasized how remote the city is from the reserve: in *Coyote City*, it takes the characters a day to cover the distance; in *The Rez Sisters*, they calculate that it will take them at least six hours for the journey if they drive fast. However, it would seem that this huge space in between the reserve and the city is not perceived as hostile. For instance, when the rez sisters are stopped on the way by a flat tire and two of them wander off the highway, they meet Nanabush, a trickster. It is as if the space beyond

---

[6] Yi-Fu Tuan, *Topophilia: A Study of Environmental Perception, Attitudes, And Values* (1974; New York: Columbia UP, 1990): 210.

the city is still their space, or at least not alien. In other words, there are no apparent changes suggested when the characters cross the reserve boundary, whereas entering the city space does have consequences. In this context, the boundary gains a different shade of meaning: as perceived by the reserve Natives, it encloses and isolates not the reserve, as was intended by the colonizer, but the city.

However, the actual crossing of this boundary is not depicted at all in the two plays. The journey itself, on the other hand, is given considerable attention. For instance, in *The Rez Sisters,* the characters' drive to Toronto is filled with sleep and intimate conversations among the travellers, safely ensconced within the familiar space of the car. Moreover, the women choose to travel at night when little can be seen through the window and in this way almost avoid coming face-to-face with the city. They prefer to plunge into it with their eyes closed: many fall asleep, metaphorically going blind as if shying away from any possible insight. In reality, the nightlights of the metropolis makes it impossible not to notice the entrance. In Highway's play, however, Emily and Zhaboonigan joke, then slap hands in the car and, as we learn from the stage directions,

> *Instantly*, the house lights come on full blast. The Bingo Master – the most beautiful man in the world – comes running up center aisle, cordless mike in hand, dressed to kill: tails, rhinestones, and all. The entire theatre is now the bingo palace. We are in: Toronto!!!! (100; emphasis mine)

Four exclamation marks echo the great expectations that have compelled the rez sisters to the city. Furthermore, the women are suddenly not just within the city, but within what constitutes its most essential part to them: the bingo palace. Nothing else is of any interest. There are not even any comments about the impressions the metropolis must have made on these women from a small rural community. Highway takes his characters straight into the middle of the long-desired action. Naturally, the bingo game follows – THE BIGGEST BINGO IN THE WORLD of their dreams – and very quickly Toronto fails them. They lose – none of them wins the fantasized half a million dollars. Moreover, they lose one of their number, as Marie–Adele, who has cancer, succumbs to her illness right in the bingo palace. After this, "the stage area, by means of 'lighting magic', slowly returns to its Wasaychigan Hill appearance" (stage direction, 103).

The 'slow' versus 'instant' change of place, experienced by the audience, suggests disappointment: the loss of excitement, of hopes and of enthusiasm. Other than that, there are neither impressions of the trip described nor memories shared. And yet, the white space has made its impact on the characters. It is detectable in Philomena's exquisite bathroom – one of the most private places in a house – in her brand-new toilet bowl, in Annie's association with Fritz the Katz, the already mentioned singer from Toronto, and in Pelajia's lost desire to leave the reserve for the city.

In a similar way, the characters of *Coyote City* are suddenly within the city: Lena and Thomas walk along the street, Boo and Martha enter a bar, the Silver Dollar, where Lena is to meet Johnny. However, in this play the effects of the crossing of the city boundary are more explicit. Clarisse, the Indian prostitute whom Thomas and Lena meet on the street, changes the latter's appearance. Instead of her usual blue jeans, Lena puts on a sexy dress and lets Clarisse make up her face for the first time in her life. By doing this, she is indirectly compared to her aunt, who has been living in the city for quite a while and has changed to the extent that her sister, Lena and Boo's mother Martha, no longer considers her a relative:

BOO:	I think we've arrived. […] We could call Auntie up.
MARTHA:	No, I have to look for Lena.
BOO:	She'd help. She's our family. Martha: How can you tell? All that stuff that woman puts on her face, she looks like a corpse. (52)

Thus, by putting on make-up, Lena, once "fresh from the bush" (9), in Johnny's words, enters the realm of the artificial: she puts on a mask, assumes a different role, starts playing a different identity, that of the girl on the street. In this way, she adjusts to the city rules as understood by Clarisse, Lena's first and major instructor here. Later, unrecognized and in this way rejected by Johnny, Lena will try to remove the make-up and recover her former self, only to ask Clarisse to fix it in order to join her in the city, determined to start looking for Johnny once again (97–98).

If Lena's behaviour is intuitive, her companion Thomas demonstrates a keen awareness of the different rules that govern city space. For instance, when Lena tries to find out about the location of the bar where she is to meet Johnny, and shouts: "Hey. Hey mister. Do you know thc way – ?", Thomas immediately stops her by saying:

> You can't approach white people like that. We could get in trouble. They'll summon the police. They don't want to see Indians. Lena, they don't like us. They'll put us down into the gutter. They'll keep us in the darkness there. (42–43)

The key word here is undoubtedly "see." It voices the idea of invisibility, imposed upon Native people by the colonizer, so that their only choice is to assimilate to the dominant white majority or stay away. Thomas's speech betrays the colonized person's obedience to such imposed invisibility, the invisibility that offers relative safety (stay out of their way and they will not be able to make you feel inferior). However, the white mister who scares Thomas so much never appears on stage, remaining an absence without a voice, a reference without a referent. The audience does not *see* him, just as it does not see *any* white people at all in the city to which Thomas and Lena, as well as the rez sisters, come. It is as if, by some sort of reversal, it is now white people who are the invisible ones in this fictional Toronto. Even the Bingo Master in *The Rez Sisters* turns out to be not a white person, but Nanabush, a trickster who has put on a mask as well. By contrast, Johnny, who is actually a ghost, is present and visible. So is Thomas, who dies and turns into a ghost at the end of the play. Thus, the city the characters have come to is indeed "full of emptiness," as Thomas has stated, although in a different way. The Native people have intruded into the white city to encounter not a single white person.

The only other character present here is a trickster, a central figure in the "dream world of North American Indian mythology" (xii), a "transformer–culture hero,"[7] an instructor who teaches behaviour and survival,

---

[7] Ricketts, quoted in Dee Horne, *Contemporary American Indian Writing: Unsettling Literature* (New York: Peter Lang, 1999): 128.

even if often through counter-example,[8] a constant presence who offers support, even if sometimes creating confusion. In *The Rez Sisters*, it was the bird-like Nanabush who followed the characters into the Bingo Palace and even assumed the guise of the Bingo Master, in this way outrageously intruding into white space and even controlling it – running the game. In *Coyote City*, Coyote, although physically absent on stage and in the city, is nevertheless constantly referred to in the story that Boo and Johnny keep telling throughout the play. It is an old Indian story Johnny had heard in the West as a child, recounting Coyote's pursuit of his dead wife and how he is finally allowed to enter the lodge of the dead and re-unite with his wife there.

This story echoes Lena's quest for her dead beloved, where the boundary between the world of the living and the world of the dead is blurred once again. Johnny himself, a ghost in the play's present, can be seen as a trickster-like figure precisely because of his ability to enter the world of the living. Not only is he able to phone Lena, but he is also seen by both Lena and the sceptical Boo, even engaging the latter in conversation. In fact, it is Johnny-the-ghost who governs the action of the play, ordering Lena to come to Toronto, then standing her up, thereby triggering off the whole chain of events that follow.[9] Consequently, the spatial rules of the city of shadows and ghosts become more important than those of the white city they are in; hence the suggestive title of the play, *Coyote City*. Just as Coyote misbehaves in the lodge of the dead and loses his wife forever, Johnny does not (want to) recognize the changed – misbehaved? – Lena, and fails to establish contact. Moreover, Lena once again refuses to listen to the Coyote story, now told by Boo, dismissing it as "fairytale

---

[8] Horne, *Contemporary American Indian Writing*, 129.

[9] See also Mark Shackleton's discussion of the play, in which he underscores Johnny's trickster-like function of a storyteller. In this role, however, Johnny is seen as a "selfish and opportunistic Coyote," telling tales without due reverence and appreciation, only to impress women or get certain favours; "Can Weesageechak Keep Dancing? The Importance of Trickster Figures in the Work of Native Earth Dramatists, 1986–2000," in *Performing National Identities: International Perspectives on Contemporary Canadian Theatre*, ed. Sherrill Grace & Albert-Reiner Glaap (Vancouver: Talonbooks, 2003): 280–81.

bullshit" that has no relation to her (29, 93). Consequently, she loses Johnny and, the coyote city having disappeared, she is herself lost in the white city, joining Clarisse on the street.

In *The Rez Sisters*, the trickster is also omnipresent. Even Philomena's toilet-bowl, her desired prize, whose purpose is to make her even more of a city lady, is related to Nanabush in a peculiar way. Peter Dickinson draws attention to the scene at the beginning of the play in which Nanabush defecates on Marie–Adele's white fence.[10] The toilet-bowl being a place of excrement, Philomena's white purchase becomes quite straightforwardly linked to the trickster. Themselves transgressors of all possible boundaries, the tricksters in these plays by Highway and Moses thus ease the characters' entrance into a different space – into the Other – by transforming it (or its elements) into a configuration whose rules, if obeyed and followed, can guarantee safety and fulfilment.

To conclude, both plays allow their characters to enter the alien space of the city, unsettling the precise boundary-line between white and Native spaces. The two worlds intersect, rejecting the imposed immobilization of people and their identities and allowing for the possibility of change, development, and becoming. How such possibilities will be used is another question, but the influence – not necessarily positive – of a space on an individual and, by extension, on the individual's culture of origin is illustrated quite explicitly.

❧

---

[10] Peter Dickinson, *Here is Queer: Nationalisms, Sexualities, and the Literatures of Canada* (Toronto: U of Toronto P, 1999): 181.

WORKS CITED

Ashcroft, Bill. *Post-Colonial Transformation* (London: Routledge, 2001).

Dickinson, Peter. *Here is Queer: Nationalisms, Sexualities, and the Literatures of Canada* (Toronto: U of Toronto P, 1999).

Highway, Tomson. *The Rez Sisters* (Calgary, Alberta: Fifth House, 1988).

Horne, Dee. *Contemporary American Indian Writing: Unsettling Literature* (New York: Peter Lang, 1999).

Lefebvre, Henri. *The Production of Space*, tr. Donald Nicholson–Smith (Oxford: Blackwell, 1991).

Massey, Doreen. *Space, Place and Gender* (Cambridge: Polity, 1994).

Moses, Daniel David. *Coyote City. Coyote City and The City of Shadows: Two Plays by Daniel David Moses* (Toronto: Imago, 2000): 5–101.

New, W.H. *Borderlands: How We Talk about Canada* (Vancouver: U of British Columbia P, 1998).

Shackleton, Mark. "Can Weesageechak Keep Dancing? The Importance of Trickster Figures in the Work of Native Earth Dramatists, 1986–2000," in *Performing National Identities: International Perspectives on Contemporary Canadian Theatre*, ed. Sherrill Grace & Albert–Reiner Glaap (Vancouver: Talonbooks, 2003): 278–88.

Tuan, Yi-Fu. *Topophilia: A Study of Environmental Perception, Attitudes, and Values* (1974; New York: Columbia UP, 1990).

❧

III

❧ Poetic Sites of Intertextuality

I Think I Could Turn Awhile

GEOFF PAGE

1.
I think I could turn awhile and write like the Americans,
they are so at ease in their syllables, irregular as eyelids,
various as the sea.
They do not hear the iamb ticking, tetchy with its small demands.
Their pronouns are huger than Texas.
I too would find my metaphysics
as I sliced my sedan through a long prairie night.
The turkey sheds of Minnesota, the slanted dusk of Iowa,
the breakers on the Big Sur coast and the stillness in the Rockies
would each be a part of my redemption.
I too would be an heir of Whitman
despite all his curious shyness with women.
I'd rummage through his catalogues, those holy repetitions,
hearing the King James Bible singing
through cirrus the size of all the eastern states
drifting by splendidly over my head.

2.
But somehow after
half a book
I know that I

would then turn back.
That rhetoric is
someone else's;
it works with very
different vowels.
I'd hear the clipped
iambics calling,
my template just
below the line.
I'd feel the need for
tighter turns,
a tiredness with the
larger flourish,
their drumroll of a
flag unfurled.
'That would be good,'
as Frost surmised,
'both going and coming back',
back to something
leaner, drier,
back to something
lower-key:
the chicken sheds of
Wallabadah …
a summer on the
Clarence maybe …

❧

How to Really Forget

❧ David Dabydeen's "Creative Amnesia"

Erik Falk

In the preface to "Turner", a poetic 're-writing' of J.M.W. Turner's painting "Slavers Throwing Overboard the Dead and Dying, Typhoon Coming On," David Dabydeen writes that the focus of the poem is the "submerged head of the African" in Turner's painting. Cleansed by the ocean, he longs to "begin anew in the sea but he is too trapped by grievous memory to escape history [...] The desire for transfiguration or newness or creative amnesia is frustrated."[1] This essay aims at outlining a few aspects of the "creative amnesia" Dabydeen mentions and the obstacles it encounters, but also points to its momentary success.[2] It will do so through a reading of two of his works: the poem "Turner," and his second novel, *Disappearance*.[3] My argument, apart

---

[1] David Dabydeen, *Turner: New & Selected Poems* (London: Jonathan Cape, 1995): ix–x. Further page references are in the main text.

[2] I do this in full awareness of the sometimes complicated relationship between the different 'texts' coexisting in Dabydeen's work. For a presentation of the various texts as a series of "masks" that unsettle the authority of, as well as hide the self, see Mark McWatt, "His True-True Face: Masking and Revelation in David Dabydeen's *Slave Song*," in Kevin Grant, *The Art of David Dabydeen* (Leeds: Peepal Tree, 1997): 15–26.

[3] The retrograde movement of my reading, from the 1995 poem to the 1993 novel, should not be taken as tacit value-judgment. My suggestion is, rather, that the problem of "creative amnesia" is, in Dabydeen's writing, investigated in various fictional-historical settings and situations.

from the implication that "amnesia" is a persistent concern in Dabydeen's writing, will be that the loss of memory, history and identity at stake in the texts in no way equals absence, but in itself constitutes a history that must, ultimately, be 'forgotten' for a new and unpredictable future to be possible. This paradoxical amnesia is, I will suggest, a form of production that always occurs in relation to something (or someone) else. In the novel, as we shall see, this relational and productive amnesia appears as 'connection'.

If the poem, as Karen McIntyre writes, "allows for a critical negotiation of the problematics of identity, history and creativity,"[4] the first thing to note is that these appear deeply entangled in the text. The speaker, a nameless African slave afloat in the sea,[5] claims he cannot remember his mother, only to describe her in some detail:

> … and I forgot
> The face of my mother, the plaid cloth
> Tied around her neck, the scars on her forehead,
> The silver nose-ring which I tugged, made her start
> Nearly rolling me from the her lap but catching me ... (18)

Inversely, his sisters, first, supposedly, presented as vivid memory – "we stoop under the belly / Of the cow and I can see I am just / Taller than its haunches, and when my sisters / Kneel their heads reach its knees" (2) – are shown to be figments of the imagination: "Shall I [...] invent a sister, and another"; "The first of my sisters, stout, extravagant / I have named Rima. / I endow her with a clear voice, fingers / that coax melody from the crudest instrument" (37). Similarly, animals have been "given fresh

---

[4] Karen McIntyre, "Necrophilia or Stillbirth? David Dabydeen's *Turner* as the Embodiment of Postcolonial Creative," in *The Art of David Dabydeen*, 142.

[5] The question of whose 'voice' is represented in the poem is, in fact, not so easily decided. Tobias Döring argues that the undecidability of voice is the poem's refusal of prosopopoeia and so constitutes an important and integral aspect of Dabydeen's aesthetic. Döring's observation, however, concerns the whole of the poem, and does not preclude the possibility of the African being the speaker in certain passages. Döring, *Caribbean-English Passages: Intertextuality in a Postcolonial Tradition* (London: Routledge, 2002): 147.

names" (1), yet are painted in such detail that they acquire the appearance of real memory. In the poem, there is a confusion of memory and invention because what is forgotten is present – in the text of the poem and in the mind of the speaker. Forgetfulness has the appearance of memory, and memory that of fiction, because of the representation they share. Loss, consequently, is not absence, but uncertainty of reference. And reference, of course, is what grounds the distinction between "identity, history and creativity." Loss is not only a form of presence, however; it is a state of uncertainty that is actively caused:

> [Turner's] tongue spurted strange potions upon ours
> Which left us dazed, which made us forget
> The very sound of our speech ...
> And we repeated in a trance the words
> That shuddered from him: *blessed, angelic,*
> *Sublime* (38)

Through an act of linguistic substitution, Turner forces his language upon the slave, makes it take the place of the mother-tongue. The speaker is made to forget former affiliations through this substitution. With the new language come new names, new phenomena, and a new identity: "*blessed, angelic, / Sublime.*" The act, moreover, is anything but metaphorical; it is directed against and executed upon the body. Linguistic domination is a form of sexual exploitation: Turner plants his "hook" in the flesh of the slaves, who "wriggle" in an attempt to free themselves from it (38).

Loss of memory or history, then, is not the elision of representations of the past, but the destabilizing of their epistemological status. It is a state of referential uncertainty that is caused by an infliction upon the body that is itself remembered. What causes amnesia is another memory.

The seemingly paradoxical presence of what is forgotten can be illuminated by a reference to Friedrich Nietzsche.[6] In the second essay in

---

[6] The similarity between Nietzsche's philosophy of history and the poem has been noted in passing by Tobias Döring in "Chains of Memory: English-Caribbean Cross-Currents in Marina Warner's *Indigo* and David Dabydeen's *Turner*," in *Across the Lines: Intertextuality and Transcultural Communication in the New*

On the Genealogy of Morals, he writes that "forgetfulness is no mere *vis inertiae* as the superficial imagine; it is rather an active and in the strictest sense positive faculty of repression."[7] For Nietzsche, history is the opposite of freedom, which, he argues, depends on the possibility of an undefined present, the radically and unforeseen new. History is what prevents that present from coming into being. History, memory, and responsibility – and, in the final analysis, "conscience" – are all, he argues, derived from the "contractual relationship between *creditor* and *debtor*, which is as old as the idea of 'legal subjects' and in turn points back to the fundamental forms of buying, selling, barter, trade, and traffic."[8] History enslaves the subject, by making him or her indebted to a forefather or a god, and this is why freedom requires forgetfulness: "there could be no happiness, no cheerfulness, no hope, no pride, no *present*, without forgetfulness."[9]

According to Nietzsche, memory or history produces subjects by making them indebted to history in one version or other. Escaping this debt means forgetting, but as active work – as "positive [...] repression." With a slight modification of terms to suit the present context, one might say that, to Nietzsche, history is a form of colonization. It is precisely this form of continuously performing history that the poem thematizes: Turner, though the agent of an event in the past, is present in the mind of the speaker, and it is by this presence that he continues to colonialize the slave, or put him in debt. His presence also prevents representations of childhood and home from passing as real memories. As Tobias Döring writes, the slave is "constantly seduced by the self-induced images of nature and community whose comforts seem to offer him a secure sense of self. In the end, however, they are all denied" because memory is al-

---

Literatures in English, ed. Wolfgang Klooss (Cross/Cultures 32, ASNEL Papers 3; Amsterdam & Atlanta GA: Rodopi, 1998): 200.

[7] Friedrich Nietzsche, *On the Genealogy of Morals* (1887; Oxford: Oxford UP, 1998): 39.

[8] *The Genealogy of Morals*, 45.

[9] *The Genealogy of Morals*, 39. The present of which Nietzsche speaks here is precisely that unforeseen, 'open' present.

ready a "territory occupied."[10] This means, too, that images, characters, names, places, and events take on another kind of reality. Regardless of their referentiality, they are all present. And through that presence, and through their performance, they are all, and cqually, rcal. As results of past acts inscribed on the body, they are historical, but as a form of presence.

If "creative amnesia" is related to Nietzsche's "forgetfulness" in the desire to allow for a radical "present" to emerge; what is it that frustrates it in the poem? The child tossed overboard – named "Turner" – "kicks alive ... dreams of family," in the speaker. These dreams, however, are cut short:

> Later it confirmed its breed,
> Tugging my hair spitefully, startling me
> With obscene memory. 'Nigger!' it cried, seeing
> Through the sea's disguise as only children can,
> Recognising me below my skin long since
> Washed clean of the colour of sin, scab, smudge (16)

In a repetition of Turner's original exploitation and imposition – and as an illustration of Fanon's analysis of the production of black identity – the child bestows a "nigger"-identity upon the poetic persona. This identity is also the enslavement to a history: it is produced through an "obscene memory." As with the memory of "Turner," it is not the representational status of this "memory" that is important. It is not even decidedly the memory 'of' someone. On the contrary: the "nigger" is recognized *despite* the fact that the sea has bleached his skin; memory or history, rather, is imposed upon him. History, formulated in linguistic utterance, is a debt that produces the subject in the present; it is a history called into being through a speech-act that, because it creates rather than represents, is *performative.*[11]

---

[10] Döring, *Caribbean-English Passages*, 165.

[11] Performative speech-acts, Austin writes, make "something happen." Promises, the passing of laws, etc, rather than referring to a pre-existing state of things, institute: "to utter the sentence [...] is not to *describe* my doing of what

If one of the elements of the performative memory and identity discussed here is its temporal placement as present, another feature is that it is relational. It comes into being through the interaction between parties existing in the present. Whether the words "primed in my mouth," or the interpellative cry "Nigger!," memory or history, and the identity they produce, is the outcome of an interaction with an 'Other.' In the poem, this interaction takes place as a repeated domination and exploitation of the poetic persona by the different "Turners,"[12] and this is the reason why the "creative amnesia" sought is frustrated. Relational memory is, in the poem, not allowed to take any other form than that of an imposition of "obscene memory" or history on the slave. The alternative inventions, memories, and fictions will not be supported by the 'Other'. There is "no future" to them, because the child "frantically […] tries to die" after naming "the gods, / The earth and its globe of stars" 'Nigger'" (39). The speaker is thus left suspended in a universe where everything is named "Nigger," suspended, that is, in a state of loss *and* limitation that is the opposite of Nietzsche's "present": a "slave to nothingness":

> frantically it tries to die,
> To leave me beadless, nothing and a slave
> To nothingness, to the white enfolding
> Wings of Turner brooding over my body,
> Stopping my mouth, drowning me in the yolk
> Of myself. There is no mother, family,
> Savannah fattening with cows (39)

"Nothingness" is, as we have seen, not absence, but the submission to a memory that cannot be forgotten. It is the outcome of a series of relations in which the slave has been subjected to history and memory. The frus-

---

should be said in so doing or to state that I am doing it: it is to do it." J.L. Austin, *How to Do Things with Words* (1955; Oxford: Oxford UP, 1976): 6.

[12] The child is, Dabydeen writes in his preface, "the unconscious" of the slave. The figure of the foetus-unconscious is, Döring suggests, a *bolom* or *dwen*, part of Caribbean folk mythology; Döring, *Caribbean-English Passages*, 197. The 'Other' is in this sense not necessarily another subject; (the presence of) memories, names, subjects are all possible 'Others'.

tration of "creative amnesia" is the failure of the relation to an 'Other' that supports the forgetting.

The thematization of loss as an active presence is paralleled by the rhetorical organization of the poem. As Döring suggests, the opening lines with their metaphoric linking of childbirth and sailing show a figurative structure that re-enacts the historical dynamic operating in the trade and trauma of the Middle Passage. On one level, what is being represented is a scene of parturition, with the pains of a labouring mother evoked at the moment of abortive birth. On another level, the imagery derives from the inventory of navigation.[13]

The observation can be expanded. What is at stake is the fact that the process of associative, or 'poetic', connection re-enacts the 'historical dynamic'. The child thrown overboard "plopped into the water and soon swelled / Like a brumplak leave that bursts buckshot / From its pod," and "Like a lime-seed spat from the scurvied mouth / Of a sailor" (2, 6); in these lines, the simile becomes the vehicle for associations that confuse and disturb the distinction between levels of signification, as well as between present and past, memory and fiction. The literal and figurative levels are equally grounded, it appears, in experience or history. The distinction between them is, rather, a temporal one, with metaphor turning into a remembrance of the past. This past, however, is prohibited from turning into idyllic memory, as another metaphor again actualizes the 'present'. With the comparison of ants to slavers – "marched with tongues / Hanging out, like a gang of slavers" (4) – the experience and memory of captivity and slavery are revealed as being already incorporated into the sphere of remembered childhood. The realm of imagery and imagination is thus not independent or timeless, nor is it a pastoral anteriority. On the contrary: the distinction between literal and figurative is one that is constantly blurred by a memory or history that performs in the present.

At the level of intervention in artistic and critical discourse or tradition, the poem performs much the same feat. "Turner", Döring notes, borrows much of its vocabulary from the discourses it rewrites, and yet sets out to reverse the ideology of them. In Turner's painting, historical realities are

---

[13] Döring, *Caribbean-English Passages*, 150.

transformed into a "naturalized power" upon which the sublime is built. Dabydeen's poem, by contrast, "questions[s] the historical constructedness and power of such naturalizing conventions."[14]

On different levels, then, the poem brings into play the issue thematized, that of history as a present and performing power. Poetic theme, figurative language, traditions and discourses of art are all circumscribed and shaped by these forms of 'working' history and memory. On all levels, it may be argued, the poem is concerned with, and engaged in attempting, a "creative amnesia." The format of this article does not allow for a discussion of the various degree of success achieved by these different levels of the text or artwork. Instead, after thus using "Turner" to analyze the workings of history and memory, I will turn to the novel *Disappearance* as an example of (relatively) successful relational amnesia.

The protagonist and narrator of *Disappearance* is an engineer from Guyana recently arrived in an English village to supervise the building of a sea-wall to protect the coast. Sitting in the living-room of his English hostess, Mrs Rutherford, he is asked about his choice of profession, and this question, with which the text begins, triggers a sustained and gradual remembrance of a past he has long since let "revert to bush."[15] At the end of the text, this question of the past has unfolded virtually the whole of the narrator's life.

It is undoubtedly important that an apparently innocent question is met with a life-story. More important, however, is the fact that the story uncovered emerges both as an attempt to escape a predetermining sense of memory or history and as the unwitting and ironical repetition of it. Two quotations will suffice to illustrate this:

> It was the sea [...] that made me a civil engineer. Every cell in my brain was absorbed in addressing the sea, there was no space for the sorrow of ancestral memory [...] It frothed and babbled against the shingle heaped on the foreshore but however much it fetched towards me, threatening to drench me in contempt, there was no

---

[14] Döring, *Caribbean-English Passages*, 164.

[15] David Dabydeen, *Disappearance* (1993; London: Vintage, 1999): 60. Further page references are in the main text.

> question of withdrawal to higher ground or into silence [...] I plotted my life in relation to the life of the sea. How to shackle it with modern tools was the challenge before me, how to enslave it to my will and make it work for me. (17–18)

> 'An engineer is a man who builds a bridge over a dangerous stretch of water. An engineer is a man who builds a dam against the wild sea. An engineer makes things spick and span, he straightens out whatever is lopsided [...] an engineer is a man of grammar whereas you speak waywardly like the nigger you are!' (60)

The second quotation, part of a speech delivered in fury by a teacher to his class, reveals the tragic irony of the narrator's escape: it has been accomplished at the price of accepting a colonialist (or neocolonialist) distinction between "engineer" and "nigger," between "straightness" and "crookedness," and between master and servant. In order to flee the victimized existence of the "waywardly nigger," he has transformed himself into a master who, when employed as engineer, supervises his "coolie" workers "with the authority of a pharaoh," forcing them to work "according to the drawings I provided, the inflexible lines like poles in their ankles" (25). Escaping the fate of one history results in the unconscious repetition of another.

As in "Turner," the uncovering of personal history reveals the illusory nature of being without history. Against the painful memories of his past, the initial feeling of being "always present, always new" through having "cultivated no sense of the past" vanishes. Though perhaps with no "sense" of the past, the engineer has nevertheless tragically repeated it. And, as in the poem, the act that produces the memories is present – and presented. The conversation takes place in a room whose walls are lined with African masks that Mrs Rutherford has brought home from her many journeys:

> I was aware of the presence of the masks. They looked so full of spite, evoking vague stories of primitive violence. They forced me to connect the smudged photograph, and Swami's death, and before that, the rape of Amerindian women, malarial fever, the drowning of my Dutch predecessors and the wastage of slave bodies. (38–39)

A history – and an identity – is bestowed upon the engineer from an 'Other' (or 'Others'), in the present, and with such power that he is unable to resist it: he is "forced to connect" to a history long preceding his own. What results is a narrative that is not necessarily a truthful representation of a past. Memory is unhinged; the past is reconsidered in relation to the masks. Memory thus takes on the same problematic real-but-fictional status as in the poem; impossible to determine in terms of representational 'truth', but performing nevertheless. What is equally indisputable is the force of the 'Others' that create the connection.

The power of the enforced historical indebtedness is emphasized elsewhere in the novel. Christie, the local Irishman "plays Paddy," and Jamal, an old classmate in Guyana, earns respect from others by being the scapegoat, taking upon himself punishment for all the tricks played by his fellows.

If the issues of memory, history and identity are outlined in terms very similar to that of the poem, there is also a difference in vocabulary and imagery. In *Disappearance*, there is a recurrent use of terms related to geography and territory. Rutherford's question has the "force of a machine" and cuts its way through the narrator's past that he has let "revert to bush" (60). When Jamal breaks down under severe punishment from his teacher, he overflows with all he had "dammed up" inside him (58). A dam is also, the narrator claims, his real identity:

> deep down I knew that a dam was my identity, an obstacle I sought to put between shore and myself to assert my substantialness, my indissoluble presence, without reference to colour, culture, or age. (133–34).

Jack, Mrs Rutherford's escaped husband, finally, has a "bulldozer mentality" (75).

The metaphorization of characters corresponds not only to the story about building, projecting, rearranging nature and so on, but also to a personification of machines and nature. Watching American bulldozers equipped with "steel teeth" build a basketball pitch in his home village in Guyana, the narrator imagines the "pain [...] the earth must have felt when the bulldozer bit into it" (39, 40). Upon completion, a perfectly square pitch has been created in the midst of the forest, a square that slowly gives way to the power of nature, which bends the poles of floodlights and breaks apart the tarmac. In the comparison implied by the joint vocabulary, the question and the masks do to the engineer what the bulldozers do to the physical landscape. Whereas in "Turner" the process of identity-formation is given oral, linguistic and material dimensions, it is here explicitly, and metaphorically, territorial. The subject, and his or her history, is a material and geographical assemblage.

Regarding the self (or subjectivity) as a geography or territory comes surprisingly close to the way Gilles Deleuze and Félix Guattari have theorized it. Subjectivity, they write, is the result of forces of 'reterritorialization' and 'deterritorialization' that work upon it from the outside. Memory and history, because they provide subjectivity with an origin, a limitation, and a law, "always have a reterritorializing function."[16] This aptly describes what happens to the narrator before the masks: he is 'reterritorialized' through the Caribbean and African history imposed on him. A whole system of events, objects, and people, it is used to produce him through enforced connection by making him the present end-point of that history.

The reason for invoking Deleuze and Guattari here is not to have them make the same point on history and memory as Nietzsche. It is their way of describing the necessary 'forgetfulness' – deterritorialization – that is of interest here, and this because it always takes place in relation to, that is to say, *with*, something else: "one never deterritorializes alone; there are always at least two terms, hand–use object, mouth–breast, face–landscape. And each of the two terms reterritorializes the other."[17]

The play of the forces of deterritorialization and reterritorialization is for Deleuze and Guattari a global process. It takes place on all levels and spheres. Drawing one of their examples from biology, they argue that the mutual dependence of the wasp and the orchid in reproduction exemplifies a "shared deterritorialization":

---

[16] Gilles Deleuze & Félix Guattari, *A Thousand Plateaus* (1980; London: Continuum, 2003): 293.

[17] Deleuze & Guattari, *A Thousand Plateaus*, 174.

> The line or block of becoming that unites the wasp and the orchid produces a shared deterritorialization: of the wasp, in that it becomes a liberated piece of the orchid's reproductive system, but also of the orchid, in that it becomes the object of the orgasm in the wasp, also liberated from its own reproduction.[18]

Flower and animal, through their connection, are "changed," both becoming "less" of what they were because they transform into something new. They form an animal–flower assemblage that is neither simply one nor the other but both. This "being," which Deleuze and Guattari call a 'rhizome', and which is the instantiation of an ever-ongoing fundamental transformation they term 'becoming', is in fact the opposite of any 'being', because it has no essence, no model, and no name: "A becoming is not a correspondence between relations. But neither is it a resemblance, an imitation, or, at the limit, an identification." The wasp–orchid rhizome is created through a "block of becoming that snaps up the two" and connects them in a way that is irreducible to language (name) or filiation (descent).[19] Becomings, moreover, are

> neither dreams nor phantasies. They are perfectly real. But which reality is at issue here? For if becoming animal does not consist in playing animal, it is clear that the human being does not 'really' become an animal any more than the animal 'really' becomes something else. Becoming produces nothing other than itself.[20]

The stress on function and performance applies to my reading of the novel. It has proceeded, it seems, through a confusion of literal and metaphoric levels of the text, arguing that history is *really* a "bush" and a question *really* a "machine." But, it should be clear by now, it is not the representational but the pragmatic side of language that is the issue. It is not because the question represents a machine that the name is appropriate, but because it functions as one. If there is any resemblance at all between the two, it can be found on the level of performance.

---

[18] Deleuze & Guattari, *A Thousand Plateaus*, 293.

[19] *A Thousand Plateaus*, 238.

[20] *A Thousand Plateaus*, 238.

The productive aspect of deterritorialization and reterritorialization corresponds in the novel to "connection." We have already seen an example of a forced reterritorializing connection. But there are other kinds:

> It's all those thousands of people I passed in the taxi in London, and the thousands of brick buildings joined seamlessly in which they lived seamless lives. I stared at everything and everybody, wondering whether there was a meaning to them, whether their lives had stories, whether I could connect with them. (74)

If the narrator phrases his exclusion as a semiotic or hermeneutic one, Mrs Rutherford's response is made in quite different terms: "How much sex have you had in all your years?" (75). She goes on to tease him:

> just the sheer thrill of nerves as you slide your hand up her thighs, the whiteness to it, the strange hungry flesh, the down of fine blond hair. And don't do it mechanically, don't gouge her flesh as if you were digging one of your canals. Soft, surprisingly oblique touches, insinuating and playful. Isn't that the way to seek out England's story and make the connection you want? (76)

Sex, when "insinuating and playful," when without goal and the "bulldozer mentality" of her husband's, is, Mrs Rutherford suggests, a way of "connecting." Flesh, touch, and playfulness are the components of the 'reading' Rutherford proposes. At a late moment in the text, after much effort to learn the real story of Curtis, his campaign to save the village, his politics and the nature of his relation to Mrs Rutherford, the narrator exclaims that he is "fed up with second-hand information" and professes his desire to "connect [...] with something real and solid":

> 'I'm beginning to think nothing exists in England. Everything is a reported story. You can't know anything for certain. Take Jack. There's not a trace of him, here, yet we keep mentioning his name. Take Curtis. He's a photograph in a newspaper and a lot of descriptions, that's all. As to the villagers, I've rarely seen any of them in real life. They might as well be Christie's ghosts.'
>
> 'But they are ghosts. There's only me and you and the sea-wall left, the only concrete certainties.' (157)

Here, too, a material form of connection, one that involves the "concrete certainties," appears to be a way to get to know.

Unlike the connection that produces a reterritorialized and historicized subject, the ones examined here will deterritorialize. Or, to put it in more Deleuzo-Guattarian terms, the configuration and degree of de- and reterritorialization are different. They are examples of connections that will break down the homogeneity of "England" or local history, into concrete and disparate elements, and form new assemblages. They are errant, without goal, and "concrete." Like reterritorialization, these forms of connection are productive and relational, but what they produce are "shared deterritorializations" (that reterritorialize in a new way), 'rhizomatic' 'beings' that are nameless because they do not exist prior to their actual expression or formation.

The territoriality of self is played out on the textual level as well. The narrator remains unnamed through the narrative, and so, paradoxically, is endowed with a 'history', while preserving a generic dimension. As this history is revealed to be nothing else than the sum of de- and reterritorializations, the pronoun becomes a contested site, a territory. "I" does not refer to a subject independent of, or preceding, the forces that shape it; it does not represent a memory or history. It marks, rather, a place in which subjectivity is constantly produced, shattered, and transformed.

It is here, in this productive deterritorialization, that I want to see Dabydeen's "creative amnesia." It is an "amnesia" that comes about through the productive connection to something else in the present, a connection that is concrete, playful and aimless. It is production because what is 'lost' is not absent but present though representationally uncertain; it is inventive because new and unforeseen connections may execute this forgetting, and because the results will always be something other than history or memory. Sex, though perhaps exemplary in its bodyliness, is only one example of this kind of "concrete" connection. Indeed, as we have seen in "Turner," sex might as well be used to reterritorialize the 'Other'. In *Disappearance*, Jack's sexual exploitation of African women, and the narrator's of a cafeteria assistant are examples of this.

If sex is exemplary because it includes the body, it is also the case that utterances, words, and narratives cannot be separated from this corporeal, material realm. Language, in "Turner," is "spurted […] on the mouth," or is the interpellative cry of "Nigger"; in *Disappearance* it is a question that works like a machine. Language, though not physical in the same way as a body, has as "concrete" a presence as an African mask, a basketball pitch, or a body.[21]

In *Disappearance*, such a deterritorializing connection takes place, paradoxically as it may seem in light of the reterritorialization discussed above, between the narrator and Mrs Rutherford. When the narrator is about to leave, Mrs Rutherford ponders the "new connection" between them constituted by their shared year of 'independence'; hers personal, his national. The connection is also formed in the mind of the narrator, who feels "drawn [...] to her" because of it (175–76). As Mrs Rutherford presents him with a necklace for his mother – a necklace whose wholeness invokes the broken string of beads in "Turner"[22] – the connection acquires another dimension. Constituted by shared experience, the exchange of a gift, and linguistically labelled, the connection has, however, already been present in other forms. By sharing a house and habits, and exchanging

---

[21] Indeed, the distinction between word and world, between sign and referent, is what Deleuze and Guattari's critique of representation aims at. Signs and objects exist "on the same level," they write:

> If noncorporeal attributes [words or utterances] apply to bodies, if there are good grounds for making a distinction between the incorporeal expressed 'to become red' and the corporeal quality 'red,' etc., it has nothing to [do] with representation. We cannot even say that the body or state of things is the 'referent' of the sign. In expressing the noncorporeal attribute, and by that token attributing it to the body, one is not representing or referring but *intervening* in a way; it is a speech act [… an utterance] does not speak 'of' things; it speaks *on the same level as* states of things and states of content" (*A Thousand Plateaus*, 86–87).

The common distinction between sign and referent disregards the fact that statements attribute qualities to, and thereby change, the objects "about" which the statement were made. For an overview of their critique of the presumptions of language as representation, see, for instance, André–Pierre Colombat, "Deleuze and Signs," in *Deleuze and Literature* (Edinburgh: Edinburgh UP, 2000): 15–33, and Ronald Bogue, *Deleuze on Literature* (London & New York: Routledge 2003), esp. ch. 2 and 3.

[22] Chronologically, of course, the reverse is true.

stories, the narrator and Mrs Rutherford have already formed a rhizomatic assemblage. They are the "concrete" elements of which the connection is created. Language and stories are part of this composite not because they represent, or necessarily lead to an 'understanding' of the Other, but because they are actively present, and performative.

It is according to this logic of productive amnesia that the narrator states his intention to return home to work – "There's always some emergency there that needs to be worked at" (174); and to 'forget' by creating "new beginnings" (179). The formulation, which echoes and inverses Turner's "slave to / Nothingness," captures, I think, the seemingly paradoxical nature of memory, history and amnesia that I have been trying to map. The poetic persona in the poem finds himself trapped in an unproductive oscillation between a forgetting that is really a remembrance and the prevention of a deterritorializing connection. The engineer, on the other hand, will return home not in order to face "ancestry" and history, but to create. "Amnesia," then, is not only an alternative to sentimentalist mourning for a lost history, but a strategic intervention in the history that created the loss. To return home is not to shoulder history but to challenge it, and this challenge will, if it is to be successful, inevitably and necessarily take the form of production, of material and concrete new connections.

❧

WORKS CITED

Austin, J.L. *How to Do Things with Words* (1955; Oxford: Oxford UP, 1976).

Bogue, Ronald. *Deleuze on Literature* (London & New York: Routledge, 2003).

Colombat, André–Pierre. "Deleuze and Signs," in *Deleuze and Literature*, ed. Ian Buchanan & John Marks (Edinburgh: Edinburgh UP, 2000): 15–33.

Dabydeen, David. *Turner: New & Selected Poems* (London: Jonathan Cape, 1995).

——. *Disappearance* (1993; London: Vintage, 1999).

Deleuze, Gilles, & Félix Guattari. *A Thousand Plateaus* (1980; London: Continuum, 2003).

Döring, Tobias. *Caribbean-English Passages: Intertextuality in a Postcolonial Tradition* (London: Routledge, 2002).

——. "Chains of Memory: English-Caribbean Cross-Currents in Marina Warner's *Indigo* and David Dabydeen's *Turner*," in *Across the Lines: Intertextuality and Transcultural Communication in the New Literatures in English*, ed. Wolfgang Klooss (Cross/Cultures 32, ASNEL Papers 3; Amsterdam & Atlanta GA: Rodopi, 1998): 191–204.

Grant, Kevin, ed. *The Art of David Dabydeen* (Leeds: Peepal Tree, 1997).

McIntyre, Karen. "Necrophilia or Stillbirth: David Dabydeen's *Turner* as the Embodiment of Postcolonial Creative" (1997), in *The Art of David Dabydeen*, ed. Grant, 141–58.

McWatt, Mark. "His True-True Self: Masking and Revelation in David Dabydeen's *Slave Song*," (1997), in *The Art of David Dabydeen*, ed. Grant, 15–26.

Nietzsche, Friedrich. *On the Genealogy of Morals* (1887; Oxford: Oxford UP, 1998).

❧

Many Masks, Big Houses

❧ Yeats and the Construction of an Irish Identity

CHARLES ARMSTRONG

COUNTLESS AUTHORS have written with insight about masks. This is hardly surprising, as the literary form may itself be said to necessarily involve a form of assumed identity. More rarely does one find authors who actually have themselves become masks. Arguably, this is the fate of William Butler Yeats: his personal identity seems to have become inextricably linked with Ireland's national identity. In many ways, his is a mask which both repulses and attracts contemporary Ireland, and yet which it is very hard to rid oneself of in order to reveal the lineaments of a brave new nation.

The historian Roy Foster claims that an elision between Yeats's biography and the history of Ireland is arguable, since the poet is an "emblematic figure" whose life intersects with all the central issues of Irish history from the late nineteenth century to the early twentieth.[1] Furthermore, current Ireland, he claims, is in many ways the creation of Yeats: Foster believes the freedom of opinion and national autonomy of the nation are inheritances bequeathed by Yeats, Lady Gregory and their circle. For others, the legacy of Yeats appears to be something far more sinister. Although not unequivocal, Seamus Deane dubs him a "colonial" writer, due to the far-reaching effects of the poet's sympathies with the Protestant

[1] R.F. Foster, *The Irish Story: Telling Tales and Making It Up In Ireland* (Harmondsworth: Penguin, 2001): 121.

Ascendancy.[2] Less partisan critics of Yeats believe that the violent and sectarian struggle between Protestantism and Catholicism to be found in the poet's writings is a reminder of tribal struggles hopefully left behind by the now cosmopolitan Republic of Ireland in the south. While some postcolonial critics are inclined to banish the literature of settler or Second-World countries beyond the pale of the postcolonial field, these critics resist this conflation for their own reasons. For them, the postcolonial fixations and fascinations of Yeats are precisely what make him dated for the new, postnational dispensation of contemporary Ireland.

Thus the memory of Yeats is a contentious one, and is felt to be both liberating and oppressive in his own home country. Yet what about Yeats's own masks? If one turns to the shifting and complex scene of Yeats's own writings, the issue of masks is so central that its signification becomes both ubiquitous and elusive. In this essay, I want to sketch some of the workings of Yeats's masks, with special reference back to questions concerning the issues of nationalism and Anglo-Irish identity already touched upon.

It is a commonplace of postcolonial criticism, as of gender criticism, that not only the oppressor but also the oppressed is inhibited or damaged by the ideological deformation resulting from oppressive representational regimes. Colonization frequently involves not only that the subjected be forced to adhere to a stereotype of the exotic but marginalized Other, but also that the colonizing powers-that-be put on a stiff upper lip – indeed, one big, stiff mask. Yeats's case is interesting not only because he gives a nuanced account of this process of self-alienation, but also because there is some uncertainty whether he should be placed in the camp of the dominating or the subjected powers, or whether he is of essence a more liminal figure.

Edward Said's reading of Yeats as poet of "decolonization" has already been criticized in some quarters for being overly simplistic; the same might also be said of his dismissal of Yeats's metaphysics as a form

---

[2] Seamus Deane, *Celtic Revivals: Essays in Modern Irish Literature, 1880–1980* (London: Faber & Faber, 1985): 49.

of escapism unrelated to his politics.[3] The mask plays an important role in Yeats's metaphysical thought, and its elaboration there is intrinsically linked with the poet's complex confrontation with the question of Ireland's national identity. In the most sustained presentation of Yeats's metaphysics, *A Vision*, the mask is one of the four faculties assigned to each incarnation or phase of life. Each individual has a will, a creative mind, a body of fate and a mask assigned to its particular phase. The importance of the mask is that it brings out the oppositional or agonistic nature of the resulting system. In one explanatory comment, Yeats underscores the significantly *theatrical* underpinnings of his scheme as follows:

> When I wish for some general idea which will describe the Great Wheel as an individual life I go to the *Commedia dell' Arte* or improvised drama of Italy. The stage-manager, or *Daimon*, offers his actor an inherited scenario, the *Body of Fate*, and a *Mask* or rôle as unlike as possible to his natural ego or *Will*, and leaves him to improvise through his *Creative Mind* the dialogue and details of the plot.[4]

Although Yeats reworks this conceit somewhat, when considering a primary or communal life rather than the antithetical and individual existence, the mask still has the same function. It relates the self to its own inverse or anti-self as an object of desire, as Yeats's organicism entails that a true form of unity always will entail the unification of opposites. This is true both of individual persons and of historical eras, and is the rationale for the way in which *A Vision* balances oppositions such as body vs soul and individuality vs the collective in its detailed map of the 28

---

[3] "Yeats's full system of cycles, pernes, and gyres in any case seems important only as it symbolizes his understandable attempts to lay hold of an extremely distant and extremely orderly reality felt as a refuge from the colonial turbulence before his eyes"; Edward W. Said, "Yeats and Decolonization," in Terry Eagleton, Fredric Jameson & Edward W. Said, *Nationalism, Colonialism, and Literature* (Minneapolis: U of Minnesota P, 1990): 93. For criticism of Said's general interpretation of Yeats, see Marjorie Howes, *Yeats's Nations: Gender, Class, and Irishness* (Cambridge: Cambridge UP, 1996): 13–14.

[4] Yeats, *A Vision* (1937; London: Papermac, 1981): 83–84.

phases of the moon. Thus Yeats conceives of himself as inhabiting phase 17, a phase which is just beyond the kind of sensuous unity of being desired by subjective artists. This phase is yet not purely subjective, for, like all other phases, it has its mask, an inversion of its own given nature: in this case, a mask which is characterized by the "simplification through intensity" linked to the opposite, more objective side of Yeats's lunar scheme.[5] His application of the system with regard to historical development similarly uses the notion of opposites to argue that a more hierarchical and violent one will soon follow his own democratic age.

Although the immediate catalyst for *A Vision* was the automatic writing of Yeats's wife, George Hyde–Lees, it generally has close links with his prior writings. This is certainly true with regard to the specific issue of the mask. In his classic study, *Yeats: The Man and the Masks*, Richard Ellmann linked the poet's strategic early use of impersonal self-representations with youthful diffidence.[6] More interestingly, there are close links to romantic theories of imagination in those early writings, as the variety of possible identities available to the poet connects the mask to something akin to Keats's theory of negative capability. In diary entries dating back to 1909, Yeats writes that the poet may "become the most romantic of all characters" if there is a willingness to "play with all masks."[7] The adoption of a wide variety of identities is an indication of an imagination unlimited in its creativity. Yet there is, of course, a potential risk here, of depleting one's powers too indiscriminately and widely. In the novella *John Sherman*, the young Yeats puts this fairly bluntly:

> Blessed are the unsympathetic. They preserve their characters in an iron bottle while the most of us poor mortals are going about the planet vainly searching for any kind of shell to contain us and evaporating the while.[8]

---

[5] Yeats, *A Vision*, 142.

[6] See Richard Ellmann, *Yeats: The Man and the Masks* (New York: W.W. Norton, 1999): 174.

[7] Yeats, *Memoirs*, ed. Denis Donoghue (New York: Macmillan, 1972): 152.

[8] Yeats, *John Sherman and Dhoya*, ed. Richard J. Finneran (New York: Macmillan, 1991): 70.

Later, apprehensive perhaps of precisely this kind of dissipation, Yeats becomes both more selective and more wary. In *A Vision*, he distinguishes firmly between the true and false masks of all of the twenty-eight phases of the moon, and in the poem "A Dialogue of Self and Soul" he lets the self ask the following question:

> How in the name of Heaven can he escape
> That defiling and disfigured shape
> The mirror of malicious eyes
> Casts upon his eyes until at last
> He thinks that shape must be his shape? (II, 10–14)

Numerous different agents may lie behind the projection of this "defiling and disfigured shape," one obvious instance being the clichéd images of Irish Paddies and potato-eaters that have long been the staple of the English imagination.

Yet one might easily oversimplify Yeats's rebellion here against such a false mask or self-representation: there is a temptation to (a) exclusively identify this as a matter of Irish and English identities, and (b) to unequivocally analyse it according to the familiar, neo-Hegelian power struggles of oppressor and oppressed evident in classic versions of postcolonialism.[9] Yeats certainly felt the pressure of English caricatures, yet confronted them in oblique fashion. In "A General Introduction for my Work," he remarks on the ambivalence of his relationship to England, encapsulating it in the remark that "my hatred tortures me with love, my love with hate. I am like the Tibetan monk who dreams at his initiation that he is eaten by a wild beast and learns on waking that he himself is eater and eaten."[10] As this statement is made as late as in 1937, it certainly illustrates the fact that Yeats's position remains complex throughout – and also that Englishness is for him both an alienating Other and part of his own identity. A similar ambivalence haunts "Easter, 1916," which – although it celebrates the transformation of the Irish revolutionaries from comic to tragic figures –

---

[9] For a subtle example of the latter, see Homi Bhabha, "The Other Question," in *Contemporary Postcolonial Theory: A Reader*, ed. Padmini Mongia (London: Arnold, 1996): 37–54.

[10] Yeats, *Essays and Introductions* (London: Macmillan, 1961): 519.

keeps open the possibility that the terrible new beauty of the Irish Republic is built on stony hearts rather than a legitimate mask.

Despite (or perhaps because of) this position of enduring ambivalence with regard to the relationship between England and Ireland, Yeats's writings do not unequivocally cast the English as the most dominating or consistent usurpers of his own self-identity. As the first volume of Roy Foster's biography has made clear, one of the most rankling set of "malicious eyes" for Yeats belong to the Irish writer George Moore, whose autobiographical trilogy *Hail and Farewell* mercilessly lampoons the poet's aristocratic pretensions – arguably driving him further towards the anti-Catholic extremities of the later stages of his career.[11] For the later Yeats, one of the most insidious and dangerous sources of disfigured shapes is yet another one: that of the crowd. Marjorie Howes has shown how the Yeatsian symbol is in part an instrument to control and order the pernicious anonymity of the crowd,[12] and the mask has a similar regulating function.

In the 1914 poem "A Coat," the dangerous image of the self projected by the crowd is figured by a "coat / Covered with embroideries / Out of old mythologies / From heel to throat" (1–4). As this coat has been appropriated by a group the speaker calls "fools" (5), he sees no other possibility than "In walking naked" (10). Here we can glimpse the rudiments of the veritable war of masks embarked upon by Yeats during the later stages of his career. It is a war in which the crowd is closely linked with the Catholic establishment of Ireland: in the poem "Church and State," for instance, the religious authorities are said to be equivalent to "the mob that howls at the door" (10). When Yeats grapples with this opponent for his coat or self-representation, a rather complex interaction results. It is important to realize that the mask is here not just something that is imposed upon, or assumed by, a victim. Richard Ellmann once pointed out that the Yeatsian "mask is a weapon of attack."[13] More precisely, one

---

[11] For instances, see Roy Foster, *W.B. Yeats: A Life*, vol. 1: *The Apprentice Mage* (Oxford: Oxford UP, 1998): 450–52 and 507–509.

[12] See Howes, *Yeats's Nations*, 66–101.

[13] Ellmann, *Yeats: The Man and the Masks*, 176.

might state that both parties of this polemic utilize masks, or disfiguring representations, as both defensive and offensive measures. While the Church denounces Yeats for being an un-Irish and licentious reprobate, he mercilessly satirizes them back, constructing parodistical images of the Papacy and its representatives. What is at stake is not just the public image of Yeats in Ireland, but also the limits and grounds of the more general 'Irishness' of the new Free State.

In the automatic script that constitutes the basis of *A Vision*, it is suggested that a mask might function as "a protection in one case a revelation in the other."[14] The personae adopted by Yeats in his dramatic monologues – most significantly in extended sequences such as those featuring Crazy Jane – may be interpreted as protective masks, enabling Yeats to take liberties with both the Catholic establishment and other opponents.[15] They are also linked with Yeats's notion that transcendent moods use individuals as vessels for their own instantiation: poems such as "The Mask" and "Before the World was Made" link the mask to fetishism and an eroticism of revelation. The speaker of "Before the World was Made" paints her face in order to achieve her own deeper self: "No vanity's displayed," she says, "I'm looking for the face I had / Before the world was made" (6–8).

Thus the mask functions in manifold ways in Yeats's poetry – as weapon, heraldic shield, and instrument of revelation. It facilitates both hate and love, emotions that for this poet are always closely intertwined. Ridding oneself completely of such self-representations is not really possible, if one is to believe Yeats's theory of the mask. Whether it is personal or political, an identity must always be clothed, or structured, in

---

[14] Yeats, *Yeats's Vision Papers*, vol. 1: *The Automatic Script: 5 November 1917–18 June 1918*, ed. Steve L. Adams, Barbara J. Frieling & Sandra L. Sprayberry (Houndmills: Macmillan, 1992): 162. From this rather suggestive comment derives the more formal and limited idea of that primary masks are "imitative" (and linked to service), while antithetical ones are "created" and self-expressive; Yeats *A Vision* (1937; London: Papermac, 1981): 84.

[15] On Crazy Jane and the Catholic establishment, see Elizabeth Butler Cullingford, *Gender and History in Yeats's Love Poetry* (Syracuse NY: Syracuse UP, 1996): 227–44.

forms of representation – and the lack of a conscious choice on this matter leads merely to the uncritical adoption of the ideology of the *doxa*. Yeats spells this out as early as in January 1909: "Active virtue, as distinguished from the passive acceptance of a code, is therefore theatrical, consciously dramatic, the wearing of a mask."[16]

Insofar as the mask is something "consciously dramatic," this theatricality is linked to Yeats's adoption of Eastern practices. His borrowing of the Japanese Noh theatre's use of masks does not entail a wholesale mimesis of the Eastern theatre's conventions but, rather, a selective appropriation utilized in the transcendence of the realist paradigm inherited from Ibsen and Shaw.[17] This appropriation is also at work, behind the scenes, in the formation of the theory of the mask formulated in *A Vision*.[18] Yet Yeats never settles on a straightforward view of exactly *how* a mask transcends the given. Especially striking is an ambivalence with regard to the role of memory, which is related to the uneasy way in which Yeats's theory of masks is both part of a nationalistic narrative and a supposedly atemporal theory of a common, transcendental realm.

Some of the most important late poems can be read as stagings of the conflict of these timeless and time-bound representations of the self. In "The Tower," for instance, Yeats's speaker constructs a poetic will, fashioning both a personal and a national identity on the basis of several chosen exemplars. Each of these exemplars is a possible mask, in the sense of an artistic superego or ideal, and is meant to function as a contrast to the false self-representation, or "caricature" (I, 2), forced upon the speaker by his old age. Despite evoking the names of such worthy Protestant forerunners as Burke and Grattan, both representatives of what Yeats elsewhere called "one of the great stocks of Europe,"[19] the poet also chooses to dwell upon the fictional character Red Hanrahan, who stems from Yeats's short stories of the 1890s. The choice of a purely fictional and self-created mask illustrates how the poet can articulate a self-re-

---

[16] Yeats, *Memoirs*, ed. Denis Donoghue (New York: Macmillan, 1972): 151.

[17] Cf. Masaru Sekine & Christopher Murray, *Yeats and the Noh: A Comparative Study* (Savage MD: Barnes & Noble, 1990).

[18] Cf. *A Vision* (1937; London: Papermac, 1981): 270.

[19] Yeats, *The Senate Speeches of W.B. Yeats*, 99.

presentation that is not straightforwardly empirical, but rather (in Yeats's own words) "a superhuman / Mirror-resembling dream" (III, 44–45).

The politics of "The Tower" are complex, partly because it combines a will to identify with the Protestant Ascendancy with a desire to transcend the entire postcolonial trauma of Ireland. In the final section of the poem, Yeats declares his preference for a people that were "Bound [...] /Neither to slaves that were spat on, /Nor to tyrants that spat" (III, 10–11). Rather than seeking to apply a slave–master dialectic, the poet tries to find a mask that leaves such a dialectic behind. Yet the very use of Yeats's own tower, Thoor Ballylee, as an emblematic locality thrusts the poem back into the struggles it seeks to transcend. The tower's military history plunges this and other linked poems – such as "Meditations in Time of Civil War" – back into the Anglo-Irish fray.

Both the manner in which the tower is frequently envisaged as a potential ruin and the close geographical and ideological nexus with Lady Gregory's neighbouring Coole Park link it with the politics of the Big House. The Big Houses of the landed gentry are more obviously ideological phenomena than the mask, but their deployment in Yeats's writings is related. Both of these are the accoutrements of the self, outside appendages that function as disciplining and inspiring façades for an otherwise vulnerable and unprotected interiority. Both are also subject to contingencies, accidents, and external threats: as one may be denied a mask, or given a false one, the Big Houses are threatened by familial degeneration or ruin. The anticipation of the fall of Lady Gregory's proud mansion in "Coole Park, 1929" is a case in point. In a rather different way, the same goes for the manner in which the proud "old Georgian mansion" of Lisadell, close to Yeats's home town of Sligo on the West of Ireland, is broached in the poem "In Memory of Eva Gore–Booth and Con Markiewicz." The political apostasy of the Gore–Booth sisters, renouncing their Ascendancy roots for a strident revolutionary, is implicitly cast as a threat to the stately mansion that gave them their beauty and dignity. In such poems, there is no doubt an element of tragedy. But tragedy is, of course, itself a matter of masks – and for Yeats there was no greater or more profound mask than that of the dramatic hero's tragic joy.

Thus there is an element of irony in Yeats's most conservative and backward-looking poems: his laments for the Protestant Ascendancy, and their marginalization on the Irish scene, is itself a sombre mask which the poet's own thought invites and relishes. We are thus returned to the theatrical spectacle where warring factions are mutually interdependent – hatred torturing with love, love with hate. The question of Irish nationalism provides this poet with perhaps his greatest stage, but it is by no means his only one. Yeats's survival and canonization rests on the mutual amplification of his various assumed identities of nation-builder, aesthetic modernist and mystic sage – to name but three of his most obvious masks. The question of an Irish identity will surely remain a crucial issue in Yeatsian criticism. But it will always have to take into account such countering statements as the following, from "A General Introduction for my Work":

> I am no Nationalist, except in Ireland for passing reasons; State and Nation are the work of intellect, and when you consider what comes before and after them they are, as Victor Hugo said of something or other, not worth the blade of grass God gives for the nest of the linnet.[20]

☙

[20] Yeats, *Essays and Introductions*, 526.

Works Cited

Bhabha, Homi K. "The Other Question," in *Contemporary Postcolonial Theory: A Reader*, ed. Padmini Mongia (London: Arnold, 1996): 37–54.

Cullingford, Elizabeth Butler. *Gender and History in Yeats's Love Poetry* (Syracuse NY: Syracuse UP, 1996).

Deane, Seamus. *Celtic Revivals: Essays in Modern Irish Literature, 1880–1980* (London: Faber & Faber, 1985).

Ellmann, Richard. *Yeats: The Man and the Masks* (1948; New York: W.W. Norton, 1999).

Foster, R.F. *W.B. Yeats: A Life*, vol. 1: *The Apprentice Mage* (Oxford: Oxford UP, 1998).

Foster, R.F. *The Irish Story: Telling Tales and Making It Up In Ireland* (Harmondsworth: Penguin, 2001).

Howes, Marjorie. *Yeats's Nations: Gender, Class, and Irishness* (Cambridge: Cambridge UP, 1996).

Said, Edward W. "Yeats and Decolonization," in Terry Eagleton, Fredric Jameson & Edward W. Said, *Nationalism, Colonialism, and Literature* (Minneapolis: U of Minnesota P, 1990): 220–39.

Sekine, Masaru, & Christopher Murray. *Yeats and the Noh: A Comparative Study* (Savage MD: Barnes & Noble, 1990).

Yeats, W.B. *The Senate Speeches of W.B. Yeats*, ed. Donald R. Pearce (Bloomington: Indiana UP, 1960).

——. *Essays and Introductions* (London: Macmillan, 1961).

——. *Memoirs*, ed. Denis Donoghue (New York: Macmillan, 1972).

——. *A Vision* (1937; London: Papermac, 1981).

——. *John Sherman and Dhoya*, ed. Richard J. Finneran (New York: Macmillan, 1991).

——. *Yeats's Vision Papers*, vol. 1: *The Automatic Script: 5 November 1917–18 June 1918*, ed. Steve L. Adams, Barbara J. Frieling & Sandra L. Sprayberry (Houndmills: Macmillan, 1992).

❧

Transtextual Conceptualizations of Northern Ireland

❧ Paul Muldoon vs Seamus Heaney

RUBEN MOI

Independence movements in many corners of the world looked to William Butler Yeats and Michael Collins for artistic inspiration and guerrilla tactics during the first part of the twentieth century. Although Yeats still holds a firm position in contemporary poetics and the critical discourses of emancipation, his representations of Northern/Ireland have been complemented by the paroxysm of poetic activity of exceptional quality and variety that coincided with the recurrence of the historical conflict in Northern Ireland in the late 1960s.[1] During the same period, the emergence of Foucault, Lyotard and Derrida provided the poetics and ancient hostilities of Northern/Ireland with new modes of intellectual analyses. Today Seamus Heaney, the poet, playwright, critic, editor, Ralph Waldo Emerson Poet in Residence at Harvard, Oxford Professor of Poetry 1989–94, and 1995 Nobel Laureate, holds the most prestigious position on the global stage of poetry. His artistic élan and pre-

[1] For a discussion of Yeats' poetic in a postcolonial context, see Terry Eagleton, Fredric Jameson, Edward Said & Seamus Deane, *Nationalism, Colonialism, Literature* (Minneapolis: U of Minnesota P, 1990). For recent monographs on Yeats, see Terence Brown, *The Life of W.B. Yeats* (Oxford: Blackwell, 1999), and the two comprehensive and critically acclaimed volumes of Roy Foster, *W.B. Yeats: A Life* (Oxford: Oxford UP, 1997, 2003).

eminent status tend to precondition the imaginative presentation of Northern Ireland in contemporary poetry, and its concomitant evaluations.[2]

Already in 1982, Morrison and Motion, in their anthology of contemporary poetry (which also includes Heaney's sixteen-year-younger Northern-Irish colleague Paul Muldoon), elevate Heaney as the "most important new poet of the last fifteen years," articulate deficiently "the spirit of postmodernism," and state that "the new spirit in British poetry began to make itself felt in Northern Ireland during the late 1960s and early 70s."[3] Although their spirit of postmodernism fits Muldoon better than Heaney, the two English poet–critics assign Heaney the most prominent position in their selection of contemporary poets, which includes five other poets from Northern Ireland: Muldoon, Derek Mahon, Michael Longley, Tom Paulin and Maedbh McGuckian. The conceptualizations of Northern Ireland in the poetics of these seven poets reveal significant similarities and differences; this article intends to examine the transtextualities between Paul Muldoon and Seamus Heaney.

Paul Muldoon, the poet, playwright, children's writer, librettist, pop lyricist, translator of Gaelic, critic, editor, Princeton Professor of Creative Writing and Oxford Professor of Poetry 1999–2004, recently acclaimed as "the most significant English-language poet born since the Second World War,"[4] appears as a distinct alternative to Heaney's aesthetic and conceptualizations of Northern Ireland. Heaney published twelve volumes of poetry (not counting his creative translations) between *Death of a Naturalist* in 1966 and *District & Circle* in 2006. Within more or less the same time-span, Paul Muldoon published ten volumes between his debut

---

[2] The reception of Heaney's poetry is, of course, much more nuanced and contested than the dominant positions simplified here. For a selection of varied approaches to the dispute over the politics and aesthetics of his poetry, see *Seamus Heaney*, ed. Michael Allen (Basingstoke: Macmillan, 1997).

[3] Blake Morrison & Andrew Motion, ed. *Penguin Book of Contemporary British Poetry* (London: Faber & Faber, 1982): 12, 13, 20.

[4] This accolade stems from the *Times Literary Supplement*, but now appears in most promotions of Muldoon. Quoted in Bill Raglie, "Paul Muldoon's Latest: A Master Poet Writ(h)es Again," *MacWeekly* 85.6, http://www.macalester.edu/weekly/101802/arts3.html (accessed 10 October 2003).

collection *New Weather* in 1973 and *Horse Latitudes* in 2006. The Nobel Committee awarded Heaney the laurels "for works of lyrical beauty and ethical depth, which exalt everyday miracles and the living past."[5] Conversely, Muldoon's deconstructive poetic oppugns fiercely established ideas of aesthetic consolation and moral consuetude in despiritualized forms of experimentalism that cannot be exempted from linguistic mediation, and that attempt to conceive of unrealized, and perhaps unrealizable, futures. Inasmuch as Muldoon's poetry can be read as a running critique of Heaney's poetic, many problematic questions arise. By conducting a transtextual reading of two poems by Muldoon – "Meeting the British" and "The Bangle (Slight Return)" – this essay intends to suggest a few answers to the question: How can Paul Muldoon's critical engagement with Heaney's radical aesthetic have any emancipatory qualities?

Muldoon's *Meeting the British* aligns textual undecideabilities with historical conditioning and social formations. The title announces confrontation and conciliation where Muldoon's preceding titles – *New Weather* (1973), *Mules* (1977), *Why Brownlee Left* (1980), *Quoof* (1983) – adumbrate alterations, liminalities, departures and enigma. In Northern Ireland in 1987, the title would have overwhelmingly negative associations for the nationalist contingent, and appear less powerful to the loyalist community. Like the majority of the poems in the volume, the title-poem is historically grounded in a specific time and place. "Meeting the British" recounts, from the viewpoint of the Ottawa Indians, how the British finally crushed Pontiac's rebellion in 1763 by employing what the cover-blurb calls "the first recorded case of germ warfare."

> We met the British in the dead of winter.
> The sky was lavender
> and the snow lavender-blue.
> I could hear, far below,

---

[5] *Nobel e-Museum*, http://nobelprize.org/literature/laureates/1995/press.html (accessed 10 October 2003).

the sound of two streams coming together
(both were frozen over)

and, no less strange,
myself calling out in French

across that forest-
clearing. Neither General Jeffrey Amherst

nor Colonel Henry Bouquet
could stomach our willow-tobacco.

As for the unusual
scent when the Colonel shook out his hand-

kerchief: *C'est la lavande,*
une fleur mauve comme le ciel.

They gave us six fishhooks
and two blankets embroidered with smallpox.[6]

This encounter between cultures annihilates romantic ideas of rebellious animus, facile nature imagery, and fascination with the exotic and the unknown. The situation of settlement domesticates any insurrectionary spirit, just as the perfidious plan of massacre reveals extreme xenophobia. Indications of cultural unification by the confluence of the two streams are shattered by linguistic and ritual alienation. Similarly, the negotiator becomes estranged to himself by adopting French as a spurious lingua franca, and the peace-pipe becomes a token of aggravation and contention. The romantic import of lavender soon shifts to a sign of a self-absorbed imperialist civilization, just as the symbols of cultural exchange turn out to be insidious gifts of genocide, revealing the colonial heart of darkness and the intent to 'exterminate the brutes'. Deferral of meaning in the "hand- / kerchief" displaces any cordial handshake with a solipsistic gesture. This spectacular word-distribution mimes its own enjambment, and interjects a sardonic irony that reinforces the poem's cynical mood

---

[6] Paul Muldoon, *Meeting the British* (London: Faber & Faber, 1987): 16.

and sense of division. The representation of the triangular entanglement by carefully paired couplets anticipates on a formal level the exclusion of any third segment. A lack of any native vocabulary in the poem indicates the silencing of the Indians, just as the confrontation of the French and the English implies unresolved differences. In this view, the poem proposes an analogy to a standard nationalist account of Irish history and the situation in Northern Ireland as endless rapacious exploitation, shrewd systematic suppression and unscrupulous eradication of the Celtic language, culture and population by the merciless and inhuman Brits.

This particular meeting with the British yields itself freely to traditional postcolonial interpretations of the historical relations between England and Northern/Ireland. The juxtaposition of imperialist suppression by the British of the natives on two different continents is evident. This continues Muldoon's analogous method of presenting the Irish Troubles through the tragic fates of native Amerindians that he first makes use of in "The Year of the Sloes, for Ishi" in *New Weather*, employs again in more antithetical fashion in "The More a Man Has the More a Man Wants" in *Quoof*, and exploits comprehensively in the debacle of Romanticism and philosophies in the next volume, the postmodernist showcase *Madoc* (1990). In recent collections, *Hay* (1998) and *Moy Sand and Gravel* (2002), the history, culture and fate of the Jews serve similar purposes. However, these powerful analogies are not simplistic accounts of British brutalism in Northern/Ireland or reductionist appropriation of alterity for propagandist purposes by the Northern/Irish. The Amerindian genocide and the holocaust relativize the historical suppression and the contemporary situation of the dispossessed in Northern/Ireland. Such a global perspective of human tragedy and disaster and the concomitant stance of self-evaluation appear irreconcilable with some traditions of Republicanism.

"Meeting the British" constitutes a poetic document that records the annihilation of an Amerindian civilization, indicts British imperialism in Northern/Ireland, and questions the accounts of British imperialism colported by some Northern/Irish agendas. This confrontational attitude in "Meeting the British," which both represents and refracts the hostility of a large minority in Northern Ireland in the year of its publication, is balanced by the variety of multicultural conciliations of Irish – Anglican,

Anglo – Irish, European and American literature, music, gastronomy, visual arts and media in *Meeting the British*.

Interestingly, in the year of *Meeting the British*, 1987, Heaney also attends to the negotiations of the many frontiers of land and language in *The Haw Lantern*. In "Terminus," his search for solutions retains hope of some uncontested ground in Northern Ireland where neutral mediation is possible:

> Two buckets were easier carried than one.
> I grew up in between.
> ....
> Baronies, parishes met where I was born.
> When I stood on the central stepping stone
>
> I was the last earl on horseback in midstream
> Still parleying, in earshot of his peers.[7]

In contrast to Heaney's equipoise, Muldoon's "Meeting the British" questions the possibility of mediation and middle positions, and reveals the negotiations as a cynical sham predetermined by imperialist foreclosure. French is not a neutral medium of communication, but an instrument of colonial politics. As the language of one of the involved European parties, it can only have reached the status of mediation by procedures of colonialism. Consequently, the native go-between is not an unknowing betrayer, but already a linguistic hostage of the invaders, as the discourse of *parlement* has already accommodated the parley. In Muldoon's poem, triangular relations entangle the issues beyond the simplicities of binary oppositions, and introduce the problematic position of the third party, the other Other. The parley is enclosed within contesting languages that are predicated upon the notions of logic, language and truth. No shift from one language to another or the tentative employment of a lingua franca can escape these strictures. Every language, French, English and others, is exorbitant, its position as orbit always already orbitory to other languages, other signification systems, other sets of values. Outside this system it is impossible to resort to the concept of another language, or history for that

[7] Seamus Heaney, *The Haw Lantern* (London: Faber & Faber, 1987): 5.

matter, without re-inscribing many of the same procedures of specific systematic strategy. In “Meeting the British” and *Meeting the British*, then, the parley is played out in the paradoxes of the supplementary double. In the poem, the go-between takes the general’s place but can never be his equal.

Processes of substitution parallel the problems of linguistic supplementarity and representation in general. The employment of individuals and words makes impossible any appeal to notions of neutral communication or any general object. The negotiator’s ignorance of the exorbitant and differential movements of his own speech and position becomes instrumental to the destructive results. Any promotion of the individual speaking subject to the status of objectivity is illusory, since the notion of objectivity is always already re-inscribed with specific bi-directional directives of language and value hierarchies. Consequently, an attempt to escape the circumscribed situation in one fell swoop by leaping out of it only amounts to an inevitable and immediate fall back into the same system. Illusions of the objective and the universal are predicated upon linguistic pristineness that ignores inter-orbital spheres in which the general *parole* is always already determined by shifting discourses that vie for domination. The individual utterance at a singular moment enters immediately into the discourse of time and language.

The viscous and many vital encounters in “Meeting the British,” and Muldoon’s multi-purpose employment of Amerindian and Jewish culture also oppose Heaney’s adoption in *Wintering Out* and *North* of the famous bog people – the well-preserved bodies, victims of ancient ritual killings, that were exhumed, particularly in Denmark, during the 1950s and 1960s – as symbols adequate to the contemporary predicaments of Northern Ireland.[8] Heaney’s striking metaphors, which stirred the artistic and public imagination and provoked so much fierce debate, convert the difference of ancient sacrificial religion and dastardly barbarity to the sameness of the contemporary conflict. Muldoon’s analogies reserve elements of differ-

---

[8] For Heaney’s own comments on the significance of these exhumed bodies to his poetry in the early and mid-1970s, see his “Feeling into Words” in *Preoccupations* (London: Faber & Faber, 1980): 41–61.

ence and difficulty, and resist the wholesale cognitive accommodation of the unknown and problematic.

❧

Both Heaney and Muldoon are scholars of classicism, but they diverge in their enactment of the literary heritage as a template for the contemporary poetics and politics of Northern/Ireland. A juxtaposition of Heaney's "Mycenae Lookout" from *The Spirit Level* in 1996 and Muldoon's "The Bangle (Slight Return)" from *Hay* in 1998 exemplifies their resemblances and dissimilarities. Heaney enacts in his "Mycenae Lookout" the tragedy of Agamemnon's return to Mycenae. In this he focuses on the return of the victors of the Trojan battle to family feuds and vengeful murders at home as an analogy for Northern Ireland at a time of ceasefire. Such a constellation of classical legend and contemporary crisis is familiar from the mythic method of modernism,[9] and the multifarious prosody and form of the poem's five sections takes its template from Yeats's "Meditations in Time of Civil War." In "Mycenae Lookout" Heaney presents a poignant meditation upon guilt and atonement, and a striking anticipation of internecine strife within the communities of Northern Ireland prior to the event of the Peace Treaty of Good Friday 1998.

As opposed to Heaney, Muldoon exploits Virgil's *Aeneid* in his poem; thus he focuses on the uncertain future of the defeated at flight from the ruins of Troy. In Muldoon's multigeneric poem, several disintegrating narratives intertwine with his characteristic, depleted sonnets to gesture towards alternative lives in a process that concentrates conspicuously on its own creativity. Virgil's *Aeneid* coalesces with the persona's culinary night in Paris, and an imaginative realization of an aborted journey to Australia intended by Muldoon's own father.[10] These narrative strands

---

[9] The *locus classicus* for the definition of the mythic method as a manner of providing shape and significance to postwar chaos is Eliot's review of Joyce's *Ulysses*, "*Ulysses*, Order and Myth," in *Selected Prose of T.S. Eliot*, ed. Frank Kermode (London: Faber & Faber, 1975): 175–79.

[10] For Muldoon's meditations on the arbitrary nature of decisions and the possibilities of alternative lives, based on his father's (non)-experiences, see "Paul Muldoon Writes," *Poetry Book Society Bulletin* 106 (Autumn 1980): 1.

commingle in a mêlée in which the fictive and the actual become impossible to distinguish, and finally narration and language cancel themselves completely in a semiotic swirl.

> The beauty of it is that your da and the other phantasm
> no more set foot in Queensland
> than the cat that got the cream
> might look at a king.
> ....
> No Mastercard. No mainferre. No slopes of Montparnasse.
> ....
> 'For "errata", 'Virgil smiled, 'read "corrigenda".'
> He looked straight through me to Lysander and Hermia.
> 'For "Mathilda" read Matilda".
>
> For "lass" read "less".
> Time nor tide wait for a wink
> from the aura
>
> of Ailsa Craig. For "Menalaus" read "Menelaus".
> For "dinkum" read "dink".
> For "Wooroonooran", my darlings, read "Wirra Wirra".'[11]

Muldoon's choice of Aeneas as a metaphorical figure for contemporary Northern Ireland, the supervention of the myth upon a semi-biographical persona, and the fictitious realization of the unrealized voyage of Muldoon's father present a complex of classical myth, autobiographical uncertainty and past possibility that contrasts strongly with Heaney's employment of post-Trojan legends as a trope for Northern Ireland at the time. Muldoon's mytho bio poieic intricacies oppose Heaney's unmediated representation and introspective focus on internal strife, and disperse Virgil's epic into idiosyncratic multidiscursivity. Metaphorically, Muldoon's poem gestures towards departures and new possibilities as opposed to Heaney's poignant but recidivist reallocation of all too familiar troubles. In its opposition to Heaney's "Mycenae Lookout," in its subversion of the mythic method, and in its deconstructed sonnets, subtle

[11] Paul Muldoon, *Hay* (London: Faber & Faber, 1998): 139–40.

sound systems, multi-narratives and celebration of ludic linguistics, the poem also renovates the High-Modernist quest for order, which desired to elevate the structures of art to a socially redemptive role in an era of postwar annihilation and cultural disintegration. A modernist quest for order is supplanted by postmodernist deconstructive creativity. On a formal Heaney and Muldoon - end level, Heaney's poem enacts retrospection and unity, whereas Muldoon's projects the uncertainties and the heterogeneities of an unknown future.

❧

In reference and attitude, Muldoon's transtextualities absorb Heaney's poetic achievement yet question its ideological basis, remonstrate against many presuppositions established by the status of Heaney's poetic, and undercut representations of social bifurcation and communal solipsism. His often oblique and ambiguous treatments of traditional nationalist topics, and his incorporation of these in an international perspective, conduct a marginalization of nationalist concerns from within. These deconstructions are not disintegration; on the contrary, they conceive of excluded possibilities in aesthetic presentations and cognitive structures. Transitions into a poetic, personal and political future based on the varied, but ultimately schismatic, visions of Heaney only would amputate from the very start the imaginings of the unknowable and the plural identifications of the individual and the social beyond partition.

These Northern/Irish issues – the dimension which delimits this essay, and which is articulated with most salience in Muldoon's first four collections and his second-last volume to date, *Moy Sand and Gravel* – subsist as only one of the many fractals of his prismatic poetic. Another fractal reveals how, in the swirls of postmodernist semiotics, Muldoon's adlinguisticity gives impetus to endless experimentation with language itself. Such linguistic dissolutions do not necessarily produce nihilism. As Muldoon's poetry illustrates lucidly, it generates artistic creativity, energizing a new aesthetic and new identifications.

Furthermore, Muldoon's disseminations interact with polemical exchange on the conceptualization of Northern Ireland in Northern/Ireland, England, America, Europe and the wider world. His deconstructions of poetry, self-imaginings and structural dichotomization invite revaluations of stereotypes and boundaries from the locally and diasporically emergent. Northern Ireland is not simply Ireland's, England's or any continent's opposite, but also an integral part of their artistic drive, imaginative formations and social concord. Divergent discursions of these kinds – endemic to Muldoon's poetry and frequently resistant to established frames of interpretation – complicate conventions and generate new conceptualizations, definitions and contexts of Northern Ireland.

Muldoon's transtextualities operate deconstructively on the shifting margins of poetics and politics in a wider world. His aesthetic pluralities do not produce the known or retain any collective nostalgia; rather, they conjure the unknown of a future that has not, and cannot yet, present itself. In these events, Muldoon's critical inspection of formal processes in the making, his redefining and refining of written and intellectual sensibility, and his opening up of aesthetic entities to complex differentiation possibly contribute irenically to communities continuously negotiating themselves precariously into aleatoric futures, in Northern/Ireland as well as other complex communities developing their contested history, society and language.

Nevertheless: if Muldoon's transtextualities have, in their critical employment, elevated the nexus of postmodernist discourses to the status of a new dominant in the evolving endeavours to conceptualize the human concerns of Northern Ireland, new aesthetic and hermeneutic projects present themselves. As the mixed population of Northern Ireland moves from conflict to conciliation, how will this development affect the poetics of Heaney and Muldoon? What new writers and hermeneutics will contribute to the processes of a future?

❧

WORKS CITED

Allen, Michael, ed. *Seamus Heaney* (Basingstoke: Macmillan, 1997).

Brown, Terence, *The Life of W.B. Yeats: A Critical Biography* (Oxford: Blackwell, 1999).

Deane, Seamus, Terry Eagleton, Fredric Jameson & Edward Said. *Nationalism, Colonialism, Literature* (Minneapolis: U of Minnesota P, 1990).

Eliot, T.S. "*Ulysses*, Order and Myth" (1923), in *Selected Prose of T. S. Eliot*, ed. Frank Kermode (London: Faber & Faber, 1975): 175–78.

Foster, Roy. *W.B. Yeats: A Life*, 2 vols. (Oxford: Oxford UP, 1997, 2003).

Heaney, Seamus. "Feeling into Words," in Heaney, *Preoccupations* (London: Faber & Faber, 1980): 41–61.

——. *The Haw Lantern* (London: Faber & Faber, 1987).

——. *Preoccupations* (London: Faber & Faber, 1980).

Morrison, Blake, & Andrew Motion, ed. *The Penguin Book of Contemporary British Poetry* (London: Faber & Faber, 1982).

Muldoon, Paul. *Meeting the British* (London: Faber & Faber, 1987).

——. *Hay* (London: Faber & Faber, 1998).

——. "Paul Muldoon Writes...," *Poetry Book Society Bulletin* 106 (Autumn 1980).

Nobel E-Museum Available from http://www.nobel.se/literature/laureates/1995 /press.html [accessed March 31 2004].

Raglie, Bill. "Paul Muldoon's Latest: A Master Poet Writ(h)es Again," *Mac-Weekly* 85.6 (18 October 2002). Available from http://www.macalester.edu /weekly /101802/arts3.html [accessed March 31 2004].

❧

(Un)Masking Possibilities

❧ Bigger Thomas, Invisible Man, and Scooter

JACQUELYNNE MODESTE

INTERTEXTUALITY IS A TERM that documents the artistic influences, or literary conversations, that occur between writers of the same or different generations and genres. The term is especially useful in delineating the possibilities made manifest in scholarly depictions of the blues. For the purpose of this discussion, the literary conversation takes as its subject Richard Wright's *Native Son* (1940), Ralph Ellison's *Invisible Man* (1952), and Albert Murray's *The Seven League Boots* (1995). The dialogue is focused on the function of art and the tools available for the artist in the creation of imaginative fiction.

Believing the work of the artist is political, Richard Wright creates Bigger Thomas, a violent, aggressive, nearly sub-human being who views the religious traditions of his mother's generation as wholly insufficient for grappling with the pressing questions of his day. In Wright's depiction, Communism or some similar collective action is viewed as a practical solution to the problems facing those living in dire conditions. Or, in Bigger's words, "one way to end fear and shame was to make all those black people act together."[1] Serving as the ideological bridge between Wright's and Murray's novels, Ralph Ellison's text concedes Wright's point that something other than, or more than, religion is needed to combat the despair that shrouds the lives of so many.

---

[1] Richard Wright, *Native Son* (New York: Harper & Row, 1940): 190.

However, Ellison does not think Wright's novel has achieved the artistic synthesis after which he himself strives. Ellison says that Wright's novel "represents a *take-off* in a *leap* which promises to carry over a whole tradition," and that Wright's *Native Son* has merely "*suggested* a path which [fellow writers] might follow to reach maturity."[2] In accordance with Ellison's view that the USA represents a synthesis of cultural influences, his protagonist maintains periodic links with a variety of cultural traditions. In agreement with Ellison's aesthetic viewpoint that one must forge his identity amidst his own traditions, Murray's Scooter is steeped in the traditions of his community and his conscious and contemporary sense of self is forged within the parameters of cultural conventions. This article will examine Wright's *Native Son* and Murray's *The Seven League Boots* by using Ellison's *Invisible Man* to demonstrate the continuum of thought that establishes Wright's and Murray's novels as literary polar opposites, in order to indicate how a rejection of cultural traditions casts one as an outsider in his own community, reinforces negative self-images, and constricts possibility, whereas cultural connections can serve to promote group consciousness and serve as platforms of opportunity upon which individual potential can be realized.[3]

Formal Structures

Analysis of several key features in the three novels provides insight into the aesthetic foundation of each text. The title of Wright's novel and the characterization of his protagonist connote a lack of human agency, dependency, and the intellectual, emotional, and psychological immaturity of a child. As a native son, Bigger dreams of doing bigger things, but is constricted by the very nature of his being and the urban ghetto in which he lives. The epigraph that opens *Native Son* is taken from the book of Job, "Even today is my complaint rebellious, My stroke is heavier than

---

[2] Ralph Ellison, "Book Review of *Native Son*," in *Richard Wright: Critical Perspectives Past and Present*, ed. Henry Louis Gates, Jr., & Anthony Kwame Appiah (New York: Amistad, 1993): 11 (emphases mine).

[3] Ralph Ellison's text will be dealt with only marginally here, in order to place emphasis on Wright's and Murray's novels. Ellison's participation in this literary dialogue will be dealt with fully in my book-length project on this topic.

my groaning," and is a statement that posits Bigger among the realm of God's persecuted.[4] As a victim of circumstances he cannot control, Bigger is like Job, a reactionary figure meant to suffer perpetually. Reversing this ideology and as if speaking to Bigger, Invisible Man asserts: "I am not complaining, nor am I protesting either."[5] Rather, Ellison's narrator is a self-proclaimed invisible man who boldly declares his manhood in the title of Ellison's text and asserts his adulthood and autonomy in the tradition of Frederick Douglass, thereby linking himself to a history and culture of proud individualism and heroism.[6]

Compounding the self-assertion of Ellison's narrator, Scooter in Murray's book does not name himself, but is given a name by his community as an expression of its adoration for the promising youth.[7] The title, *The Seven League Boots*, is reminiscent of the popular fairy-tale *Puss in Boots*, made popular by Charles Perrault, in which a wily talking cat acquires untold riches for his poverty-stricken master. As Murray's title suggests, his novel is one of incredible experiences and chance happenings that test Scooter's ability to negotiate the extraordinary circumstances with which he is faced. Murray broadens the scope of action depicted in Ellison's novel by extending the potential for individual achievement into the realm of fantasy.[8] *The Seven League Boots* opens with a line by Franz Kafka

---

[4] Wright, *Native Son*, epigraph.

[5] Ralph Ellison, *Invisible Man* (New York: Random House, 1952): 3.

[6] Both Ellison's novel and Frederick Douglass's 1845 *Narrative* (Douglass, *Narrative of the Life of Frederick Douglass, an American Slave: written by himself* [Garden City NY: Doubleday Anchor, 1989]) begin with opening paragraphs that assert the speaker's individual selfhood.

[7] Such naming practices are continuations of African naming rituals. Eugene D. Genovese notes: "Africans commonly would name a child […] after a particular personality trait discerned immediately"; Genovese, *Roll, Jordan, Roll: The World the Slaves Made* (New York: Vintage, 1976): 448. Scooter was given his name as a small child in Murray's *Train Whistle Guitar* when he started 'scooting around', moving from place to place before he learned to walk. Similarly, the name Schoolboy was given to Scooter when his academic proclivities became clear to community members.

[8] While the events experienced by the Invisible Man are fantastic it is not clear at the moment of each occurrence that these events benefit the narrator. Only by

that suggests the complexity, grand-scale adventure, and mystery of Scooter's journey. "The castle was hidden, veiled in mist and darkness, nor was there even a glimmer of light to show that a castle was there." The alleged castle is hidden and may not even be real, but Scooter will pursue it without even a "glimmer of light" to guide him. Contrasting with the stylistic basis of Ellison's novel, Murray's use of allegory juxtaposes the light of self-awareness within Scooter with the 1,369 bulbs that force light upon Ellison's Invisible Man. The premise established at the onset of each novel demonstrates stylistically textual constriction, mediation, and expansion respectively, thus placing Murray's *The Seven League Boots* at the literary polar opposite of Wright's *Native Son*. Scooter represents all that Bigger dreamed of being and all that Invisible Man tried to be.[9]

The depiction of education and the idea of hope are linked in the novels of Wright, Ellison, and Murray and are key features explored in each text. Having attended school only "to the eighth grade," Bigger Thomas is ill-prepared to meet the demands of social productivity. He lacks verbal acuity and fluidity, social graces, and intellectual control over his raw emotion.[10] There is no notion of hope contained in Wright's novel, because hope requires imagination and Bigger's world is too narrow for that. In his lamentation about life, Bigger feels the weight of his oppression in the white world – these people "don't let us do *nothing*."[11] Lacking formal education and guidance from within his community, Bigger inhabits a world that is culturally and intellectually narrow. He has no method for demonstrating his value to himself or his community, for testing or proving his intellect, because he is not cognizant of the world around him. Bigger is acutely focused only on his despair.

---

novel's end can these bizarre events be seen as useful in the narrator's journey toward self-awareness.

[9] In presenting protagonists who represent heterogeneity in male character types, the novels of Wright, Ellison, and Murray stylistically revise the literary image of the black male. This type of gender-specific study is the subject of several critical essays in *Callaloo* 26.3, and I shall explore this topic in depth in my book-length study of Murray's work.

[10] Wright, *Native Son*, 48.

[11] *Native Son*, 22. Emphasis in original.

The characterization of Invisible Man as an educated, hopeful protagonist refutes, stylistically, Wright's Bigger Thomas. Invisible Man is a precocious youngster who excels in high school, graduates, receives a college scholarship, and travels to new geographic and psychological destinations. Formal education broadens Invisible Man's world-view by providing him with new opportunities. At each juncture of change, literally with the onset of each new chapter, Ellison's protagonist is engaged anew intellectually, physically, and psychologically. By willfully asserting his intellect to grapple with each new reality, Invisible Man transforms the chaos of his environment into meaningful insights coupled with a consciousness of physical action.

Similarly, Scooter's education makes possible the transformation of the myriad opportunities and anxieties he faces in Murray's *The Seven League Boots.* When Scooter takes his first cross-country and first transatlantic flight there is no one to guide him through his new adventure. He is anxious, but neutralizes his angst by delving into his memory and unmasking images that help transform his fears into reassurance. Revealing his hometown as more than a typical Confederate town, Scooter unveils its complexity. Unique in its human diversity, the Mobile of Scooter's recollection is the "City of Five Flags (Spanish, English, French, Confederate, and American)" and "was not only an international seaport into which ships and seamen came from all over the world," but also had a thriving downtown area whose streets were crowded with "people representing so many of the languages and customs and even costumes of so many of the lands that Miss Lexine Metcalf's" third-grade geography class had introduced.[12] Scooter believes his encounters in Europe will have the same cosmopolitan atmosphere as Mobile but in a different geographical terrain. Murray's book depicts hope as an attitude of self-affirmation forged through an amalgamation of down-home training, formal academic instruction, cultural awareness, and general common sense.

---

[12] Albert Murray, *The Seven League Boots* (New York: Vintage, 1995): 263.

Variety of Experience

Integration and segregation are concepts that help shape Wright's, Ellison's and Murray's novels. Bigger, Invisible Man, and Scooter migrate from the American South to the urban North, yet each author's depiction of life in the city is markedly different. In Wright's version, Bigger's substandard housing and inferior, truncated education are symptoms of his abject poverty. Having left the south at an early age, Bigger has "become estranged from the religion and the folk culture of his race," suggesting that Bigger has no foundation upon which to rely as he matures.[13] Segregated by law, Bigger separates himself from a community that might have provided him with a sense of the wealth he could have acquired from his cultural heritage. He never has conversations with any community elders. He is culturally illiterate because unaware of local heroes and wise elders whose examples or advice he might follow. Bigger views the spirituals sung by his mother, the prayers she recites, and the weak attempts of Mary and Jan to render an authentic Negro spiritual as inadequate to convey the depth and complexity of his misfortune.[14] His torment is transformed only into violence. As Wright explains,

> the civilization which had given birth to Bigger contained no spiritual sustenance, had created no culture which could hold and claim [his] allegiance and faith, had sensitized him and left him stranded.[15]

When Bigger tells Mary and Jan that he cannot sing, he functionally separates himself from the spirituals and culture that sustained his mother's generation and those previous.[16]

Invisible Man has bitter experiences with integration. As an emerging college student he participates in a battle royal held for the entertainment of well-respected local whites because, like Bigger Thomas, he is poor and does this as a way to earn money. While he is delivering his gradua-

---

[13] Wright, *Native Son*, xiii.

[14] *Native Son*, 14, 37, and 77.

[15] *Native Son*, xix.

[16] *Native Son*, 76.

tion speech at the community event, Invisible Man is beaten and bloodied, humiliated and mocked. The naked white woman who dances before the group of boys participating in the event reveals the intimacy of each boy's shame. Invisible Man's trust in Brother Jack is shattered when he becomes aware of his mentor's glass eye. Invisible Man never comes to terms with the despair he feels regarding whites, but instead of resorting to violence or timidity, he relies on his own cultural background for sustenance – for instance, by listening to Louis Armstrong's music in the hole or eating a yam – and on his intellect to transform his anxiety, and create for himself a mental, if not physical, safe haven. Ellison's views on life are made manifest in the self-characterization of his protagonist, "I think I felt more complexity in life, and my background made me aware of a larger area of possibility."[17]

In Murray's novel, integration is used to transform ideology and place Scooter in control of his destiny. Like Bigger and Invisible Man, Scooter lives within a segregated world and is poor. His experiences with the white world have been typically marked by fear and violence. As a young man in *The Seven League Boots*, Scooter has numerous opportunities to engage in intimate relations with traditionally forbidden white women. By heeding the advice of more experienced band members, Scooter transforms his fear of sex and its consequences, and decides that intercourse with white women is "as much a part of [his] birthright as anything else out here."[18] Scooter, having erased the colour line, views all women as the same and thus approachable in the neutral and relatively safe realm of heterosexual relations. The fear of sexual interaction across the colour line and the associated violence and eroticism of lynching is inverted in Murray's novel as white women hotly pursue sexual relations with Scooter and other black band members. By revealing the least common denominator between men and women as gender rather than colour and in making women the sexual aggressors, Murray reverses the image of the black male rapist (Bigger), aligns men in a pact of masculine heterosexuality,

---

[17] Ralph Ellison, "That Same Pleasure, That Same Pain," in in Ellison, *Shadow and Act* (New York, Vintage, 1972): 15.

[18] Murray, *Seven League Boots*, 69.

and unmasks the reality and power of female sexual desire.[19] Scooter's fear of the integration/segregation dichotomy is transformed thanks to the advice of his elders, employing down-home carnal knowledge, and his sophisticated sexual experiences gained in a local brothel during his college years.

Rejection

Wright's novel demonstrates the chaos that results from a rejection of heritage, a lack of communal knowledge, and the outright destruction of a religious past, culminating in Bigger's killing of Mary Dalton. Like her biblical namesake, Mary is regarded as the holiest of all women. By portraying Mary Dalton as a wild child who gets drunk, defies her parents, and engages sexually with her boyfriend, Wright defiles the image of the Holy Mother. Touching the "soft swelling of her breasts," Wright sexualizes and scandalizes the interaction Bigger has with the Virgin Mother, reducing her to a flesh-and-blood human capable only of fulfilling man's carnal desires.[20] Bigger does not simply kill Mary, he suffocates her, cuts off her head, shoves her into the furnace, and then burns her, systematically eliminating her from this world. However, Mary's legacy, religion, endures. Her bones are revealed and Bigger is captured, serves time, and is sentenced to death for his crime.

Bigger's rejection of culture is illustrated in his relationship with Bessie Mears. The would-be alliance between Bigger and Bessie is destructive. Bigger's rape and murder of Bessie is indicative of his rejection of black culture, mothering, and women in general. He goes to Bessie to confess his crime and to solicit her help in his mission. He is tense and anxious when he arrives at Bessie's house, and he wants a drink. Sensing his need, Bessie tells him, "Naw; no whiskey. You need hot milk."[21] However, when the milk on the stove boils over and scorches, Bigger

---

[19] There is a lot of work to be done regarding gender studies using Murray's series as a launch-pad. In later projects I plan to address gender themes and many more as they relate to Murray's fiction and the blues ontology.

[20] Wright, *Native Son*, 82.

[21] *Native Son*, 212.

drinks it anyway, finding comfort in it because such harshness has been his life. As a leading lady of the blues, Bessie Smith was known and adored by millions. In raping and murdering Bessie even after taking her milk as nourishment, Wright's protagonist symbolically eliminates a black cultural icon and metonym for a whole tradition. Bigger resolutely breaks with the past by eliminating Bessie, her presence, and her reigning influence as old, useless, and incapable of nourishing his generation. As she "clenched her hands in front of her and rocked to and fro with her eyes closed upon gushing tears," Bessie and her prayers represent all that Bigger despises.[22] Yet Bessie's timid demeanour and her personal despair resonate with the intimacy of the blues. She wails, "God only knows why I ever let you treat me this way… All you ever did since we been knowing each other was to get me drunk so's you could have me," and yet she resigns herself to staying with Bigger, the man she loves, and to whose fate she believes hers is linked.[23] Bigger violates Bessie and after murdering her he shoves her body into an airshaft, only to realize "that was a dumb thing to do" because with her he had thrown away all the money he had, his last resource.[24] Stereotypically linked with passivity because of her religious beliefs, Bessie represents all women, and in killing her Bigger eliminates what he believes to be a useless element in society. In his flight from black tradition, Bessie is a necessary casualty. Yet Bigger's awareness of having done something stupid suggests that he realizes there must be some good to Bessie. Lacking the intellect and personal depth to explore such issues, however, he cannot reconcile the paradox of how to simultaneously keep Bessie and advance his own newly emerging worldview.

With Mary and Bessie dead, Wright's novel can advance an aesthetic philosophy that metaphorically shatters the masks of the seemingly 'weak' or 'passive' forms of self-expression offered by the blues and religion. These deaths, however, contribute to Bigger's inability to forge a

---

[22] Wright, *Native Son*, 215.

[23] *Native Son*, 215.

[24] *Native Son*, 224.

new path; he has functionally done away with his philosophical foundation.

Acceptance

Demonstrating his embrace of heritage, Murray's *The Seven League Boots* unmasks black women as the vehicles of history. Much like to Bigger's Bessie, Gaynelle Whitlow is a native southerner who has come to the big city to make it on her own. She maintains her own apartment and is financially independent. Like Bessie, Gaynelle provides the male protagonist with a source of sexual comfort and emotional release. Scooter is compelled to Gaynelle's side by a deep longing and is similarly drawn by thoughts of his beloved, Eunice Townsend. Gaynelle is Scooter's only female confidante. The Hollywood mansion of his millionaire actress girlfriend, Jewel Templeton, is full of material comforts and boasts an incredible view of the California hillside, but it is, alas, in no way superior to the "second floor apartment" with "hassocks and three fanback rattan chairs" in Gaynelle's cosy abode.[25] When Gaynelle tells Scooter she is eager to settle in and listen to "a stack of dirty low-down blues and get in the kitchen and cook me a good old home folks meal and sit right down and eat it barefooted," his mouth waters, his loins throb, and his belly aches for the taste of home.[26] Scooter's sexual relations with Gaynelle complicate the intimacy between the two and place their interaction definitively outside the realm of platonic or maternal relations. Sexualizing the male–female relationship exudes the intimacy of blues music and its passionate and bittersweet side. Murray states: "Nothing is more aphrodisiac than the blues."[27] As the first teachers of children and the physical and sexual complement to men, black women assume the role of transmitters of culture, framers of identity, and intimate confidantes in Murray's novels, and so must not be destroyed.

---

[25] Murray, *Seven League Boots*, 235.

[26] *Seven League Boots*, 233.

[27] Albert Murray, *From the Briarpatch File: On Context, Procedure, and American Identity* (New York: Pantheon, 2001).

Guiding Philosophy

Native Son suggests the plausibility of using Communism or fascism as a guiding philosophy rather than religion in order to address practically the issues of poverty, labour, and class. If any hope is expressed in Wright's novel, it is that of political revolution. However, divorcing Communism or fascism from the cultural traditions of the country in which it is meant to be realized creates a void in its practical application; the ideologies remain abstract concepts, not concrete experiences. While these ideologies may be useful in changing the outward manifestations of dire circumstances, they are inadequate for meeting the pressures that are daily inflicted upon one's psyche. Revolutionary change takes time and requires diligence and often painstaking, minute steps towards a goal that is likely to remain unrealized in the course of one's lifetime. The transformation imagined in the longterm does little or nothing to transform the psychology of deprivation. In Bigger's case, any measure of change requires overt, organized, thoughtful human agency, and his lack of agency leaves him wholly unable to meet these demands. Wright's novel offers no meaningful change in either mental state or physical, economic, or social condition because, as stated in the novel's epigraph, "Even today is my complaint rebellious."[28] This misses the point of revolutionary change and positions Wright's novel squarely within the realm of protest or rebellious writing that gestures toward but achieves no long-term productive goals. As Murray states,

> Protest is something that you must always be extremely careful about, because it can degenerate so easily into the self-righteousness of those who regard themselves as victims rather than people of potential and thus become more emotional than insightful and corrective.[29]

Wright denies Bigger the opportunity for self-affirmation, a vital tenet of the blues as expressed in literary form, and so denies the possibility of revolutionary change. Rebellion, as Murray asserts, "is sometimes only a

---

[28] Wright, *Native Son*, epigraph.

[29] Murray, *From the Briarpatch File*, 20.

matter of rejecting or even destroying established procedures and institutions," whereas "the primary concern of revolution is not destruction but the creation of better procedures and institutions."[30] Viewed in the light of the blues, Wright's version of political ideology is tantamount to religious zeal and is escapist, because it offers no method for transforming one's psyche – the first step in revolution.

Taken as a whole, the organizing themes of Ellison's and Murray's novels stylistically parallel the structure of jazz music. Each novel begins with and focuses acutely on the individual, his angst, its mediation and transformation within arenas of ever-expanding opportunities. Each novel pays homage to the cultural traditions of African Americans and depicts such connections as vital to the development of the protagonist and his efforts towards self-assertion and affirmation. Bigger Thomas never achieves the catharsis of self-realization as Ellison's narrator does, but neither protagonist begins his journey from a position of self-assurance, as does Murray's Scooter. Enveloped in the support of his community and self-assured, Scooter is poised for grand-scale adventures that could not be realized by either Bigger or Invisible Man. *Invisible Man* and *The Seven League Boots* are titles that indicate human agency and the fascination and wonderment of dreaming endlessly and traversing vast psychological and, in Murray's case, geographical terrain. As the foundation for jazz music, the blues radiate individuality through the agency of the performer, and the songs are endowed with the breadth and complexity of human experience. Invisible Man's textual journeys are of the deeply personal variety and are often bizarre, while Scooter's are made up of predictable events that emerge from his already possessing the self-assurance after which Invisible Man strives.

Education, linked textually to the idea of hope in both Ellison's and Murray's novels, is the metaphoric fulcrum between the blues and jazz traditions. While blues artists needed no formal training, legendary jazz musicians, the sort depicted in Murray's novels, were trained formally, were literate musically, and performed nationally and abroad as 'ambassadors' of American culture. Similarly, in Ellison and Murray's texts, for-

[30] Murray, *From the Briarpatch File*, 18.

mal education is necessary to extend the scope of one's experiences. Invisible Man and Scooter use formal academic training to advance personal goals even as they grapple with or rely on communal knowledge as a guiding element in the creation of identity. While integration and segregation played an insignificant role in the bluesman's craft and artistry – he could always create songs for himself, by himself, and the question of audience might be incidental – the integration/segregation dichotomy was vital for the jazz musician, who, as part of an ensemble, relied on an audience in order to receive payment for his effort and had often to cross the colour line in order to sustain professional vitality. Ellison and Murray's novels indicate the need to overcome colour-line angst in order to maximize individual potentialities. Musicians prove their talent by satisfying audiences, maintaining an active tour schedule, performing at larger venues, and by receiving more pay. Like these musicians, Scooter is 'going places' professionally and personally. Ellison and Murray's protagonists use mobility as an exercise in liberation. Despite the Jim Crow of his era, Invisible Man is psychologically free to pursue the goal of attaining mental clarity, and he does so, in part, by migrating from the South to the North. Each author remains true to his upbringing in the American South, and, like world-class musicians, each protagonist uses his past in the development of his individual voice. Modelled after the blues and jazz, Ellison and Murray's novels provide insight into the myriad possibilities made manifest in a stylistic shaping of the complexities of sound.

Resurrection

Murray and Ellison have created novels which identify, articulate, and extend the blues as a frame of mind and which set themselves up in opposition to Wright's *Native Son* textually on this most fundamental level. Both Murray and Ellison's novels suggest that, in knowing oneself, one must delve deep into the cultural origins of one's being. According to Murray's text, if one is like Scooter and reared in the blues, one is also the progenitor of a heroic legacy. Rather than being disengaged like Wright's Bigger Thomas, Scooter follows the tradition of community elders whose determination to persevere "in spite of, and even in terms of, the ugliness and meanness inherent in the human condition" condition him similarly to make the "best of a bad situation."[31] The centrality of improvisation in blues music, and in blues-based narratives like Ellison's and Murray's, indicates adherence to a particular legacy alongside the maintenance and/or creation and assertion of an individual voice. While Murray's aesthetic take on conveying the blues in print may differ from Ellison's, the two methods form a unified ideology and are variations or improvisations on the same tradition. As Ellison states, "Those who know their native culture and love it unchauvinistically are never lost when they encounter the unfamiliar";[32] Invisible Man hovers on the brink of losing his way but always regains his composure. Similarly, Scooter navigates his way through each scenario with admirable self-assurance. Exuding a profound sense of shame and rage, Bigger Thomas is perpetually lost in his encounters with the unfamiliar.

The blues as a musical genre, however, is not about violence but about freedom of self-expression, and as such it is intimately tied to self-affirmation, love, and democracy. Bigger's outright rejection of the blues is anti-democratic, because it denies individuals the right to self-expression and the ability to realize possibilities that actually exist despite one's conditions or circumstances. This is where Murray and Ellison might argue, and I would agree, that Wright's novel falls short. As Ellison asserts, "the blues, the spirituals, the jazz, the dance – was what we had in place of freedom" and it should/could have provided Bigger with a foundation strong enough to transform his anger into practical form by allowing him to envision liberty despite his circumstances.[33] As Murray states,

> The most fundamental as well as the most obvious shortcoming of Bigger Thomas [...] is that he is an exaggerated oversimplification of both the complexity as well as the potential of Negro life in the United States.[34]

---

[31] Albert Murray, *The Hero and the Blues* (New York: Vintage, 1973): 36.

[32] Ralph Ellison. "Living With Music," in *Shadow and Act*, 1972.

[33] Ralph Ellison, "Blues People," in *Shadow and Act*, 255.

[34] Murray, *The Hero and the Blues*, 94–95.

Wright's novel ends with the protagonist's impending death – a logical and long-awaited outcome for the intellectual and emotional death that has existed all along. Ellison's novel ends on a hopeful if uncertain note, and this is precisely Ellison's point: life is uncertain. While Invisible Man is eager to embark upon above-ground adventures and test his new sense of self, there is no promise of a problem-free environment, clarity or not. Murray's novel ends similarly, with Scooter, fingers crossed, waiting for whatever comes next, but hopeful, because he envisions finally securing the castle, metaphorically speaking, of which he has always dreamed. Like the blues, Ellison's and Murray's novels illuminate life's fascinating complexities and contradictions, thus releasing from its masked condition the human agency that is frustrated by Wright's artistic endeavour.

WORKS CITED

Douglass, Frederick. *Narrative of the Life of Frederick Douglass, an American Slave: written by himself* (Garden City NY: Doubleday Anchor, 1989).

Ellison, Ralph. *Invisible Man* (New York: Random House, 1952).

——. *Shadow and Act* (New York: Vintage, 1972).

Gates, Henry Louis, Jr., & Anthony Kwame Appiah, ed. *Richard Wright: Critical Perspectives Past and Present* (New York: Amistad, 1993).

Genovese, Eugene D. *Roll, Jordan, Roll: The World the Slaves Made* (New York: Vintage, 1976).

Murray, Albert. *From the Briarpatch File: On Context, Procedure, and American Identity* (New York: Pantheon, 2001).

——. *The Hero and the Blues* (New York: Vintage, 1973).

——. *The Seven League Boots* (New York: Vintage, 1995).

——. *Train Whistle Guitar* (Boston MA: Northeastern UP, 1974).

Wright, Richard. *Native Son* (New York: Harper & Row, 1940).

❧

Notes on Contributors

CHARLES I. ARMSTRONG is an associate professor in the English department of the University of Bergen, and a former visiting scholar at Wolfson College, Cambridge. He is the author of *Romantic Organicism: From Idealist Origins to Ambivalent Afterlife* (2003) and a number of articles on modern literary romanticism and twentieth-century poetry, and is the co-editor (with Øyunn Hestetun) of *Postcolonial Dislocations: Travel, History, and the Ironies of Narrative* (2006).

KRISTINA AURYLAITĖ is a teaching assistant in the Department of English Philology, Vytautas Magnus University, Lithuania, and a doctoral candidate in the Department of English, Bergen University, Norway. Her dissertation "Power and Space in Native Canadian Literature" explores racialized spatial constructions in contemporary Native Canadian drama and fiction. Her main research areas are contemporary multicultural Canadian literature, postcolonial theory, drama and performance studies.

DAVID BELL currently works in the English Department, Lund University, Sweden. He has also been a Nordic Guest Researcher at the Nordic Africa Institute, Uppsala. Among his research interests are British working-class writing and contemporary South African fiction. His publications include *Ardent Propaganda* (1995), *Latitude 63o N* (ed. 2002), and *Joseph Conrad's "Nigger of the Narcissus"* (ed. 2002); in progress is a co-edited publication on the work of the South African writer Zakes Mda.

ERIK FALK is a doctoral student in English at Karlstad University, Sweden. His dissertation deals with the negotiation and production of history in the works of David Dabydeen, Abdulrazak Gurnah, and Yvonne Vera.

ALAN FREEMAN is an assistant professor of Literature in English at Yeditepe University in Istanbul. His research focuses on the modern writing, especially fiction, of his native Scotland; his publications in this area include *Imagined Worlds: Fiction by Scottish Women* 1900–1935 (2005).

ASBJØRN GRØNSTAD is a postdoctoral fellow in the Department of Media, University of Bergen. Previous publications include articles on film history and theory and American and European cinema. He is co-editor (with Lene Johannessen) of a collection of essays on a nineteenth-century Minneapolis writer, *To Become the Self One Is: A Critical Companion to Drude Krog Janson's "A Saloonkeeper's Daughter"* (2005). He is presently at work on two projects, "Illicit Images" and "Rethinking the Pictorial Turn: The Ekphrastic American Novel."

LENE M. JOHANNESSEN is associate professor in the English Department, University of Bergen. Her research interests and fields of publication are American, Chicano, and postcolonial literatures and cultures, theories of language, and the politics and theories of identity. A book-length study, Reading from Thresholds: The Aesthetic of Time in Chicano Literature, is forthcoming, as well as the collection *Considering Class: Essays on the Discourse of the American Dream* (co-edited with Kevin Cahill). Her current book project is titled "The Architectonics of Memory in Exile and Migration" and explores the tropology of the migratory in American literature.

UTE KAUER has a doctorate in English literature. She has taught at the University of Marburg, Germany, and currently works as a school-teacher. She has published books and articles on narration and gender, South African literature, and on the English novel from the eighteenth century to the present.

SUSAN KNUTSON is Professor of Literature and Dean of Arts and Sciences at the Université Sainte-Anne, a small francophone university in Church Point serving the Acadian population of Nova Scotia. The author of numerous articles and the book-length study *Narrative in the Feminine: Daphne Marlatt and Nicole Brossard* (2000), she is currently working on a study of how and why Canadian authors re-encode canonical literary texts, particularly Shakespeare.

EVELYN LUTWAMA is a part-time lecturer in the Department of Women and Gender Studies, Makerere University, Uganda. After taking a B.A. degree in Drama and Philosophy and a Diploma in Music, Dance and Drama at Makerere University, she obtained her M.Phil. degree in Gender and Development from the University of Bergen, Norway. She is now actively involved in the growing field of gender, theatre and development studies.

JACQUELYNNE MODESTE, who teaches in the Department of English, Hampton University, earned a B.A. in English literature from the University of Massachusetts at Amherst; an M.A. in American Studies from Columbia University; and a doctorate (2004) in American studies from the College of William and Mary, Williamsburg, Virginia, with a dissertation on "The Blues and Jazz in Albert Murray's Fiction: A Study in the Tradition of Stylization." Her current research explores the notion of cultural legitimacy, democracy and cultural diplomacy.

RUBEN MOI lectures at the University of Tromsø, Norway, and has published widely on English and Irish literature in both English and Norwegian journals. He holds a doctorate in Anglo-Irish literature from the University of Bergen and an M.A. in English literature from the University of Edinburgh, and is the author of *Crossing the Lines: The Postmodernisms of Paul Muldoon's Poetics* (2004).

ANNE NOTHOF is a professor of English at Athabasca University in Alberta, Canada. She has developed and taught distance education courses in post-colonial literature and drama, women in literature, history of drama, Canadian drama, and genre studies. She has published widely in international academic journals, and is the editor of an essay collection on Sharon Pollock as well as a collection of Pollock's plays. She is a board member and editor for NeWest Press in Edmonton, and past president of the Association for Canadian Theatre Research.

WENCHE OMMUNDSEN is Professor of English literatures in the School of Communication and Creative Arts at Wollongong University, Australia. She has published widely on postmodern fiction and literary theory, and on multi-cultural and diasporic writing, including *Metafictions* (1993), *From a Distance: Australian Literature and Cultural Displacement* (1996), *Appreciating Difference: Writing Postcolonial Literary History* (1998), and *Bastard Moon: Essays on Chinese-Australian Writing* (2001). She is currently working on two projects funded by the Australian Research Council: "Australian Lliterature and Public Culture," and "Building Cultural Citizenship: Multiculturalism and Children's Literature."

GEOFF PAGE has published sixteen collections of poetry as well as two novels, two verse novels, and several other works, including anthologies, translations and a biography of the jazz musician Bernie McGann. He retired at the end of 2001 after being in charge of the English Department at Narrabundah College in the ACT, a position he had held since 1974. He has won several awards, including the Queensland Premier's Prize for Poetry and the 2001 Patrick White Literary Award.

ULLA RAHBEK lectures at the University of Copenhagen. She has written a doctoral dissertation on Caryl Phillips, and articles on Black British literature and culture, Australian literature, and postcolonial issues.

PRISCILLA RINGROSE is a graduate of Glasgow and Edinburgh Universities and currently an associate professor in globalization studies in the humanities at the University of Trondheim, NTNU, Norway. She has published articles on North African francophone literature, 'beur' literature, and identity politics in the context of globalization. She is currently working on masculinity in Middle-Eastern literatures, and has recently published *Assia Djebar: In Dialogue with Feminisms* (Rodopi, 2006).

ANNE HOLDEN RØNNING has recently retired as associate professor of English literature at the University of Bergen. She is the author of *Hidden and Visible Suffrage: Emancipation and the Edwardian woman in Galsworthy, Wells, and Forster* (1995), and has co-edited several books, including *A Sense of Difference: Women's Writing* (1995; with Marit Berge), *Feminismens Klassikere* (1994; with Toril Hanssen), *Dialoguing on Genres* (2001; with Ulf Lie), and *Identities and Masks: Colonial and Postcolonial Studies* (2001; with Jakob Lothe and Peter Young). She has published on women's literature and postcolonial writing, especially from Australia and New Zealand. She is currently completing a study of the New Zealand writer Yvonne du Fresne.

JOHAN SCHIMANSKI, an associate professor of comparative literature at the University of Tromsø, has worked on eighteenth-century literary forgeries, literature in Welsh, science fiction, genre theory, lyric poetry, national identity, arctic discourse, and postcolonialism. At present he is working on a book on 'border poetics' and narrative descriptions of border-crossings. He has published *A Poetics of the Border: Nation and Genre in Islwyn Ffowc Elis, Wythnos yng Nghymru Fydd* (2006) and the collection *Border Poetics De-Limited*, edited with Stephen Wolfe (2006).

❧

Index